COMPANY VOLUNTARY ARRANGEMENTS

ELGAR CORPORATE AND INSOLVENCY LAW AND PRACTICE

Series Editors: Andrew Keay, *Emeritus Professor of Corporate and Commercial Law, University of Leeds, UK* and *Chief Insolvency and Companies Court Judge* Nicholas Briggs

The Elgar Corporate and Insolvency Law and Practice series is a library of works by leading practitioners and scholars covering discrete areas of law in the field. Each title will be analytical in approach, highlighting and unpicking the legal issues that are most critical and relevant to practice. Designed to be detailed, focused reference works, the books in this series aim to offer an authoritative statement on the law and practice in key topics within the fields of company law, corporate governance, corporate insolvency and personal insolvency.

Presented in a format that allows for ease of navigation to a particular point of law, each title in the series is written by specialists in their respective fields, often with insight either from private practice or from an academic perspective.

For a full list of Edward Elgar published titles, including the titles in this series, visit our website at www.e-elgar.com.

COMPANY VOLUNTARY ARRANGEMENTS

Law and Practice

ANDREW KEAY

Emeritus Professor of Corporate and Commercial Law, School of Law, University of Leeds, Academic Member, South Square, Gray's Inn, UK and Barrister (unregistered)

PETER WALTON

Emeritus Professor of Insolvency Law, Wolverhampton Law School, University of Wolverhampton and Academic Member, South Square, Gray's Inn, UK

ELGAR CORPORATE AND INSOLVENCY LAW AND PRACTICE

Edward Elgar PUBLISHING

Cheltenham, UK • Northampton, MA, USA

Published by

Edward Elgar Publishing Limited
The Lypiatts
15 Lansdown Road
Cheltenham
Glos GL50 2JA
UK

Edward Elgar Publishing, Inc.
William Pratt House
9 Dewey Court
Northampton
Massachusetts 01060
USA

Authorised representative in the EU for GPSR queries only: Easy Access System Europe – Mustamäe tee 50, 10621 Tallinn, Estonia, gpsr.requests@easproject.com

A catalogue record for this book is available from the British Library

Library of Congress Control Number: 2025940892

This book is available electronically in the **Elgar**online
Law subject collection
https://doi.org/10.4337/9781035325658

ISBN 978 1 0353 2564 1 (cased)
ISBN 978 1 0353 2565 8 (eBook)
ISBN 978 1 0353 7131 0 (ePub)

CONTENTS

EXTENDED CONTENTS

PREFACE

This book was originally the idea of our friend Chris Umfreville who, together with Pete Walton and Lezelle Jacobs, had completed a research report in 2018 for R3 on how Company Voluntary Arrangements ('CVAs') operated in practice. Chris subsequently gained well-deserved career advancement at Aston University and so was unable to see the book through. Andrew Keay most graciously stepped in. Pete Walton is eternally grateful to Andrew for agreeing, one final time, to work with him on a project.

The book is intended to provide a useful and readable guide to CVAs. The options available to financially distressed companies have increased in recent years with the introduction by the Corporate Insolvency and Governance Act 2020 of the standalone Moratorium procedure and the court-sanctioned restructuring plan. Due to a number of developments, not least the pandemic, the continued use of pre-packaged administration and the (partial) re-introduction of HMRC's preferential creditor status, the numbers of CVAs have declined in recent years. There are fewer companies who are willing and able to attempt a genuine corporate rescue (as opposed to the transfer of the company's business to another entity).

CVAs can, and often are, a cost-effective way to rescue a financially distressed company. We are grateful to R3 who have permitted us to reproduce their CVA Standard Conditions for CVAs, created as the economy came out of the pandemic, and intended to encourage the use of CVAs.

The book deals with some of the historical background to the introduction of CVAs. It looks at the legal nature of CVAs and considers in some detail their procedural and legal requirements. It examines the role of insolvency practitioners, and other stakeholders, in commencing and running a CVA. It also considers the professional regulatory framework. It discusses how different creditors are impacted by CVAs.

We are most grateful to Tony Hawitt at Edward Elgar for his continued support and patience as the book has taken shape. Pete Walton would like to thank specifically his wife, Rev Debs, for her particular brand of practical assistance.

We have stated the law as it is available to us at 1st January 2025.

Andrew Keay
Peter Walton

TABLE OF CASES

TABLE OF STATUTES

TABLE OF STATUTORY INSTRUMENTS

TABLE OF STATEMENTS OF INSOLVENCY PRACTICE

1

HISTORY AND NATURE OF COMPANY VOLUNTARY ARRANGEMENTS

A. INTRODUCTION

1.001 It is usually helpful in understanding current law and practice to have a good idea as to how the law has developed over the years. Lessons are often learnt which have informed new reforms. Some aspects of the current law may seem somewhat anomalous or unusually worded. The reasons are often found in its historical development. A grasp of the historical development of law may lead to a better understanding of the current law and also a clearer focus on how, if at all, it might be improved.

1.002 In the first part of this chapter, we will look historically at the types of agreements that companies have been able to enter into with their creditors. Not surprisingly, as companies registered under the Companies Acts only became a realistic possibility in the latter half of the nineteenth century, the approach to creditor arrangements in the corporate sphere has traditionally borrowed from the types of arrangements available to individual debtors. This remains the case with voluntary arrangements – the corporate version effectively being a copy of the individual version. In the second part of the chapter, we will consider the legal nature of voluntary arrangements and how the courts have explained or described them. It is hoped that a consideration of the history of voluntary arrangements and their legal nature will assist in following the exposition of the law and practice in subsequent chapters.

1.003 The problem often facing a debtor who cannot pay its debts in full is that Common Law has always held that a creditor cannot generally, effectively agree to accept a part of a sum due to them in discharge of the whole debt. As all students who have studied contract law are aware, payment of a lesser sum than the amount due does not, without more, discharge an outstanding debt.[1] The payment of only part of a debt is not supported by consideration for the relinquishing of the balance of the debt. A number of exceptions apply to this general rule. For example, if the agreement of the creditor is embodied in a deed, the Common Law views the seal on the deed as providing consideration, and so the debt is effectively discharged.[2]

1.004 Further, at Common Law, in the case of a composition arrangement (where creditors agree to accept less than full payment of their debts) between the debtor and all or several of their creditors, the mutual agreement between the creditors to accept less than their debts supplies the requisite consideration as between the debtor and each creditor.[3] This type of arrangement may involve a promise from the debtor to pay money, may involve a third party acting as surety for such payments, and/or may involve the transfer of property to a trustee who may have the power to realise that property on behalf of the creditors. The weakness of any such agreement is that it only binds those creditors who agree.

1.005 Over the centuries, there have been different approaches to creating a workable system to permit a debtor to reach an accommodation with their creditors. Cases where debtors agree with their creditors that those creditors will accept less than the full amount of the debt owed are traditionally referred to as a composition of debts. In cases where creditors agree to wait to receive

---

1 This rule was stated authoritatively by the House of Lords in *Foakes v Beer* (1884) 9 App Cas 605 and is based upon the decision in *Pinnell's Case* (1602) 5 Co Rep 117a, 77 ER 237. The rule was recently affirmed by the Supreme Court in *MWB Business Exchange Centres Ltd v Rock Advertising Ltd* [2018] 4 All ER 21, although statements that the rule might benefit from being revisited, articulated in *Foakes*, continue to be made judicially.

2 Another exception is where payment of a lesser sum is accompanied at the same time with the transfer of a chattel or article. The creditor is seen as accepting the collateral benefits by way of 'accord and satisfaction' or some other practical benefit, and cannot thereafter sue for the original debt. The concept was explained by Sir George Jessel MR in *Couldery v Bartrum* (1881) 19 Ch D 394, 399: 'According to English Common Law a creditor might accept anything in satisfaction of his debt except a less amount of money. He might take a horse, or a canary, or a tomtit if he chose, and that was accord and satisfaction; but, by a most extraordinary peculiarity of the English Common Law, he could not take 19s. 6d. in the pound.'

3 *Couldery v Bartrum* 19 Ch D 394, 399–400.

full payment, perhaps by accepting a longer-term instalment option, such an agreement was historically referred to as a scheme of arrangement.[4] Creditors may agree to a combination of these two options, so that they receive less than full payment over a longer period of time than originally agreed. In addition, in the context of companies, it is often agreed that creditors will exchange their debt for shares in the company (a 'debt-equity swap').

Whatever the details of the suggested agreement with creditors, a debtor (and their creditors) wants the agreement to be enforceable so that everyone has at least some certainty in the short or medium term. The law governing such agreements has developed to provide two main avenues – one actively considered and sanctioned by the court, and one largely under the control of the creditors (with the court only being used as a backstop if there are problems). The main problem with court-managed settlements is that they are usually time-consuming and expensive. Out-of-court agreements are usually quicker and cheaper but, lacking any initial sanction or approval by the court, they have historically often been found to be subject to a lack of transparency and have been used fraudulently. They are also subject to attack in the courts which creates uncertainty. It may not be safe to assume such an out-of-court agreement is to be fully relied upon by the parties until the time has lapsed for a dissenting party to bring an action in court disputing its validity. There may be this uncertain period where the parties are left in a form of 'limbo'. **1.006**

The following provides a brief historical outline as to how the law has approached and regulated debt arrangements. The story involves repeated attempts to get the balance of the law right. There has, for many years, been a perceived need to provide the means to have an effective debt relief mechanism for debtors to reach an enforceable agreement with their creditors. The mechanism needs to balance the needs of the debtor with the rights of the creditors. The origins of such agreements pre-date modern company law and so initially concerned individual debtors (whether or not in business). When companies registered under the Companies Acts became relatively common at the end of the nineteenth century, company law adopted and adapted the rules applicable to individual debtors into the corporate context. As we will see, the creation of the modern law on Company Voluntary Arrangements ('CVAs') was a corporate version of the amendments recommended for individual debtors (Individual Voluntary Arrangements – 'IVAs') by the *Report of the Review* **1.007**

4 Today, the term 'scheme of arrangement' is given an unrestricted meaning and can cover extensive variations of rights: *Discovery (Northampton) Ltd v Debenhams Retail Ltd* [2019] EWHC 2441 (Ch) at [29].

Committee on Insolvency Law and Practice ('the Cork Report')[5] which came into effect in the Insolvency Act 1986.

B. HISTORY OF CREDITOR ARRANGEMENTS

1. Introduction

1.008 An individual debtor has, for hundreds of years, been subject to the bankruptcy jurisdiction of the courts. In order to avoid bankruptcy, debtors would often propose an alternative to their creditors. The alternative might be outside any court process or might be proposed quite late in the day when the debtor was already subject to the bankruptcy court's jurisdiction. The Muir Mackenzie Report on Bankruptcy Law in 1908[6] observed that there were practically two methods in which the property of an insolvent debtor could be applied in satisfaction of their debts and which provided a temporary or permanent protection from ordinary legal process by creditors – proceedings under the bankruptcy laws or proceedings under voluntary Deeds of Arrangements with creditors.[7]

1.009 The arrangement suggested by the debtor might entail the whole (or part) of the debtor's assets being transferred to a trustee who would be empowered to sell the assets in order to raise funds to pay creditors. Alternatively, the debtor might remain in possession of their assets and, for example, continue their trade or profession with the intention of making periodical payments from their earnings to creditors.

1.010 Historically, any transfer, outside a court process, of an individual debtor's estate for the benefit of their creditors, often in the form of a Deed of Arrangement, suffered from the significant weakness that it was, in itself, often grounds for the debtor's bankruptcy (it was termed an 'act of bankruptcy' under the former bankruptcy legislation).[8] By the end of the nineteenth century, where an individual debtor ran a business, the Deed of Arrangement often took the form of what was labelled an Inspectorship Deed, which did not usually qualify as an act of bankruptcy as technically there was no assignment of the business within the terms of the Bankruptcy Acts. There was instead an intention to carry on the debtor's business in order to make sufficient profits

---

5 (1982) Cmnd 8558. The Cork Report was followed by a White Paper in 1984, *A Revised Framework for Insolvency Law* (1984) Cmnd 9175, which ultimately led to the Insolvency Act 1986.

6 *Bankruptcy Law and its Administration* (Report to the Board of Trade) (1908) Cd 4068 ('the Muir Mackenzie Report').

7 Ibid., at para 6.

8 See Deeds of Arrangement Act 1914, s 24 and Bankruptcy Act 1914, s 4.

to pay dividends to the debtor's creditors (whether as a continuing business or as a gradual winding down of the business without purchasing new stock). The deed in question would require various controls over what the debtor was able to do and would enable the trustee to terminate the arrangement if the debtor failed to live up to their obligations under it. Even where a Deed of Arrangement (either by way of composition or otherwise) was entered into, it only bound those creditors who had executed it. It did not bind any minority of creditors who did not agree to it. Such creditors remained at liberty to apply for the debtor's bankruptcy or to take other legal action such as suing and enforcing judgment.

2. Individual debtors

(a) Court-sanctioned arrangements

Various Bankruptcy Acts have provided a statutory mechanism for debtors to **1.011** avoid, or stay, their bankruptcy by means of a court-approved arrangement or composition. For example, section 185 of the Bankruptcy Act 1861 provided for a debtor who had been adjudicated bankrupt by the court to reach a form of arrangement with their creditors requiring a three-quarters majority in value and number of the creditors to approve the proposal. In order to become effective, and to stay the bankruptcy, the court needed to confirm the arrangement.[9] A similar court-based procedure is found in the Bankruptcy Act 1869,[10] a procedure under section 125 labelled 'liquidation by arrangement'. A debtor, subject to a bankruptcy petition, could avoid being adjudicated bankrupt if their creditors (this time by a majority in number and a three-quarters majority in value) and the court agreed to the arrangement. Due to dishonesty and malpractices, the 1869 procedure fell into disrepute. The inherent flexibility of the 1869 regime was its weakness in that it was frequently taken advantage of by unscrupulous debtors and creditors. The Bankruptcy Act 1883 replaced it with a more formal system of compositions and schemes of arrangement. These provisions continued largely unamended until 1986 through, for example, sections 16 and 21 of the Bankruptcy Act 1914. In general terms, such provisions required the court to sanction an arrangement which the creditors had approved, usually by a three-quarters in value majority.[11]

The bankruptcy system under the Bankruptcy Acts of 1883 and 1914 differed **1.012** from previous systems in that the court made a form of preliminary bankruptcy

9 Bankruptcy Act 1861 (24 & 25 Vict c 134), s 186.
10 33 & 33 Vict c 71.
11 Cork Report at [362].

order, known as a receiving order, under which a government official, the Official Receiver, assumed control over the estate of the debtor (whose conduct became the subject of investigation). After a receiving order was made, the debtor's creditors met and the debtor could make a proposal for a composition or arrangement with them. If accepted by the creditors and approved by the court, it became effective. The debtor would thereby avoid being adjudicated bankrupt. This process was only possible after the investigation had been completed. If no composition or arrangement was approved (or proposed), the debtor was adjudicated bankrupt (which unfortunately occurred in the large majority of cases).[12]

(b) Out-of-court arrangements

1.013 Outside the Bankruptcy Act 1883 (and later the Bankruptcy Act 1914), a Deed of Arrangement depended entirely upon negotiation and arrangement between the debtor and their creditors privately. The debtor was outside the bankruptcy system, and there was no investigation of the debtor's conduct, no official audit of the debtor's accounts or control over the trustees who conducted the administration of the estate under the agreed arrangement.

1.014 A voluntary Deed of Arrangement by a debtor to a trustee for the benefit of the debtor's creditors obtained its validity and efficacy not from statute but from the conveyance of property made by the debtor. The trust was binding and effective if and when any creditors expressly or impliedly assented to the Deed.[13] It was therefore possible for a debtor to assign all their property to an untrustworthy person on trusts of the debtor's own creation and, provided one or more creditors assented to the Deed, it was recognised by the court.[14]

1.015 Fairly limited statutory provisions applicable to such Deeds of Arrangements were introduced:

1. the Deed had to be registered within seven days; otherwise, it was absolutely void;[15]

12 See Muir Mackenzie Report at [7]–[8]. At [86], the Report explained a number of prohibitive restrictions on the use of the statutory scheme; e.g., under s 8 Bankruptcy Act 1890, the power to offer a composition or arrangement was effectively limited to cases where at least 10 shillings in the £ (50 per cent of the debt) was being offered to the creditors.

13 See Muir Mackenzie Report at [128] citing *Johns v James* (1878) 8 Ch D 744 and *Siggers v Evans* (1855) 5 El & Bl 367, 119 ER 518.

14 Muir Mackenzie Report at [127].

15 Deeds of Arrangement Act 1914, s 2.

2. the trustee was required once a year to send accounts to the Board of Trade (for statistical purposes only – the accounts were not audited);[16] and
3. the execution of a deed over all the debtor's property for the benefit of all the debtor's creditors generally was an act of bankruptcy and if the debtor was made bankrupt on the petition of a non-assenting creditor within three months of the Deed's date, it was void against the trustee in bankruptcy and the creditors in general. One practical consequence of this was that the Deed itself could not be safely acted under (for the statutory period of three months after its execution) as it could be avoided in the subsequent bankruptcy.[17]

The statutory provisions were seen as providing only limited protection for creditors. There was no statutory provision requiring any investigation of the debtor's conduct, testing the character of the Deed's trustee, giving the creditors any power over who the trustee was to be, or for any audit of the trustee's accounts.[18] **1.016**

However, where a debtor at a meeting of creditors executed a Deed assigning their property to a trustee of repute approved by the creditors, on trusts which they approved, the Deed often worked to the satisfaction of those concerned, with the main disadvantage being that the Deed could be upset in subsequent bankruptcy proceedings brought by dissenting creditors.[19] Various recommendations were made to improve confidence in such Deeds; for example, the suggestion that a significant majority of creditors should be needed to approve a Deed before it could be effective, and secondly, for a professional bond to be paid by any trustee of the Deed equal to the value of the assets available to creditors.[20] **1.017**

Although at one time popular, especially with sole traders, where they provided a more efficient way to realise a business than in bankruptcy, the numbers of Deeds of Arrangement dwindled. This was partly due to the lack of confidence in the robustness of the process but probably more due to the increased incorporation of small- and medium-sized entities ('SMEs'). By 1979, only 44 Deeds were entered into. Ten years earlier, the figure had been 255.[21] By **1.018**

16 Ibid., s 13.
17 Ibid., s 24. See also Muir Mackenzie Report at [128] and the Cork Report at [350]–[353].
18 Muir Mackenzie Report at [129]. Making a trustee under such an arrangement liable for their administration of the trust fund required Chancery proceedings by creditors, which were expensive and likely to be dilatory [130]. There was evidence of large-scale frauds being perpetrated against a debtor's creditors by unscrupulous trustees [131].
19 Muir Mackenzie Report at [132]–[133].
20 Ibid., at [136] et seq.
21 Cork Report at [358]–[359].

the time Deeds of Arrangement were finally abolished in 2015,[22] there had been years where none had been executed and in other years there had been only a solitary deed.

1.019 Deeds of Arrangement had outlived their utility. Due to the risk of bankruptcy still hanging over the head of the debtor, they were not favoured by debtors. Creditors often had little confidence in the process due to the lack of regulation of the activities of trustees appointed under Deeds. Trustees themselves were in a weak position in terms of the powers they had to investigate prior conduct by the debtor and to act effectively in light of their findings.[23]

1.020 It was the Cork Committee's recognition that there was an important social need to provide a satisfactory alternative to bankruptcy proceedings, which led it to recommend the introduction of the IVA.[24] Cork recognised the likely benefits of an out-of-court procedure to keep costs down and encourage swift action, but emphasised the need to have suitable regulation to ensure confidence. There would need to be a heavy responsibility placed upon the professional competence, independence and integrity of the insolvency practitioner acting as nominee and supervisor of the voluntary arrangement.[25] There would always be the need to have a right to apply to court if a creditor was not in at least as advantageous a position as they would have been in a bankruptcy. As we will see below, these fundamental principles were also recommended for CVAs.[26]

---

22 They were abolished when paras 1–3 of Sch 6 to the Deregulation Act 2015 repealed the Deeds of Arrangement Act 1914.

23 Cork Report at [358].

24 Cork Report at [359]. The Cork IVA recommendations were somewhat unusually based upon creditors' voluntary liquidation, this being an unusual occurrence of personal insolvency law reform borrowing from corporate insolvency (at [363]).

25 Cork Report at [364].

26 It is interesting to note that although the Cork Committee recommended the introduction of IVAs and CVAs as a statutory procedure, enabling an insolvent debtor to agree with their creditors on an agreement leading to the discharge of their debts, the version which made it into the Insolvency Act 1986 differs in several regards from that suggested by Cork. The requisite percentage of creditors whose agreement is sought, the powers of the supervisor to revisit antecedent transactions and a requirement for a committee of creditors are some of the areas where there was some divergence (see Cork Report at [381], [388] and [377]). Other significant characteristics remained, e.g., the ability for creditors bound by the majority vote to apply to the court if they would be worse off under the terms of the voluntary arrangement (at [362]). In addition, the Cork recommendation that preferential and secured creditors should not be affected without their consent was essentially retained (at [386]).

3. Companies

(a) Court-sanctioned arrangements

The Cork Committee explained how companies were able to enter into a binding arrangement with their creditors under the Companies Act 1948 (CA 1948).[27] Although in theory a company had three statutory options, in reality, two of those were illusory in the case of financially distressed companies. Section 287 of the CA 1948 enabled a liquidator, with sanction of a special resolution of the company, to transfer the business of a company to another company. The transfer did not affect the rights of the creditors. The power only applied where the transferor company was solvent and so was not relevant to Cork's deliberations. In practice, the procedure available under section 306 of the CA 1948 was a dead letter as it required the consent of three-quarters in number and value of *all* the company's creditors, not just those creditors who were present and voting at a creditors' meeting. This made it unworkable. **1.021**

As the Cork Committee commented, it was 'an irony' that Schemes of Arrangement under section 206 of the CA 1948 (the predecessor of today's Part 26 of the Companies Act 2006), which applied to all companies whether or not they were being wound up, were introduced in the latter part of the nineteenth century for the benefit only of companies in the course of being wound up.[28] This restriction was lifted by the Companies Act 1907[29] so that a company did not first have to enter liquidation to propose a scheme. Although at the time of the Cork deliberations,[30] such schemes were frequently entered into by solvent companies, they were only rarely used by insolvent companies. They were and remain an expensive option for distressed companies. An initial court hearing is needed for the court to convene meetings of classes of creditors. Assuming the classes of creditors approve the scheme (by a majority of three-quarters in value and a simple majority in number), the company must then return to court for a further hearing to request the court's sanction. **1.022**

---

27 Cork Report at [400] et seq.

28 Ibid., at [404]. The power to propose a scheme originates from ss 159 and 160 of the Companies Act 1862, but it was of limited use as a sanctioned scheme did not bind a dissenting creditor (see *Re Dominion of Canada Freehold Estate and Timber Co Ltd* (1886) 55 LT 347, 351). Only in 1870 was it possible for a majority of creditors within a class to bind a dissenting minority.

29 See Companies Act 1907, s 38.

30 The statutory scheme of arrangement provisions were effectively replicated throughout the twentieth century up to the present day: s 24 Companies Act 1900, s 120 Companies Act 1908, s 153 Companies Act 1929, s 206 Companies Act 1948, s 425 Companies Act 1985 and Part 26 Companies Act 2006.

1.023 The Companies Act scheme of arrangement appears to be a procedure imported from bankruptcy law. As Vaughan-Williams J commented in *Re London Chartered Bank of Australia*:[31]

> The scheme of arrangement under the Act of 1870 is – as I have had occasion to point out in several cases – an alternative mode of liquidation which the law allows the statutory majority of creditors to substitute for the pending winding-up, whether voluntary or under the Court, just as the Bankruptcy Act, 1869, allowed the creditors the substituted liquidation by arrangement under section 125 … for a pending bankruptcy.

1.024 The corporate scheme of arrangement, therefore, originates from the equivalent provision in bankruptcy. It was originally seen as a type of liquidation but became available outside liquidation. It allows for the requisite majority of each consenting class of creditors to bind any dissenting minority at a class meeting. It does not allow for a class that dissents to be bound by the scheme, even if all other classes vote in favour. It requires each class of creditors to approve the scheme before the court considers granting its sanction. If effective, it discharges the debts covered by the scheme.

1.025 Some of the problems relating to schemes of arrangement identified by the Cork Committee have latterly been addressed by the Corporate Insolvency and Governance Act ('CIGA') 2020.[32] It is now possible (within limits) for a company looking to reach an agreement with its creditors to acquire the benefit of a moratorium on actions while it prepares and proposes its arrangement (see below Chapter 3 for an explanation as to how the standalone Moratorium works under Sch A1 of the Act). One problem not identified by Cork but subsequently seen as a genuine hurdle was the difficulty faced when one class of creditor withheld its consent to the scheme in the hope of more beneficial treatment being offered. The introduction of the restructuring plan by CIGA 2020 (found in Part 26A of the Companies Act 2006), and the power of the court to cram down a dissenting class (subject to certain safeguards) has been a success in addressing this concern.[33]

---

31 [1893] 3 Ch 540, 546.

32 See Cork Report at [405] et seq.

33 See the Government's *Post Implementation Review of CIGA 2020* dated 21 February 2023 and the research supporting the Review: P Walton and L Jacobs, *Corporate Insolvency and Governance Act 2020 – Final Evaluation Report*, November 2022 and P Walton and L Jacobs, *Corporate Insolvency and Governance Act 2020 – Interim Report*, March 2022. Classes of creditors must approve a restructuring plan by three-quarters in value. There is no requirement for a majority in number as there is with schemes. The requirement for a convening hearing and later a sanction hearing is effectively the same for both schemes and restructuring plans.

Whether a scheme of arrangement or a restructuring plan is used, the problems of substantial formality and complexity (and associated costs) remain a concern.[34] Realistically, schemes and restructuring plans are out of reach for most SMEs due to the time and cost involved in obtaining creditor approval and court sanction. **1.026**

(b) Out-of-court arrangements

There was (and is) nothing preventing a company from entering into a Deed of Arrangement with its creditors. Such Deeds were never subject to the provisions of the now repealed Deeds of Arrangement Acts as they were executed by corporate bodies that fell outside the Acts.[35] As with Deeds executed by individuals, they only bound creditors who consented. Non-assenting creditors could continue to enforce their rights against the company, including petitioning for its liquidation. There is no evidence that they were ever used by companies. Prior to 1986, there was no viable out-of-court statutory procedure available to a distressed company. **1.027**

4. The Cork Committee and the Insolvency Act 1986

The Cork Committee, as well as recommending the introduction of administration,[36] also proposed the CVA. The CVA was seen as an adaptation of the IVA procedure, which Cork recommended for individual debtors.[37] As Cork explained, if a company needed a moratorium on actions in order to prepare a CVA proposal, it would be possible first to enter administration. In terms of the CVA procedure itself, the court was not to be involved in the formulation of the proposal and its presentation to creditors. The company directors (or administrator) would propose a CVA and would be obliged to provide creditors with full information about the proposal and the company's financial position. The creditors would be able to control which insolvency practitioner was appointed to supervise the CVA and, of course, to vote on the proposal itself. If approved, the majority decision would bind a dissenting minority. The introduction of a system of licensing insolvency practitioners, following the Cork recommendations, was seen as crucial to the success of the CVA. The history of creditor arrangements had shown that many previous attempts to develop an effective and trusted mechanism for such agreements had often foundered on the lack of independence and regulation of those **1.028**

34 Ibid.
35 *Re Rileys Ltd* [1903] 2 Ch 590.
36 Cork Report, Chapter 9.
37 Ibid., at [428]–[430].

acting as trustees for the parties involved. It was considered that the facility to promote such arrangements without the obligation to go to the court would prove valuable to SME companies urgently seeking a straightforward composition or moratorium.

1.029 The Cork recommendations were broadly adopted by the then government and the CVA was introduced as Part 1 of the Insolvency Act 1986, where, subject to various amendments over the years, it remains today. The procedure to enter into a CVA is explained in detail in Chapter 2, although it may be useful at this stage to have a general overview of the procedure.

1.030 A CVA may be entered into by a company if it remains under the control of its directors or if it is in administration or liquidation. The company does not have to be insolvent.[38] The proposal is made to both the company's creditors and members and must be for a composition of debts or a scheme of arrangement of its affairs. The proposal must provide for it to be supervised by a qualified insolvency practitioner. A CVA cannot affect the rights of secured creditors without their consent or affect the priority of any preferential creditors. The CVA must be approved by a majority of at least three-quarters in value responding to the notice of a creditors' decision to consider the CVA. The decision binds a dissenting minority. As can be seen from this outline, the CVA has learnt the lessons of history. It allows a large majority of unsecured creditors to bind a dissenting minority. It is considered and supervised by an independent professional but with a backstop power to apply to the court if there is a problem. The procedure is designed to operate outside the court (unless a problem arises) and so set-up and operating costs should be far less than under the court-sanctioned possibilities under the Companies Act 2006.

1.031 Although the members of the company also vote on the proposal, section 4A of the Insolvency Act 1986 provides that the decision of the creditors to approve the CVA will override any resolution of the members to the contrary (subject to a right in the members to apply to the court). If approved, the CVA immediately has the effect of binding every creditor who was entitled to vote on the proposal (whether or not they did vote and whether or not they actually had notice of the creditors' decision), as if they were a party to the CVA. A creditor (or member) may apply to the court claiming that any approved CVA unfairly

---

38 Insolvency Act 1986, s 1(3). The procedure differs depending on whether the proposal is by the directors or by an administrator or liquidator. There is no power for a receiver or special manager under s 177 of the 1986 Act to make a proposal: he or she would need to get the directors to do so.

prejudices their interests or on the grounds that there was a material irregularity in its approval.

Although there are some statutory requirements as to what must be included in a CVA proposal, much is left to the company and its advisers to decide how to frame it. Its inherent flexibility is often seen as one of its strengths. Despite its flexible nature, there is some benefit to having workable precedents in circulation to allow for certainty, encourage use and to keep costs down. In an effort to encourage distressed SME companies to consider a CVA as a rescue mechanism, specifically in the aftermath of the pandemic but more generally as well, R3 (the Association of Business Recovery Professionals) has drafted Standard Terms and Conditions for an SME CVA which it has kindly agreed to have replicated in this publication (see the Appendix at the end of the book). As we will see, in order to understand how CVAs work in practice, it is useful to understand the contractual terms commonly found within them. The R3 Standard Terms and Conditions are a useful tool in drafting and understanding how CVAs work. **1.032**

5. Moratorium

It has long been thought that a CVA would benefit from the company being able to enter first into a moratorium on creditor actions, thus providing the company with a breathing space in which to put its proposal together and to request the creditors' approval. Although it has been possible since the 1986 Act came into force, and remains possible, for a company first to enter administration and take advantage of the moratorium[39] which is the hallmark of administration, this use of the two procedures in tandem is relatively rare in practice.[40] This is partly due to the ability of many companies to negotiate a short standstill agreement with their creditors informally and partly due to the expense of entering both administration and a CVA. It is often seen as prohibitively expensive to pay the fees and costs of both processes, especially for SME companies. **1.033**

A bespoke CVA-specific moratorium was introduced by the Insolvency Act 2000 and brought into force as Schedule A1 to the 1986 Act. It was rarely used in practice and became effectively a dead letter by the time it was abolished by CIGA 2020. It has been replaced by a more general standalone Moratorium **1.034**

---

39 Insolvency Act 1986, Sch B1, paras 42 and 43.

40 See P Walton, C Umfreville and L Jacobs, *Company Voluntary Arrangements: Evaluating Success and Failure* (May 2018).

under Part A1 of the 1986 Act which may be used, and is being used, as a precursor to a CVA (or other rescue attempt). The Part A1 Moratorium is considered below in Chapter 3.

C. LEGAL NATURE OF A CVA

1.035 A CVA is clearly an agreement between a company and its creditors. The exact nature of it has been described a number of times by the courts, but no single definitive explanation of its nature has yet been made. Relevant case law includes both cases considering CVAs and decisions on IVAs, as the basis for both types of arrangement is essentially the same. Voluntary arrangements have been variously called a contract, a trust and a statutory binding. The binding of a whole class (usually the unsecured creditors) to a contractual arrangement by the vote of only part of the class (a 75 per cent majority is needed), without the need for a court order, has been referred to as 'statutory magic'.[41] Previous types of formal agreements by a debtor with their creditors, such as under the Deeds of Arrangement Act 1914, were accepted as contractual in nature even though the party who held the assets subject to the deed and who carried out the terms of the deed was labelled the trustee.[42]

1.036 A starting point for our discussion might be *Re McKeen*[43] which concerned the effect of a bankruptcy order on a pre-existing IVA. The petition had been brought by a creditor not bound by the IVA. Morritt J decided that the IVA survived the bankruptcy order. The creditors who were parties to the IVA were 'bound by a contract imposed under statute'.[44] As the IVA had not provided for its termination in the event of bankruptcy, the matter fell to be decided upon the construction of the Act. The Act was silent as to the fate of an IVA in this situation. A bankrupt's estate was subject to the rights any other person had in the property comprising the estate. The trustee in bankruptcy held the bankrupt's estate subject to the rights of the creditors under the IVA. Morritt J regarded the IVA as taking effect as a form of statutory contract where there was 'no restriction on the proposals which a debtor may put forward to his creditors'.[45] There was freedom of contract to include any provision; for example, the creditors may agree to a provision which excludes them from sharing

41 *Narandas-Girdhar v Bradstock* [2016] 1 WLR 2366 at [35] per Briggs LJ.
42 Cork Report at [144].
43 [1995] BCC 412.
44 Ibid., at 416.
45 Ibid., at 415.

in any property acquired after the date of the IVA. There was no mention in the arrangement itself that the supervisor was to hold property on trust for the creditors. The terms of the IVA provided for the assets comprised in the arrangement to be applied for the benefit of the creditors bound by the IVA. Their rights under the IVA were contractual and bound the subsequent trustee in bankruptcy.

Slightly different language was used in *RA Securities Ltd v Mercantile Credit Co Ltd*[46] by Jacob J, who referred to the CVA as a 'statutory binding' rather than a statutory contract. It is not entirely clear whether there is any practical difference between the two phrases. His Lordship utilised privity of contract principles to decide who may claim benefit from a CVA and who may not. Consistent with this approach, in *Burford Midland Properties Ltd v Marley Extrusions Ltd*[47] His Honour Judge Roger Cooke construed the CVA 'like any other commercial agreement',[48] which suggests a contractual approach to construction. 1.037

The language of trust rather than contract was used in *Re Leisure Study Group Ltd*.[49] The case involved a company subject to a CVA entering into administrative receivership. The receiver claimed to be entitled to funds held by the CVA supervisor. The terms of the arrangement provided for the company to make monthly payments to the supervisor with a distribution to be made to the creditors every three months. Harman J rejected the receiver's claim. His Lordship analysed the wording of section 1(2) of the Insolvency Act 1986 ('the Act') which defined a proposal for a voluntary arrangement to be one which provided for an insolvency practitioner 'to act in relation to a voluntary arrangement either as trustee or otherwise for the purpose of supervising its implementation'. His Lordship considered that the term 'trustee' was the most obvious and most appropriate word to use to describe what the supervisor was doing. He was holding the legal title to property on behalf of the creditors bound by the arrangement who were beneficially entitled to the property. Consequently, the company in receivership had no claim on such money. The trusts of the CVA had priority. 1.038

The decision in *Re Bradley-Hole*[50] also adopted the terminology of the trust. The terms of the IVA provided that the whole of the debtor's assets, along 1.039

46 [1994] BCC 598.
47 [1994] BCC 604.
48 Ibid., at 611.
49 [1994] 2 BCLC 65.
50 [1995] 1 WLR 1097.

with the net profits from his trading as the landlord of a public house, were to be available for the benefit of his creditors. The debtor was made bankrupt on the basis of debts incurred after the date of the IVA. The main issue before the court was whether or not the IVA had been terminated by the bankruptcy order. Rimer J accepted that the nature of the IVA was a statutory contract between the debtor and the creditors bound by the IVA. Under the terms of the arrangement, the supervisor held the assets on trust for the IVA creditors. The creditors, as beneficiaries, could compel performance of the terms of the arrangement.

1.040 In *Davis v Martin-Sklan*,[51] Blackburne J explained that the approval of the arrangement gave rise to a species of statutory contract binding the debtor and the creditors. His Lordship also referred to the trusts upon which the supervisor held money subject to the arrangement, even though there was no express provision in the arrangement declaring that the money was to be held on trust.

1.041 In *Re Halson Packaging Ltd*[52] the court had to consider the effect on funds held by the supervisors of a CVA of the company entering creditors' voluntary liquidation. The terms of the arrangement provided for the company to make monthly payments to the supervisors who would distribute the money to the creditors. The cessation of business and liquidation of the company necessarily brought the arrangement to an end in the sense that there could be no further payments made to the supervisors. Judge Maddocks decided that the CVA had expressly created a trust of the funds in favour of the creditors. There was no provision terminating this trust in the event of liquidation and so the CVA continued with regard to the assets still held by the supervisors. The trust was expressly created by the terms of the CVA. Judge Maddocks described the effect of the CVA as a contract between the creditors, and as between the creditors as a class, and the company. Absent any overriding reasons not to do so, the terms of the contract would be given effect and so the money held by the supervisors remained subject to the trust in favour of the CVA creditors and could not be claimed by the liquidator.

1.042 To similar effect the company in *Re Arthur Rathbone Kitchens Ltd*[53] entered into a CVA but was unable to keep up the monthly payments required by its terms and entered liquidation. Judge Roger Kaye QC found that although there was no express provision creating a trust of the assets in the supervisor's

51 [1995] BCC 1122.
52 [1997] BCC 993.
53 [1998] BCC 450.

hands, it was clear on construction of its terms that the CVA imposed a trust on the supervisor to deal with funds received according to the terms of the CVA.

The case law arguably appears to contain some inconsistencies of approach. Sometimes the voluntary arrangement is described as a form of statutory contract and at other times a trust or statutory binding.[54] The answer to this potential conundrum is to be found in the courts' consistency of approach in each case of construing the wording of the Act and the arrangement itself. **1.043**

The nature of a voluntary arrangement was largely settled by the Court of Appeal in *Johnson v Davies*.[55] The case involved an IVA which compromised, amongst other debts, a liability for rent. The debtor's co-debtors for that liability claimed that the release of the debtor under the IVA also released them from liability. They argued that the release of one co-debtor released all. The Court of Appeal, in a detailed account of the law relating to statutory debtor arrangements from the nineteenth century, decided upon a contractual approach. Under previous statutory forms of debt arrangements, there were clear provisions expressly stating that co-debtors were not released. Under the voluntary arrangement regime, things had changed. The answer in any particular case depended only upon a construction of the terms of the voluntary arrangement, which was referred to as a 'statutory hypothesis'. It had to be construed as if it were a 'consensual agreement' between the debtor and all the creditors bound by it. The terms of the IVA in question did not release the co-debtors (which it might have provided for[56]). In explaining the concept of a voluntary arrangement as a 'statutory hypothesis', Chadwick LJ explained that the statute: **1.044**

> does not purport, directly, to impose the arrangement on a dissenting creditor whether or not he has agreed to its terms; rather, he is bound by the arrangement as the result of a statutory hypothesis. The statutory hypothesis requires him to be treated as if he had consented to the arrangement.[57]

54 See also, e.g., *Re Zebra Industrial Projects Ltd* [2004] EWHC 549 (Ch), [2005] BPIR 1022, *Welburn v Dibb Lupton Broomhead* [2002] EWCA Civ 1601, [2003] BPIR 768 and *Welsby v Brelec Installations Ltd* [2000] 2 BCLC 576.

55 [1999] Ch 117.

56 Although, as will be seen in Chapter 2, such a clause would be subject to attack as unfairly prejudicial to the creditor.

57 [1999] Ch 117 at 129H.

1.045 In considering any knock-on effects on co-debtors, his Lordship continued:

> The consequence, as it seems to me, is that the legislature must be taken to have intended that both the question whether the debtor is discharged by the arrangement and the question whether co-debtors and sureties are discharged by the arrangement were to be answered by treating the arrangement as consensual; that is to say, by construing its terms as if they were the terms of a consensual agreement between the debtor and all those creditors who, under the statutory hypothesis, must be treated as being consenting parties.[58]

1.046 The wording of the Act states that the effect of approval of the arrangement is that it binds every person entitled to vote as if they were a party to the arrangement.[59] This has been recognised as the language of contract and results in the courts construing the terms of the arrangements as contracts. A voluntary arrangement is not a voluntary contract in that parties can be bound by an arrangement even if they do not approve its terms. This point led Jacob J in *RA Securities* to regard a voluntary arrangement as a statutory binding rather than a contract as it does not have all the consequences of a voluntary contract. Other judges seem content to call it a 'statutory contract' or an agreement which operates by analogy with a contract between the debtor and their creditors[60] which by definition distinguishes it from voluntary contracts. The 'statutory hypothesis,' whereby the court adopts a contractual analysis to interpreting voluntary arrangements, makes it unnecessary and inappropriate to consider any of the usual principles of contract formation.[61]

1.047 In *Tanner v Everitt*[62] Mann J observed that a voluntary arrangement 'is therefore contractually based, with the statute providing the consent or deemed consent of the otherwise dissenting parties'.[63] It is not based upon the actual consent of creditors (as a number of creditors may in fact dissent) and so is based upon deemed consent under the statutory mechanism. Although it is to be interpreted using contractual principles, it is not subject to all the rules of contract law such as offer, acceptance and consideration.[64]

1.048 The approach in *Johnson v Davies* as to the nature of a voluntary arrangement was further explained by Etherton J in the context of a CVA:[65]

---

58 Ibid., at 138B–D.

59 Subsections 5(2) (CVAs) and 260(2) (IVAs).

60 *Lloyds Bank plc v Ellicott* [2002] EWCA Civ 1333, [2003] BPIR 632.

61 *Re SHB Realisations Ltd* [2018] EWHC 402 (Ch), [2018] BPIR 818.

62 [2004] EWHC 1130 (Ch).

63 Ibid., at [71].

64 See, in particular the explanation in *Re SHB Realisations Ltd* [2018] EWHC 402 (Ch), [2018] BPIR 818 at [28]–[29].

65 *Prudential Assurance Company Ltd v PRG Powerhouse Ltd* [2007] EWHC 1002 (Ch).

> The hypothetical agreement is a bilateral agreement between each creditor and the company. Section 1(1) of the IA refers to the intention to make a proposal 'to the company and *its* creditors for a composition in satisfaction of *its* debts or a scheme of arrangement of *its* affairs' ...
>
> In short, each creditor is a party to the arrangement by virtue of being, and in the capacity of, a creditor of the company. It is the company and not any third party which has the benefit of and can enforce the rights and obligations conferred by the CVA. This interpretation of the statutory provisions is supported by the case law.'[66]

His Honour Judge Simon Barker QC commented in *Re Rhino Enterprises Properties Ltd*:[67] 'at most, CVAs are a form of quasi-contract, for some purposes seemingly or apparently treated as if contracts, but in fact in all cases not actual contracts.'[68] **1.049**

On the basis of this reasoning, the learned judge concluded that a CVA was not a contract for the purposes of the Contract (Rights of Third Parties) Act 1999. Although a CVA has contractual effect, it is not a normal contract and so not every principle of contract law applies to it.[69] **1.050**

Often the terms of the voluntary arrangement provide either expressly or by implication[70] for the supervisor to hold assets under the arrangement on trust for the creditors.[71] In the absence of any such express or implied provision, Harman J in *Leisure Study* construed section 1(2) of the Act as leading prima facie to a conclusion that the supervisor is acting in relation to the voluntary arrangement as trustee. The subsection refers to the insolvency practitioner acting in relation to the arrangement 'as trustee or otherwise for the purpose of supervising its implementation'. **1.051**

Although the supervisor may act as a trustee, the Act expressly recognises the possibility that they may also act in some other capacity for the purpose of supervising the voluntary arrangement. Under rules 2.39 and 8.25 of the Insolvency (England and Wales) Rules 2016,[72] after the approval of a voluntary arrangement, the company and the debtor respectively must 'do all that is required to put the supervisor in possession of the assets included' in the **1.052**

---

66 Ibid., at [46]–[47].

67 [2020] EWHC 2370 (Ch).

68 Ibid., at [84].

69 See also *Re SHB Realisations Ltd* [2018] EWHC 402 (Ch), [2018] BPIR 818, where this reasoning led the court to conclude that the law of penalties did not apply to CVAs.

70 See, e.g., *Re Arthur Rathbone Kitchens Ltd* [1998] BCC 450.

71 See, e.g., the IVA case, *Green v Wright* [2017] EWCA Civ 111, [2017] BPIR 430, where the Court of Appeal decided that the debtor's historic PPI claims, which were realised after the successful completion of the IVA, were still subject to the trust created by the IVA, years after the completion of the IVA.

72 SI 2016/1024.

arrangement. Putting the supervisor into possession is not the same as transferring title to hold on trust for the creditors. It is therefore clearly possible, depending on the terms of the arrangement, for the supervisor to be controlling the debtor's assets without necessarily being constituted as legal (or equitable) owner and trustee. This would seem to be the situation in *Re McKeen* where Morritt J recognised the IVA creditors' contractual rights as surviving the bankruptcy order even though there was no trust of the IVA assets in their favour. Although it is usually the case that the supervisor will hold on trust for the creditors, it is not necessarily so and the issue will be dependent upon the construction of the arrangement and the statutory provisions.

1.053 The responsibilities of a supervisor under a voluntary arrangement can be seen as purely contractual and statutory in nature. The supervisor's functions are to carry out the terms of the arrangement and to satisfy the provisions of the Act. If they breach the terms of the statutory contract, remedies are available under the Act. There will be no private law action available for breach of contract, breach of trust or negligence.[73] The supervisor's responsibilities range no wider than the terms of the arrangement and the Act. An aggrieved creditor (or other party with locus) must use the remedies available under section 6 of the Act.[74] The CVA is a creature of statute and remedies for breach lie in the statute.

73 *King v Anthony* [1997] BPIR 24 and *Irvine v Duff & Phelps Ltd* [2019] EWHC 2780 (Ch).

74 See, e.g., *Re Paramount Licensing Inc* [2024] EWHC 3287 (Ch) where the court, in ordering the supervisor to issue a certificate of termination under the terms of the CVA, was critical of the supervisor's conduct in failing to comply with their obligations under the CVA.

2

ENTERING INTO A CVA

A. INTRODUCTION

2.001 In this chapter, we examine the process involved in the entry of a company into a CVA. Until its revocation by the Corporate Insolvency and Governance Act 2020 ('CIGA'), a company that fell within certain criteria and was known as 'an eligible company' was able to benefit from a moratorium while a CVA proposal was being formulated. The CIGA repealed this option and introduced a new standalone Moratorium, to be known as a Part A1 Moratorium, which could be accessed by any company. Thus, any company may enter a moratorium process while a CVA proposal is being formulated. The situation that existed with moratoriums both before the enactment of the CIGA and that has existed since the CIGA was introduced is discussed in detail in the next chapter. As mentioned above, this chapter focuses on the process that must be followed for entry into a CVA and this will apply, post-CIGA, to all proposals whether or not a Moratorium has preceded the CVA process being put into effect.

2.002 Initially, the chapter considers in depth the nature of a proposal and what proposals can be put before the creditors and which can become a CVA if approved, the preparation of proposals and what a proposal must contain as well as what might be prudent or appropriate to insert in a proposal. Secondly, the chapter examines how a proposal can be initiated and by whom. Thirdly, there is a discussion of the nominee, who is the person who will endeavour to structure an arrangement that will be capable of achieving the necessary statutory majorities and will not be unfairly prejudicial to any creditor. Next, there is an examination of the meeting and decision procedure process. This involves a consideration, among other things, of the procedure, the role of a chair or convener, proxies, adjournments, modifications to proposals and, most importantly, issues relating to voting and voting rights. This is followed by a part that examines which creditors are protected from a CVA and the aftermath of any approval of a CVA, including consideration of who is bound by a CVA. The final primary part of the chapter analyses the challenges that might be initiated in respect of an approved proposal for a CVA, and it includes an examination of the powers that courts have when hearing any challenges.

2.003 Before commencing the chapter in depth, we should note that a qualified insolvency practitioner will be involved in different roles in relation to a CVA. These roles include, for the most part, providing initial advice, assisting in the preparation of the proposal to be put to creditors, discussing the debtor company's position with creditors, acting as the nominee and acting as the supervisor. It is important that practitioners differentiate clearly between the roles that they are playing and ensure that their roles are explained to the company's directors (where they are making the proposal), shareholders and creditors.[1]

Statement of Insolvency Practice ('SIP') 3.2 makes it clear that an insolvency practitioner must act professionally and with objectivity in all of the roles that he or she is playing. The SIP points out that any failure in this respect on the part of the insolvency practitioner 'may prejudice the interests of both the company and creditors and is likely to bring the practitioner and the profession into disrepute'.[2] If the insolvency practitioner or his or her firm has provided advice of an auditing nature or any other advice to the company or any of its directors or principal shareholders, he or she should not act in relation to the proposing of a CVA. **2.004**

B. THE PROPOSAL

1. Introduction

If a company is considering whether to propose a CVA to its creditors, it might be wise for it to secure a Part A1 Moratorium first so that it gives the company 'breathing space', as no insolvency or legal proceedings can then be taken against the company while it is in the process of formulating a proposal and then having it voted on. Another option, and the only viable one for companies that were not eligible for a moratorium pursuant to the now repealed section 1A of the Insolvency Act 1986 ('the Act'), is for a company to take the company into administration and for a CVA to be arranged by the administrator while the company has the benefit of the moratorium that automatically comes into effect when a company enters administration.[3] **2.005**

Often, legal proceedings are not likely to be commenced by creditors, as any CVA that is proposed will produce a better result than if the company had to enter insolvent liquidation. Thus, a significant number of CVAs have been successfully achieved with the assistance of insolvency practitioners as nominees, by persuading the creditors of the commercial case for such an arrangement and having the creditors to agree to withhold any enforcement action in the interim. **2.006**

1 Statement of Insolvency Practice ('SIP') 3.2 (Company Voluntary Arrangements), para 3.
2 Paragraph 4.
3 Insolvency Act 1986, Sch B1, paras 42 and 43.

2.007 A company might already have the benefit from a moratorium as it is either in liquidation or, more likely, in administration when the idea of a CVA is considered.

2.008 Often, before a company decides to propose a CVA, an insolvency practitioner may be asked to provide advice to the directors concerning CVAs and what form a CVA might take in the company's circumstances. The insolvency practitioner, once he or she has established that the company is in financial difficulties that need addressing, will need to consider whether the company may be able to be rescued. SIP 3.2 provides that the insolvency practitioner: 'should ensure that information and explanations about all the options available are provided to the directors, so that they can make an informed judgement as to whether a CVA is an appropriate solution for the company.'[4] Paragraph 5 of the SIP indicates that an insolvency practitioner should have: 'procedures in place to ensure that the information and explanations provided to the company and/or the directors at each stage of the process, as appropriate (that is, assessing the options available, and then preparing and implementing a CVA), are designed to set out clearly' and the paragraph goes on to set out the issues which an insolvency practitioner should address.

2.009 It should be borne in mind before constructing the proposal that the company should consider that there might be a need to change the proposal during the course of the arrangement if it is approved.

2. The essence of the proposal

2.010 The legislation permits a CVA to be proposed either during an administration or liquidation by the administrator[5] or the liquidator[6] respectively. It is highly unlikely that a CVA will be proposed by a liquidator as, among other things, most companies in such a situation would not be a good proposition to be restructured using a CVA or at all. Where a creditor's winding-up petition is pending, it may be possible for the directors to obtain from the court an adjournment of the hearing of the petition for a reasonable period to allow them to propose a voluntary arrangement. Nevertheless, Lloyd J stated in *Judd v Williams*,[7] when referring to an individual voluntary arrangement and bankruptcy, this being equivalent to a CVA and liquidation, that:

---

4 Paragraph 5.
5 Insolvency Act 1986, s 1(3)(a).
6 Ibid., s 1(3)(b).
7 [1998] BPIR 88.

> it seems to me that the prima facie right of the creditor to a bankruptcy order is one to which the court must give effect and that the practice of repeated adjournments, however understandable it may be in mercy to the debtor, is one which has profoundly unsatisfactory consequences. As a matter of policy it is unjustifiable in that, as Miss Johnston submits, it has the effect of an ad hoc imposed voluntary arrangement which could never be achieved if it were proposed directly under the relevant provisions of the Insolvency Act.[8]

Although administrators are under a duty to consider mechanisms for rescuing the company, in practice, research undertaken in the first few years following the enactment of legislation which permitted the commencement of administration extra-judicially, indicated that such rescue attempts occur in fewer than 10 per cent of administrations.[9] There is nothing to suggest that that has not continued to be the case. Administrators appear to favour a sale as a going concern of the company's business rather than a rescue of the company itself. An administrator can then distribute the proceeds of sale to the creditors.[10] It may often be easier and quicker for a company to enter into a pre-pack administration than to negotiate a CVA with its creditors (with or without a Moratorium). **2.011**

Also, and most frequently, a CVA may, where there is no liquidation or administration, be proposed by the directors where the company is not in administration or liquidation.[11] The directors can take such action if the company is subject to a Part A1 Moratorium or not subject to such a Moratorium procedure. **2.012**

According to section 1(1) of the Act, a proposal for a CVA must either be a composition in satisfaction of its debts or a scheme of arrangement of its affairs. If a proposal cannot be considered as either a composition or an arrangement, then it is a nullity. The proposal is not able to be saved even if modifications are introduced during the decision procedure and the creditors support such modifications.[12] **2.013**

A composition is an arrangement to pay a sum in lieu of a larger debt or other obligation, and when a debt is compounded, the forbearance to sue for the full amount of the debt is in exchange for a money payment or other consideration. It is an agreement between the debtor and all (or some) of the creditors **2.014**

8 Ibid., 94.

9 See A Katz and M Mumford, *Study of Administration Cases – Report to the Insolvency Service* (2006).

10 See Sch B1, para 65. Also, see *Re GHE Realisations Ltd* [2005] EWHC 2400 (Ch), [2006] 1 All ER 357.

11 Insolvency Act 1986, s 1(1).

12 *Commissioners of Inland Revenue v Bland* [2003] BPIR 1274, an individual voluntary arrangement ('IVA') case. In this case, the proposal was neither a composition nor an arrangement.

by which the creditors agree with the debtor, and, expressly or impliedly, with each other, to accept from the debtor payment of less than the amounts due to them in full satisfaction of the whole of their claims.[13] In contrast, a scheme of arrangement involves something less than the release or discharge of creditor debts.[14] This might include a moratorium[15] on the enforcement of creditor claims. For example, in *Inland Revenue Commissioners v Adam & Partners Ltd*[16] the Court of Appeal said a moratorium on the prosecution of claims for three years was valid as an arrangement, and this was even though no dividend was to be paid to any creditor under the CVA. The Court made the point that there was nothing to stop creditors from enforcing their claims after the expiration of the three years.[17] A scheme could also involve a debt-for-equity swap, that is where the creditors swap their claims against the company for interests in the company. A proposal does not cease to be a CVA within the terms of section 1 of the Act merely because it purports to affect the rights of third parties.[18] It has been held that a CVA does not constitute an 'agreement' for the purposes of section 203 of the Employment Rights Act 1996.[19]

2.015 The proposal must provide for its implementation under the supervision of a qualified insolvency practitioner ('the nominee'), either as trustee or otherwise.[20] The nominee must be a person qualified to act as an insolvency practitioner or authorised to act as nominee/supervisor in relation to the company. A nominee may be the liquidator or the administrator where the proposal is made by the liquidator or administrator respectively. Where the company is being wound up by the court, the liquidator must give notice of the proposal and the name and address of the nominee (if the nominee is not the liquidator) to the Official Receiver.[21]

2.016 The nominee will most frequently become the supervisor of a CVA and in that role will oversee the CVA's execution. The nominee is not granted powers relating to the operation and management of the company or the assets of the company. Normally, the person identified as the nominee will undertake a significant role in assisting the directors of the company in compiling the

13 *Inland Revenue Commissioners v Adam & Partners Ltd* [2001] 1 BCLC 222, [39].
14 *March Estates plc v Gunmark* [1996] 2 BCLC 1, 5; *Inland Revenue Commissioners v Adam & Partners Ltd* ibid., [40].
15 *March Estates plc* ibid.
16 *Inland Revenue Commissioners v Adam & Partners Ltd* (n 13).
17 Ibid., [43].
18 *SISU Capital Fund Ltd v Tucker* [2005] EWHC 2170 (Ch), [2006] BPIR 154.
19 *Re Britannia Heat Transfer Ltd* [2007] BCC 470, [2007] BPIR 1038.
20 Insolvency Act 1986, s 1(2).
21 Insolvency Rules 2016, r 2.5.

proposal, but nevertheless, the proposal is that of the directors (or the liquidator or administrator if proposing the CVA). The nominee is not the agent of the debtor company,[22] and the nominee must remain objective at all times. In particular, the nominee must be objective in relation to the report that he or she must file with the court concerning the proposal. In carrying out this task, it is critical that nominees maintain an independent stance, act in good faith, and only propose a CVA if they are satisfied that it will not unfairly prejudice the rights of any creditor, member or contributory of the company.[23]

Harman J in *Re A Debtor (No 222 of 1990) ex parte Bank of Ireland (No 2)*[24] summarised aspects of the nominee's role in undertaking completion of the report and as acting as chair: **2.017**

> In my judgment, the nominee both in making his report and in acting as chairman of the meeting is to be taken as having a duty (arising from the requirement in the statute that he shall report his own opinion to the court) to exercise a professional independent judgment. The fact that judgment is required to be that of a licensed insolvency practitioner emphasises the fact that the court is to receive a report from a qualified person skilled and experienced in these matters, who is exercising his own professional functions in judging whether the matter is, in his opinion, fit to go forward.[25]

R3, the trade association for the UK's insolvency and restructuring professionals, has prepared a standard form for a Proposal and may form the basis for a proposal.[26] **2.018**

3. The mandatory contents of a proposal

(a) Introduction

In broad terms, rule 2.2(1) of the Insolvency Rules 2016 ('the Rules') provides that a proposal must include identification details for the company, explain why the proposer thinks a CVA is desirable, indicate why the creditors are expected to agree to a CVA and be authenticated and dated by the proposer. According to rule 2.2(2), a proposal may only be amended, with the nominee's agreement in writing, in two situations. First, the nominee is not the **2.019**

22 *Re A Debtor (No 222 of 1990) ex parte Bank of Ireland (No 2)* [1993] BCLC 233, 235.

23 *Mourant & Co Trustees Ltd v Sixty UK Ltd (in liq)* [2010] EWHC 1890 (Ch), [2010] BPIR 1264, [2011] 1 BCLC 383, [88].

24 *Re A Debtor (No 222 of 1990) ex parte Bank of Ireland (No 2)* (n 22).

25 Ibid., 234.

26 *Standard Form Covid 19 CVA Proposal*, October 2021 and available at: https://www.r3.org.uk/technical-library/england-wales/technical-guidance/r3-standard-form-covid-19-cva-proposal/.

liquidator or administrator of the company.[27] Secondly, the nominee's report has not been filed with the court under section 2(2) of the Act.

2.020 In the proposal, creditors would normally require reasonably detailed and credible financial information concerning the company's affairs, as well as a realistic assessment of the company's future and its ability to satisfy its obligations under the proposal. Creditors will often need sufficient information to understand the company's financial and trading history.

2.021 The contents of the proposal must comply with the mandatory requirements of rule 2.3.

(b) Assets

2.022 The proposal must set out the company's assets, with an estimate of their respective values, identify which assets are charged and state the extent of the charge, which assets are to be excluded from the CVA and particulars of any property to be included in the CVA that is not owned by the company, including details of who owns such property, and the terms on which it will be available for inclusion.[28]

(c) Liabilities

2.023 The proposal is required to state the nature and amount of the company's liabilities, how the company's liabilities will be met, modified, postponed or otherwise dealt with by means of the CVA and, in particular how preferential creditors and creditors who are, or claim to be, secured will be dealt with, and how creditors who are connected with the company will be dealt with if the company is not in administration or liquidation. It should also should state whether, if the company did in fact go into administration or liquidation, there are circumstances which might give rise to claims under section 238 (transactions at an undervalue), section 239 (preferences), section 244 (extortionate credit transactions) or section 245 (floating charges invalid), and where there are circumstances that might give rise to such claims, whether, and if so what, provision will be made to indemnify the company in respect of them.[29]

27 Insolvency Rules 2016, r 2.2(3).
28 Ibid., r 2.3(1)(a)–(d).
29 Ibid., r 2.3(1)(e)–(f).

(d) Nominee's fees and expenses

The proposal must specify the amount proposed to be paid to the nominee by way of fees and expenses.[30] The Act does not specify how nominees are to be remunerated and how their costs, expenses and disbursements are to be covered. Rule 2.43 provides that the fees and expenses that may be incurred for the purposes of the CVA are: fees for the nominee's services agreed with the company (or, as the case may be, the administrator or liquidator) and disbursements made by the nominee before the decision approving the CVA takes effect under section 4A;[31] fees or expenses which are sanctioned by the terms of the CVA, or where they are not sanctioned by the terms of the CVA would be payable, or correspond to those which would be payable, in an administration or winding up.[32] SIP 9 contains guidance notes on this subject, including recommendations as to the best practice. **2.024**

(e) Supervisor

The proposal is to include: identification and contact details for the supervisor; confirmation that the supervisor is qualified to act as an insolvency practitioner in relation to the company and the name of the relevant recognised professional body which is the source of the supervisor's authorisation; how the fees and expenses of the supervisor will be determined and paid (see (d) above and r 2.43); the functions to be performed by the supervisor; where it is proposed that two or more supervisors be appointed, a statement whether acts done in connection with the CVA may be done by any one or more of them or must be done by all of them.[33] **2.025**

Added to this, there is likely to be an indication as to whether the supervisor will only handle company money and act as a conduit for funds produced by the company's business, and which is payable to creditors or whether he or she will be engaged in more than this. It is likely that a supervisor will require a specific provision which effectively excludes him or her from personal liability, such as personal liability for statutory offences.[34] **2.026**

30 Ibid., r 2.3(1)(g).
31 Ibid., r 2.43(a).
32 Ibid, r 2.43(b).
33 Ibid., r 2.3(1)(h)–(l).
34 Geoffrey Weisgard, Michael Griffiths and Louis Doyle, *Company Voluntary Arrangements and Administrations*, 3rd ed (LexisNexis, 2013), [5.34].

(f) Guarantees and proposed guarantees

2.027 The proposal needs to state whether any, and if so what, guarantees have been given in respect of the company's debts, specifying which of the guarantors are persons connected with the company, and whether any, and if so what, guarantees are proposed to be offered for the purposes of the CVA and, if so, by whom and whether security is to be given or sought.[35]

(g) Timing

2.028 The proposed duration of the CVA and the proposed dates of distributions to creditors, with estimates of their amounts, are to be stated in the proposal.[36] The arrangement may be expressed to be for a fixed period (and if the company does not fully comply with the terms within the period, the arrangement automatically, or upon the issue by the supervisor of a certificate of default, comes to an end), or to continue until such times as certain specified results are achieved. Power may be given to the supervisor and/or the creditors to extend the fixed period in certain situations. This power can normally only be exercised before the expiration of any fixed period specified in the terms of the CVA.[37]

(h) Type of proceedings

2.029 The proposal must state whether the proceedings will be COMI proceedings, establishment proceedings or proceedings to which the EU Regulation as it has effect in the law of the United Kingdom does not apply, with reasons.[38]

(i) Conduct of the business

2.030 How the business of the company will be conducted during the CVA must be explained in the proposal.[39]

(j) Further credit facilities

2.031 The proposal must give details of any further proposed credit facilities to be provided for the company, and how the debts so arising are to be paid.[40]

---

35 Insolvency Rules 2016, r 2.3(1)(m)–(n).
36 Ibid., r 2.3(1)(o)–(p).
37 *Strongmaster Ltd v Kaye* [2002] EWHC 444, [2002] BPIR 1259, 1262.
38 Insolvency Rules 2016, r 2.3(1)(q).
39 Ibid., r 2.3(1)(r).
40 Ibid., r 2.3(1)(s).

(k) Handling of funds arising

The proposal must provide: details concerning the manner in which funds held for the purposes of the CVA are to be banked, invested or otherwise dealt with pending distribution to creditors; how funds held for the purpose of payment to creditors, and not paid to creditors on the termination of the CVA, will be dealt with; how the claim of any person bound by the CVA by virtue of section 5(2)(b)(ii) will be dealt with.[41] It has been suggested that the proposal includes a provision: **2.032**

> to the effect that if any payment due to any creditor remains unclaimed for a period of (say) six months, it will revert to the company or its liquidator or administrator (as the case may be) but, whilst the arrangement is still in force, will be regarded as part of the assets comprised in the arrangement and may be invested in an interest-bearing account.[42]

(l) Moratorium

Whether a Moratorium is, or has been, in force for the company under Part A1 of the Act is to be stated as well as the date that the Moratorium came into force and (if applicable), the date it ended.[43] **2.033**

Besides the above, the proposal must contain any other matters that the proposer considers appropriate to enable members and creditors to reach an informed decision on the proposal.[44] **2.034**

(m) Details about the prescribed part

Where the proposal is made by the directors, an estimate, so far as known to them, of the value of the prescribed part (under s 176A) if the proposal for the CVA is not accepted and the company goes into liquidation (whether or not the liquidator might be required under section 176A to make the prescribed part available for the satisfaction of unsecured debts), and the value of the company's net property on the date that the estimate is made, must be given.[45] Where the proposal is made by the administrator or liquidator, the following, so far as known to the office-holder, must be included in the proposal: an estimate of the value of the prescribed part (whether or not the administrator or liquidator might be required under s 176A to make the prescribed part available for the satisfaction of unsecured debts); the value of the **2.035**

41 Ibid., r 2.3(1)(t)–(v).
42 Jeremy Kutner (ed), *Tolley's Company Law* (Lexis, 2023), [I6039].
43 Insolvency Rules 2016, r 2.3(1)(va).
44 Ibid., r 2.3(1)(x).
45 Ibid., r 2.3(2).

company's net property (as defined by s 176A(6));[46] a statement as to whether the administrator or liquidator proposes to make an application to the court under section 176A(5) and if so, the reasons for the application;[47] and details of the nature and amount of the company's preferential creditors.[48]

(n) Exclusion of information

2.036 Information may be excluded from an estimate of the value of the prescribed part (under s 176A) pursuant to either rule 2.3(2) or rule 2.3(3)(a) of the Rules if the inclusion of the information could seriously prejudice the commercial interests of the company.[49] If the exclusion of such information affects the calculation of the estimate, the proposal must include a statement to that effect.[50] Also, the nominee, the directors or any person appearing to the court to have an interest, may apply to the court for a direction that specified information be omitted from the statement of affairs as delivered to the creditors where disclosure of that information would be likely to prejudice the conduct of the CVA or might reasonably be expected to lead to violence against any person.[51]

4. Additional contents of the proposal

2.037 The matters which are required by rule 2.3 to be included in a proposal may not, obviously, cover everything that should be included to ensure that the proposal is comprehensive and addresses particularly critical issues. Other provisions may need to be inserted, depending on the positions taken by creditors and the company itself. Even full compliance with those guidelines may not be sufficient and may need to be added to or modified according to the circumstances of the case. The requirements in rule 2.3 are not meant to be exhaustive of what is included in the proposal. The following particular features of a proposal may need to be expressly addressed:[52]

(a) the roles of the directors and key employees and their future involvement in the company, including the background and financial history of the directors, where relevant;

---

46 Ibid., r 2.3(3)(a).
47 Ibid., r 2.3(3)(b).
48 Ibid., r 2.3(3)(c).
49 Ibid., r 2.3(4).
50 Ibid., r 2.3(5).
51 Ibid., r 2.7.
52 The following is taken from, or based on, para 15 of SIP 3.2 (which contains very useful guidelines as to the further information and provisions which the proposal should contain) and also draws upon Kutner (ed), *Tolley's Company Law* (n 42), [I6039].

(b) any additional specialist assistance which may be required by the company that will not be provided by any supervisor appointed, and the reason why such assistance may be necessary;
(c) any conditions that must be fulfilled before the arrangement comes into effect, such as the company entering into any particular transaction, should be stated;
(d) if the company has become, or is about to become, insolvent, why;
(e) in the situation where the company's business is continued by the existing management, an indication of the extent (if any) of the supervisor's management and/or monitoring role in relation to the business, and the provision of reliable management account and cash-flow projections. A provision might be made that empowers the company to carry on the existing business at market values;
(f) any other attempts that have been made to solve the company's financial difficulties, and the alternative options considered, both prior to and within formal insolvency by the company;
(g) if there is to be payment to the arrangement's creditor, wholly or partly from the proceeds of the sale of company assets that are not in the ordinary course of business, the company should be empowered to do so with accompanying constraints where appropriate;
(h) a comparison of the estimated outcomes of the CVA, and the outcome if the CVA is not approved;
(i) An indication that there are restrictions applied to creditors bound by the CVA from enforcing their rights, in respect of the debts due to them comprised in the proposal, against the company or its assets outside the CVA during the life of the arrangement, and only the supervisor is able to enforce any rights. Additionally, and related to this, the proposal might provide that upon premature termination the creditors are free to enforce immediately their full rights in respect of their full debts from which would be subtracted what they may have received under the arrangement;
(j) where relevant, sufficient information to support any profit and cash projections, although this is subject to any issues of commercial sensitivity;
(k) the proposal might include that all costs, expenses and liabilities properly incurred in or in connection with the putting into effect, or operation of, the arrangements and the conduct of the business are payable from arrangement assets, in priority to any sums payable to the creditors and to the supervisor in respect of their remuneration. The creditors will often require a limit on the costs that are incurred without creditor consent;
(l) an explanation of the role and powers of the supervisor. This could include a statement that while the supervisor is to exercise appropriate skill and judgement, he or she is protected against personal liability and is indemnified against any personal loss;
(m) details of any discussions that have taken place with key creditors;
(n) where it is proposed that certain creditors are to be treated differently, an explanation as to which creditors are affected, how and why, in a manner that aims to be clear and useful;
(o) an explanation of how debts are to be valued for voting purposes, in particular where the creditors include long-term or contingent liabilities;

(p) disclosure of the estimated costs of the CVA;
(q) the cost of any additional specialist assistance which will not be provided by any supervisor appointed;
(r) the identity of the source of any referral of the company to the nominee, the relationship or connection of the referrer to the company and, where any payment has been made or is proposed to the referrer, the amount and reason for that payment;
(s) details of the amounts and sources of payments, other than remuneration and expenses, made, or proposed to be made, to the nominee and the supervisor or their firms in connection, or otherwise, with the proposed CVA, directly or indirectly, and the reason(s) for the payment(s);
(t) provision for the admission of creditors for the purposes of participation in the distributions in the arrangement as opposed to voting, and it might be provided that the rules applicable to creditors' voluntary liquidation are applied;
(u) Inclusion of a provision that if there is any default by the company of its obligations under the CVA, or by any third party pursuant to the obligations, it has to fund, guarantee or provide security will not automatically terminate the arrangement and that termination is only by way of a certificate of default provided by the supervisor;
(v) an explanation of how debts, which it is proposed are compromised, will be treated should the CVA fail;
(w) the circumstances in which the CVA may fail and what constitutes a breach of the CVA;
(x) to include, to make it plain, whether the arrangement constitutes a trust over the assets of the company comprised in the arrangement, and who would be the trustee and beneficiaries thereunder;
(y) would the winding up of the company cause the premature termination of the CVA and whether such termination would end any trust over the scheme assets;
(z) whether, on the final payment under the CVA and the discharge of the liability of the company, co-debtors and sureties are also discharged;
(za) setting out what will happen to the company and any remaining assets subject to the CVA should the CVA fail;
(zb) a provision that upon the completion of the CVA, the supervisor must deliver a notice that the CVA has been fully implemented or terminated to all the members and those creditors who are bound by the arrangement. Additionally, it might be advisable to include a provision indicating that the supervisor will continue to possess all of his or her powers and functions under the proposal up to the point where it may be necessary to distribute the funds which the supervisor holds and address all outstanding matters in accordance with the CVA;
(zc) provision of a term that if the company fails to cooperate with the supervisor sufficiently, he or she may petition for a winding-up order;
(zd) it might be advisable, where there is a period in which, after the approval of the Proposal, there is a delay in the company re-commencing trading, to include a breathing-space period provision in the Proposal, that is, a provision which provides that the company will not be obliged to make any payments during

this period. The terms of R3's Proposal[53] provide for such a period. The period may begin from the time of the approval of the Proposal or at some other later point in time. This type of provision was obviously employed in the R3 Proposal to address the Covid pandemic, but it could be used outside of that, and where appropriate.

The Court of Appeal in *Cadbury Schweppes plc v Somji*[54] (dealing with an IVA) made it plain that a voluntary arrangement should be marked by 'complete transparency and good faith by the debtor',[55] and any proposed secret deals or confidential arrangements (for example, between a creditor and a third party for the creditor to vote for the arrangement in return for a payment from the third party of an amount larger than that which the creditor would receive under the voluntary arrangement) are 'as unacceptable today as they were in Victorian England'.[56] At first instance, the judge, whose decision was affirmed by the Court of Appeal, found that there had been a secret deal between the debtor and a creditor in order to influence the vote of two other creditors at the meeting called for approval of the proposal for an IVA, and that, if that fact had been known, it would have influenced the vote. A major creditor applied under section 262 of the Act (equivalent to s 6 for CVAs) for an order that the IVA be revoked on the basis that there was a material omission from the proposal presented to the creditors. Thus, it is critical that the proposal discloses any agreements that will affect the approval of the arrangement. **2.038**

The decision in *Cadbury Schweppes* might well suggest that where a secret deal or confidential arrangement is made following the date on which the proposal is sent to the creditors, and before the date of the creditors' meeting at which the proposal is approved, that arrangement should be disclosed at the approval meeting and before a vote is taken.[57] Failure to disclose such arrangements, that are material in that if the truth had been told it might well have made a material difference to the way in which the creditors would have considered and assessed the particular arrangement to which they were being invited to agree,[58] or it might well have made a material difference to the way in which the creditors would have considered and assessed the proposal, may result in a successful challenge by them under section 6 of the Act on either the ground **2.039**

53 Paragraph 4.2ff, *Standard Form Covid 19 CVA Proposal*, October 2021 and available at: https://www.r3.org.uk/technical-library/england-wales/technical-guidance/r3-standard-form-covid-19-cva-proposal/.

54 [2001] 1 WLR 615, [2001] 1 BCLC 498, [2001] BPIR 172.

55 Ibid., at [44] per Judge LJ.

56 Ibid., per Judge LJ.

57 Kutner (ed), *Tolley's Company Law* (n 42), [I6039].

58 *Re Tack* [2000] BPIR 164, 204.

of unfair prejudice or material irregularity on the one hand or the presentation of a winding-up order on the other.

2.040 The proposal needs to be formulated after taking into account the likely questions which creditors and their representatives might have.[59]

5. Restrictions on proposals

2.041 The Act and the Rules impose two major restrictions on a company's ability to enter into a proposal. First, under section 4(3) of the Act, neither the company nor the creditors are able to approve any proposal (or modification) which affects the rights of a secured creditor (within the meaning in section 248 of the Act) to enforce their security, except with the concurrence of the creditor concerned. It has been held that a landlord, with a right to forfeit, is not treated as a secured creditor for the purposes of section 4.[60] In *Thomas v Ken Thomas Ltd*[61] Neuberger LJ (as he then was) (with whom Mummery and Jacob LJJ agreed) said that: 'It does not seem as if the legislature intended a creditor with a right to forfeit should be treated in a different or better position under a CVA than any other sort of unsecured creditor.'[62]

2.042 Secondly, without the concurrence of the preferential creditor concerned, a proposal cannot be approved. Section 4(4) of the Act provides that neither the company nor the creditors are able to approve any proposal (or modification) under which: any preferential debt of the company is to be paid otherwise than in priority to such of its debts as are not preferential debts;[63] any ordinary preferential debt of the company is to be paid otherwise than in priority to any secondary preferential debts that it may have;[64] a preferential creditor of the company is to be paid an amount in respect of a preferential debt that bears to that debt a smaller proportion than is borne to another preferential debt by the amount that is to be paid in respect of that other debt;[65] a preferential creditor of the company is to be paid an amount in respect of a secondary preferential debt that bears to that debt a smaller proportion than is borne to another secondary preferential debt by the amount that is to be paid in respect of that other debt;[66] or in the case of a company which is a relevant financial

59 Weisgard et al., *Company Voluntary Arrangements and Administrations* (n 34), [5.1].
60 *Thomas v Ken Thomas Ltd* [2006] EWCA Civ 1504, [2007] BPIR 959, [43].
61 Ibid.
62 Ibid., [43].
63 Insolvency Act 1986, s 4(4)(a).
64 Ibid., s 4(4)(aa).
65 Ibid., s 4(4)(b).
66 Ibid., s 4(4)(c).

institution (see section 387A), any non-preferential debt is to be paid otherwise than in accordance with the rules in section 176AZA(2) or (3).[67]

2.043 In *Inland Revenue Commissioners v Wimbledon Football Club Ltd*[68] a company that ran a football club was under financial stress and it entered into an agreement to sell its undertaking, business and assets as a going concern. The agreement provided for the purchaser to pay all sums due to the company's 'football creditors'. These were the club's players, other clubs and the English Football League. If these creditors had not been paid, the English Football League would have been entitled to prevent the club (the company) participating further in the League. Some of the company's assets and some third-party funds paid to the company were the subject of a CVA, under which preferential creditors were expected to receive 30p in the pound. The Inland Revenue argued that this was in breach of section 4(4). This argument was rejected at first instance and on appeal. Neuberger LJ said that it was necessary to consider the commercial realities, which were that if the football creditors were not paid, then there would be no sale agreement involving a purchase of the business.[69] Participating in the League was a critical element of the business. His Lordship felt that it was important that the Revenue was benefitting from a third-party payment, which it could not usually expect.[70]

2.044 Section 387(2) provides that the relevant date for determining the existence and amount of a preferential debt (under Sch 6) is, in relation to a company which is not being wound up, where the company is in administration, the date on which the company entered administration, and where the company is not in administration, the date on which the voluntary arrangement takes effect. Section 387(3) provides the relevant date where the company is being wound up.

6. Winding-up petitions presented before approval of CVA

2.045 If a winding-up petition is presented and is heard before the approval of a CVA, the court may exercise its discretion and adjourn the hearing of the petition if it is convinced that there is a good chance that an arrangement can be put into effect. While an adjournment was denied and a bankruptcy order was

67 Ibid., s 4(4(d).
68 [2004] EWCA Civ 655, [2005] 1 BCLC 66, [2004] BPIR 700, [2004] BCC 638.
69 Ibid., [43].
70 Ibid., [53].

made in *CFL Finance Ltd v Bass*,[71] an earlier adjournment had been granted when there was evidence that an IVA was being proposed.

C. INITIATING THE PROPOSAL

2.046 As mentioned earlier, a proposal may be put to the creditors and members by the directors, or if the company is in liquidation, by the liquidator, or if the company is in administration, by the administrator. It is, naturally, critical that before the proposal is put forward and submitted to members and creditors, it is approved by the board of directors.

2.047 It should be noted that in *Inland Revenue Commissioners v Wimbledon Football Club Ltd*[72] it was said that a 'proposal' for the purposes of section 4 did not extend to an agreement or other understanding between a third party and some creditors, certainly in the situation where the money involved is not being advanced at the cost of the company.[73]

1. Proposals by the directors

2.048 Most frequently, the directors of the company will make the proposal for a CVA to the creditors on behalf of the company. In such a case, the directors should be able to provide trading and cash flow forecasts that indicate that any proposal formulated is viable.[74] The directors must submit to the proposed nominee, according to section 2(3), a document setting out the terms of the proposed voluntary arrangement and a statement of the company's affairs containing such particulars of its creditors and of its debts and other liabilities as may be prescribed, and such other information as may be prescribed. The practice is usually to deliver both the proposal and the statement of affairs together. As to what is to be included in the document providing for the terms of the proposed CVA, see rules 2(2) and 2(3).[75]

2.049 The proposal may be amended with the nominee's agreement and before the nominee's report has been filed with the court under section 2(2).[76]

71 [2019] EWHC 1839 (Ch), [2019] BPIR 1327.
72 [2004] EWCA Civ 655, [2005] 1 BCLC 66, [2004] BPIR 700, [2004] BCC 638.
73 Ibid., [59].
74 Weisgard et al., *Company Voluntary Arrangements and Administrations* (n 34), [2.12].
75 These provisions are discussed above at [2.021]–[2.036].
76 Insolvency Rules 2016, r 2.2.

The statement of affairs must contain the particulars set out in rule 2.6(1). These are: 2.050

(a) a list of the company's assets, divided into such categories as are appropriate for easy identification, and with each category given an estimated value;
(b) in the case of any property on which a claim against the company is wholly or partly secured, particulars of the claim, and of how and when the security was created;
(c) the names and addresses of the preferential creditors, with the amounts of their respective claims;
(d) the names and addresses of the unsecured creditors with the amounts of their respective claims;
(e) particulars of any debts owed by the company to persons connected with it;
(f) particulars of any debts owed to the company by persons connected with it;
(g) the names and addresses of the company's members, with details of their respective shareholdings; and
(h) any other particulars that the nominee, in writing, requires to be provided for the purposes of making the nominee's report on the proposal to the court.

The statement must be delivered to the nominee. 2.051

If a Moratorium under Part A1 of the Act is, or has been, in force for the company at any time within the period of 12 weeks ending with the day on which the statement of affairs is made up, the statement of affairs must, according to rule 2.6(1A)(1B), identify which of the debts owed by the company are 2.052

(a) Moratorium debts, and
(b) priority pre-Moratorium debts,

within the meaning given by section 174A; and 2.053

(c) rule 2.6(1)(c) has effect as if the reference to preferential creditors included references to Moratorium debts and priority pre-Moratorium debts within the meaning given by section 174A.

The statement of affairs must be made up to a date not earlier than two weeks before the date on which notice of the proposal is given to the nominee,[77] but the nominee may allow an extension of that period to the nearest practical date (not being earlier than two months before the date of notice to the nominee). If the nominee grants this extension, the nominee shall give their reasons for 2.054

77 Ibid., r 2.6(2).

doing so in their report to the court on the directors' proposal.[78] The statement of affairs must be verified by a statement of truth by at least one director.[79]

2.055 The proposal needs to be formulated after taking into account the likely questions which creditors and their representatives might have.[80]

2.056 Section 6A provides that it is an offence, punishable by imprisonment or fine or both, for a person being a past or present officer (including a shadow director) to make a false representation or commit any other fraud for the purpose of obtaining the approval of the company's members or creditors to a proposal for a voluntary arrangement.

2. Proposals by administrators

2.057 Where there is an administration, consideration may be given to a CVA as a way for the company to exit the administration. If a CVA is considered, the administrator is likely to be the proposed nominee.

2.058 Where the proposal is made by the administrator but provides for another insolvency practitioner to act as nominee, the administrator is to give notice to the intended nominee,[81] and prepare their proposal in the same manner as is required of the directors in the case of a proposal made by them. A statement of affairs conforming with rule 2.6 must be provided.

3. Proposals by liquidators

2.059 It would be most unusual to have a CVA proposed where the company is in liquidation, but it is possible.

2.060 Whether a liquidator is the nominee or another insolvency practitioner is the proposed nominee, the same rules apply as for a proposal by the administrator. There is an additional requirement in respect of a compulsory winding up, namely that the responsible insolvency practitioner must give notice of the proposal to the Official Receiver (with the name and address of the insolvency practitioner who has agreed to act as nominee where the liquidator is not the nominee).[82]

---

78 Ibid., r 2.6(3)(4).

79 Ibid., r 2.6(5)(6).

80 Weisgard et al., *Company Voluntary Arrangements and Administrations* (n 34), [5.1].

81 Insolvency Rules 2016, r 2.2.

82 Ibid., r 2.5.

D. THE NOMINEE

1. The role

Section 1(2) of the Act mandates that the proposal must provide for some person, known as 'the nominee', to act in relation to the voluntary arrangement either as trustee or otherwise for the purposes of supervising its implementation. 2.061

The nominee must be a person who is qualified to act as an insolvency practitioner or authorised to act as nominee in relation to the voluntary arrangement.[83] Section 390A allows for partial or full authorisation of insolvency practitioners. They can be authorised either in relation to corporate insolvency or personal insolvency (partial) or both (full). 2.062

It is common for the nominee to become the supervisor of a CVA once it has been approved and in that role the practitioner will oversee the operation of the CVA. However, as far as the role of nominee is concerned, the insolvency legislation does not confer any powers on a nominee concerning the the operation of the company or the assets of the debtor company. The nominee's major role is often engaging in negotiation with the creditors of the debtor company to ascertain to what terms they would agree. 2.063

It is the norm that the prospective nominee will play a significant role in advising and assisting the directors of the company in the formulation of the proposal. In fact, often the prospective nominee will take a major role in the preparation of the proposal. Having said that, it must be emphasised that the proposal is to be regarded as the directors' proposal (or that of the liquidator or administrator if they are proposing the CVA). The nominee is not the agent of the debtor company.[84] The nominee must remain objective and independent, and this is evident from the report which the nominee is required to file with the court, and the fact that the nominee must comment on the proposal. SIP 3.2, and considered in conjunction with SIP 1, sets out the principles, key compliance standards and standards of general application with which, save in exceptional circumstances, a person acting as nominee or supervisor of a CVA must comply. The nominee 'should be satisfied that it is achievable and that a fair balance is struck between the interests of the company and the creditors'.[85] 2.064

83 Insolvency Act 1986, s 1(2). Also, see s 388(1)(b).

84 *Re A Debtor (No 222 of 1990) ex parte Bank of Ireland (No 2)* (n 22), 235.

85 Paragraph 7.

2.065 Paragraph 15 of SIP 3.2 provides that the insolvency practitioner should have procedures in place to ensure that the proposal is considered objectively, and the paragraph sets out those matters that should be addressed in a proposal. Paragraph 16 provides that the nominee should have procedures in place to ensure that he or she can report objectively whether or not, in the nominee's judgment, the company's financial position is materially different from that contained in the proposal, explaining the extent to which the information has been verified, the CVA is manifestly unfair, and the CVA has a reasonable prospect of being approved and implemented. The test of 'reasonable prospect' is the same as that applied in relation to what is a real prospect that one of the purposes of administration would be achieved in court applications for administration orders.[86]

2.066 Besides being independent, nominees must act in good faith, and it is necessary that they only propose a CVA if satisfied that it will not unfairly prejudice the rights of any creditor, member or contributory of the company.[87] In *Mourant & Co Trustees Ltd v Sixty UK Ltd (in liq)*[88] Henderson J said that:

> The need for a responsible and professional attitude is even more pronounced where the CVA is structured in such a way that it is bound to be passed by the votes of creditors whose position is either unaffected or improved, and where another much smaller class of creditors is to be deprived of valuable contractual rights in reliance on the *PRG Powerhouse* principle [which had established that a CVA could lawfully be structured in a manner which would deprive a creditor landlord of the benefit of a third party guarantee of the liabilities of the tenant debtor company]. I do not say that it is necessarily impossible to propose a fair CVA of this type, but the greatest care is needed to ensure fairness to the latter class, both in the substance of what is proposed and in the procedure that is adopted.[89]

2.067 The role of the nominee is to try to structure an arrangement that will be capable of achieving the necessary statutory majorities and will not be unfairly prejudicial to any creditor.[90] In *SISU Capital Fund Ltd v Tucker*[91] Warren J explained that: 'To achieve a proposal which falls within the permissible range, the officeholder will often need to adopt a variety of approaches, including in particular acting as a mediator or broker between various groups of creditors in an attempt to see if sufficient common ground can be found.'[92]

---

86 See *Re Harris Simons Construction Ltd* (1988) 5 BCC 11, 13.
87 *Mourant & Co Trustees Ltd v Sixty UK Ltd (in liq)* (n 23), [88].
88 Ibid.
89 Ibid., [88].
90 *SISU Capital Fund Ltd v Tucker* [2005] EWHC 2170 (Ch), [2006] BPIR 154, [118].
91 Ibid.
92 Ibid., [118].

The nominee is usually in a difficult position in that he or she is to conduct an investigation but, for the most part, is not able to undertake a comprehensive one. Nevertheless, the nominee must not merely wave the proposal through. The nominee, if he or she has no reason to doubt the accuracy of the information with which he or she has been supplied, can rely on it,[93] but the prospective nominee must be properly sceptical.[94] Lindsay J explained the role of the nominee in this regard in an IVA case, *Greystoke v Hamilton-Smith*,[95] but which is also relevant to CVAs: **2.068**

> Plainly, the less inquiry the nominee undertakes, the more important, in terms of reliance upon it, becomes the fullness and candour of the information provided by the debtor. If, for whatever reason, the nominee's inquiries in questionable cases have been so restricted or unsatisfactory that the nominee would be unable to assure creditors that he had satisfied himself that those three minima were met, then he should not unequivocally report, under s 256(1)(a), that in his opinion a meeting of creditors should be summoned. Where such doubts have reasonably arisen it cannot be right for the nominee unquestioningly to accept whatever it put in front of him on the supposed basis that it is not for him but for the creditors to accept or reject the proposal; it is fundamental to the intended operation of IVAs that what the creditors vote upon is not the debtor's raw material but a proposal that, at least to the qualified extent I have described, has survived scrutiny and which, to at least that extent, has commended itself to an independent professional insolvency practitioner as proper to be put to, and capable of being not unfairly voted upon by, the creditors. Although it may be said, in the broadest terms, that the plan of the 1986 Act in relation to IVAs is 'Leave it to the creditors', it is not, in other words, *anything* that is so to be left; the formalities apart, the 'it' to be left to them by the nominee has (at least in the cases of doubt which I have described and with which I am, for the moment, concerned) to have met the three minima I have mentioned.[96]

It has been suggested that the following questions should be posed by an insolvency practitioner when considering a proposal: **2.069**

(1) Is there a profitable core business?
(2) Does the business have up-to-date financial information?
(3) Is there a business plan for the next 12 months?
(4) Is the business plan realistic bearing in mind the present financial situation?
(5) Is the present management capable of dealing with the business plan?
(6) Are resources available to meet immediate cash flow requirements?
(7) Are the major creditors likely to support a rescue plan?
(8) Is any litigation pending against the business?
(9) Can the management be trusted?

93 *Pitt v Mond* [2001] 624, 645.
94 Ibid.
95 [1997] BPIR 24.
96 Ibid., 29.

(10) How much luck is required to make the scheme work?[97]

2.070 The nominee is to endeavour, as much as possible, to ensure that a proposal is capable of being adopted and would not be unfairly prejudicial to any creditor,[98] and nominees should not put forward proposals unless they know that there is a reasonable prospect of their being adopted.[99] Warren J in *SISU Capital Fund Ltd v Tucker*[100] explained what might need to occur:

> If the officeholder can broker an agreement between *all* creditors, his task in putting forward proposals is an easy one. If, after attempting to broker a deal, he can establish consensus among a majority, he can put the consensus forward as a proposal for a voluntary arrangement – but only if he considers that it is not unfairly prejudicial to the minority.[101]

2.071 According to SIP 3.2, the insolvency practitioner should have procedures in place to ensure, taking account of the company's circumstances and the nature of the company's finances, that, where a directors' proposal is concerned, the directors have had, or receive, the appropriate advice in relation to a CVA and this should be confirmed in writing if the insolvency practitioner or their firm has not done so before.[102] It also states that sufficient information should be obtained to make an assessment of a CVA as a solution, and to enable a nominee to prepare a report, including:

i. the measures taken by the directors or others to avoid recurrence of the company's financial difficulties, if any;
ii. the likely expectations of any key creditors;
iii. the effect of the CVA on third parties where their views may have an effect on the viability of the CVA; and
iv. proportionate investigations into, and verification of, income and expenditure and assets and liabilities.[103]

2.072 Paragraph 14 (c) of the SIP states that creditors should be given adequate time to consider what is being planned regarding the CVA.

2.073 What steps are reasonable in the circumstances for a nominee to satisfy himself or herself about the proposal depends on many variables such as the strength

---

97 Weisgard et al., *Company Voluntary Arrangements and Administrations* (n 34), [1.73] and referring to questions posed by Gerald Krasner.
98 *SISU Capital Fund Ltd v Tucker* (n 18), [118].
99 Ibid., [119].
100 Ibid.
101 Ibid., [118].
102 Paragraph 14(a).
103 Paragraph 14(b).

of the grounds for questions or doubts as may have arisen, 'their materiality to the propriety or feasibility of the debtor's proposals, the quality of the debtor's answers to the nominee in intended resolution of those doubts, the ease or difficulty with which independent inquiry by the nominee may resolve any continuing doubts, the expense entailed in such further inquiry and the availability of funds to meet that expense'.[104]

It would be advisable for the nominee to be satisfied that any dominant creditor is broadly willing to support the proposal.[105] **2.074**

In *Pitt v Mond*[106] HHJ Roger Cooke (sitting as a Deputy High Court judge) said that a nominee has a duty to the debtor up to the point when the proposal is accepted. He or she will act simply as an adviser to the debtor at first and then as nominee, but as nominee he or she may still be undertaking an advisory role. Once the proposal is approved duties to the debtor would cease.[107] The judge accepted the fact that the duty to the debtor company would be a duty of care.[108] **2.075**

Finally, a nominee owes no free-standing duty, statutory or otherwise, to the creditors. Any liability could only occur where the nominee made a negligent representation when he or she was under a duty not to do so and when the nominee thereby made himself or herself liable for damages.[109] In *Prosser v Castle Sanderson (a firm)*[110] Clarke LJ (with whom Hale and Mummery LJ agreed) said that courts should be careful not to impose duties upon nominees.[111] A nominee would not be liable in relation to post-CVA debts as any duty owed by the nominee not to make a representation could only have been to creditors in respect of their existing debts and would not have extended to debts incurred after the CVA was approved.[112] **2.076**

2. The report

A critical step in the placing of a proposal before the creditors and the members is the drafting by the nominee of a report relating to the terms of the proposal. **2.077**

---

104 *Greystoke v Hamilton-Smith* [1997] BPIR 24, 28–29, per Lindsay J.
105 Weisgard et al., *Company Voluntary Arrangements and Administrations* (n 34), [2.52].
106 [2001] BPIR 624.
107 Ibid., 642.
108 Ibid.
109 *Heritage Joinery v Krasner* [1999] BPIR 683, 690.
110 [2002] BPIR 1163.
111 Ibid., [66].
112 *Heritage Joinery v Krasner* (n 109).

In the situation where the nominee is not the liquidator or administrator of the company,[113] the nominee is required by section 2(2), within 28 days (or such longer period as the court may allow) (the period of 28 days in which the nominee must submit a report to the court under s 2(2) begins on the date the nominee received the proposal as stated in the notice[114]) after they are given notice of the proposal, to submit a report to the court stating:

(a) whether, in their opinion, the proposed voluntary arrangement has a reasonable prospect of being approved and implemented;
(b) whether, in their opinion, the proposal should be considered by a meeting of the company and by the company's creditors; and
(c) if, in their opinion, it should, the date on which and time and place at which they propose a meeting of the company should be held.[115]

2.078 Pursuant to section 2(3) and for the purposes of enabling the nominee to prepare the report, the person intending to make the proposal is to submit to the nominee a document setting out the terms of the proposed voluntary arrangement (with amendments if any are authorised under r 2.2(2)), and a statement of the company's affairs containing such particulars of its creditors and of its debts and other liabilities and of its assets as may be prescribed, and such other information as may be prescribed.

2.079 A nominee who consents to act must deliver a notice of their consent to the proposer as soon as reasonably practicable after the proposal has been submitted to the nominee under section 2(3)[116] and the notice must state the date the nominee received the proposal.[117]

2.080 The proposer must also give, besides the proposal and statement of affairs, the nominee such access to the company's accounts and records as the nominee may require to enable the nominee to consider the proposal and prepare the report.[118] If it appears to the nominee that the report to the court cannot properly be prepared on the basis of information in the proposal and statement of affairs, the nominee may require the proposer to provide more information about the circumstances in which, and the reasons why, a CVA is being proposed, particulars of any previous proposals which have been made in relation

113 Insolvency Act 1986, s 2(1).
114 Insolvency Rules 2016, r 2.4(4).
115 Insolvency Act 1986, s 2(2).
116 Insolvency Rules 2016, r 2.4(2).
117 Ibid., r 2.4(3).
118 Ibid., r 2.8(4).

to the company under Part 1 of the Act, and any further information relating to the company's affairs which the nominee thinks necessary for the purposes of the report.[119]

The nominee may require the directors to inform the nominee, with respect to any person who is, or at any time in the two years preceding the directors' notice of the proposal to the nominee has been, a director or officer of the company, whether and in what circumstances (in those two years or previously) that person has: 2.081

(a) been concerned in the affairs of any other company (whether or not incorporated in England and Wales) or limited liability partnership which has been the subject of insolvency proceedings;
(b) been made bankrupt;
(c) been the subject of a debt relief order; or
(d) entered into an arrangement with creditors.[120]

When the nominee files his or her report at court under section 2(2), it must be accompanied by a copy of the proposal (with amendments if it has been amended under r 2.2(2)) and a copy of the statement of the company's affairs or a summary of it.[121] Also, the nominee must deliver a copy of the report to the company.[122] The court must endorse the nominee's report and the copy of it with the date of filing and deliver the copy to the nominee.[123] The court is effectively only being used as a filing point for reports and does not consider them unless there is cause to do so.[124] 2.082

Rule 2.9(2) provides that the report must state why the nominee considers the proposal does or does not have a reasonable prospect of being approved and implemented and why the members and the creditors should or should not be invited to consider the proposal. 2.083

Where a proposal is to be made by the administrator or the liquidator and the administrator or liquidator will be the proposed nominee, there is no requirement to submit any report or the proposal to the court prior to summoning meetings. 2.084

119 Ibid., r 2.8(2).
120 Ibid., r 2.8(3).
121 Ibid., r 2.9(1).
122 Ibid., r 2.9(4).
123 Ibid., r 2.9(3).
124 This compares with individual voluntary arrangements where the courts play a more active role.

2.085 In complying with the report process, the nominee is not to act merely as what the Insolvency Service has referred to as a 'post box'[125] for conveying the proposal but must, at least where the fullness or candour of the information given by the company has properly come into question, take reasonable steps appropriate in the circumstances to satisfy themselves that the company's true position as far as assets and liabilities does not appear to be substantially different from that which it is to be represented to the creditors to be stated, that there is a real prospect of the proposal being implemented in the manner in which the proposal represents and that the information that the nominee has provides a basis such that there is no 'already-manifest yet unavoidable prospective unfairness to any class creditors'.[126] This does not mean that the nominee is expected in every case to have personally verified every figure and tested every part of the proposal.[127]

3. Replacing the nominee

2.086 Where the nominee has failed to submit a report as required by section 2 because they have died or on an application made by that person or the nominee, in a case where it is impracticable or inappropriate for the nominee to continue to act as such, the court may direct that the nominee be replaced by another person qualified to act as an insolvency practitioner in relation to the CVA.[128]

2.087 A person (other than the nominee) who intends to apply to the court under section 2(4) for the nominee to be replaced must deliver a notice that such an application is intended to be made to the nominee at least five business days before filing the application with the court.[129] Where a person intends to apply to the court for replacement of the nominee, they must give at least five business days' notice of their application to the person intending to make the proposal for a CVA.[130] No replacement nominee will be appointed unless the replacement nominee's consent to act and their confirmation that they are qualified to act as an insolvency practitioner, or are authorised to act, is filed in court.[131]

125 *Re A Debtor (No 140 IO of 1995)* [1996] 2 BCLC 429, 434.
126 Ibid., 435.
127 Ibid.
128 Insolvency Act 1986, s 2(4).
129 Insolvency Rules 2016, r 2.10(1).
130 Ibid., r 2.10(2).
131 Ibid., r 2.10(3).

E. MEETINGS AND DECISION PROCEDURES

1. Procedure for the initiation of the company's meeting and creditors' decision procedure

In the situation where the nominee is neither the liquidator nor the administrator, and the nominee has submitted a report to the court, pursuant to section 2(2), meetings of the company and its creditors should be summoned. The nominee shall, unless the court otherwise directs, summon the meetings for the time, date and place proposed in the report.[132] **2.088**

Section 3(2) provides that where the nominee is either the administrator or the liquidator, the office-holder shall summon a meeting of the company to consider the proposal for such time, date and place as he or she thinks fit, and seek a decision from the company's creditors as to whether they approve the proposal. **2.089**

A decision of the company's creditors as to whether they approve the proposal is to be made by a qualifying decision procedure[133] (and the decision cannot be by a deemed consent procedure), and notice of the qualifying decision procedure must be given to every creditor of the company of whose claim and address the person seeking the decision is aware.[134] 'Decision procedure' means a qualifying procedure or a creditors' decision procedure as prescribed by rule 15.3.[135] The person who convenes a decision procedure is known as 'the convener.' Rule 1.2 provides that the convener is the office-holder or other person who seeks a decision in accordance with Part 15 of the Rules. **2.090**

With respect to the company meeting, the nominee must, according to rule 2.25(3)(a)–(c), deliver to every person whom the nominee believes to be a member a notice which must identify the proceedings, state the venue for the meeting and state: the effect of rule 2.35 concerning members' voting rights, the effect of rule 2.36 concerning the requisite majority of members for passing resolutions, and the effect of rule 15.35 about rights of appeal. The notice must be accompanied by: a copy of the proposal, a copy of the statement of affairs, or if the nominee thinks fit a summary including a list of creditors with the amounts of their debts, the nominee's comments on the proposal, unless the nominee is the administrator or liquidator, and details of all resolutions to **2.091**

132 Insolvency Act 1986, s 3(1).
133 Ibid., s 3(3), Insolvency Rules 2016, r 2.25(2).
134 Insolvency Act 1986, s 3(4).
135 Insolvency Rules 2016, r 15.2(1).

be voted on.[136] Also, the notice to members under rule 2.25(3) must specify the purpose of, and venue for, the meeting and be accompanied by a blank proxy.[137]

2.092 The date of the company meeting (except where the nominee is the administrator or liquidator of the company) must not be more than 28 days from the date on which the nominee's report is filed with the court under rule 2.9.[138] The nominee must have regard to the convenience of those invited to attend when fixing the venue for a meeting (including the resumption of an adjourned meeting).[139] Rule 2.30(1) provides that a notice under rule 2.25(3) summoning a meeting of the company must be delivered, at least 14 days before the day fixed for the meeting, to all the members and to every officer or former officer of the company whose presence the nominee thinks is required and all other directors of the company. Every officer or former officer who receives such a notice stating that the nominee thinks that person's attendance is required must attend the meeting.[140] Where the members are invited to consider a proposal, the consideration is presumed to have duly taken place even if not everyone to whom the notice is to be delivered receives it.[141]

2.093 With respect to the creditors, the nominee must deliver to each of them a notice in respect of the decision procedure which complies with rule 15.8, so far as is relevant.[142] As with the notice to members, the notice to the creditors must be accompanied by: a copy of the proposal, a copy of the statement of affairs, or if the nominee thinks fit a summary including a list of creditors with the amounts of their debts, the nominee's comments on the proposal, unless the nominee is the administrator or liquidator; and state how a creditor may propose a modification to the proposal, and how the nominee will deal with such a proposal for a modification.[143] The decision date must be not less than 14 days from the date of delivery of the notice to the creditors and not more than 28 days from the date the nominee's report is filed with the court under rule 2.9.[144]

136 Ibid., r 2.25(5).
137 Ibid., r 2.26(1).
138 Ibid., r 2.26(3).
139 Ibid., r 2.26(2).
140 Ibid., r 2.30(2).
141 Ibid., r 2.32.
142 Ibid., r 2.25(4).
143 Ibid., r 2.25(5).
144 Ibid., r 2.27.

The date of the decision, as far as the creditors' decision procedure is concerned, may be on the same day as, or on a different day from, the meeting of the company.[145] But if it is not, it must be made before the members' decision.[146] The members' decision on the proposal must be made no later than five business days after the creditors' decision.[147] For the purpose of this rule, the timing of the members' decision is either the date and time of the meeting of the company or, where the nominee invites members to consider the proposal by correspondence, the deadline for receipt of members' votes.[148] **2.094**

If the creditors requisition a physical meeting to consider a proposal (with or without modifications), which they are entitled to do in accordance with section 246ZE and rule 15.6,[149] the meeting must be held within 14 days of the date on which the prescribed proportion of creditors have required the meeting to take place.[150] A notice summoning a meeting of the creditors must be delivered to the creditors at least seven days before the day fixed for the meeting.[151] **2.095**

Both the notice to members and the one to creditors may also state that the results of the consideration of the proposal will be made available for viewing and downloading on a website and that no other notice will be delivered to the creditors or members.[152] Where the results of the consideration of the proposal are to be made available for viewing and downloading on a website, the nominee must comply with the requirements for the use of a website to deliver a document set out in rule 1.49(2)(a)–(c), (3) and (4) with any necessary adaptations, and rule 1.49(5)(a) applies to determine the time of delivery of the document. **2.096**

If, in response to a notice inviting members to consider the proposal by correspondence or creditors to consider the proposal other than at a meeting, a member or creditor proposes that a person other than the nominee be appointed as supervisor, that person's consent to act and confirmation of being qualified to act as an insolvency practitioner in relation to the company must be delivered to the nominee by the deadline in the notice given by correspondence or by the **2.097**

145 Ibid., r 2.28(1).
146 Ibid., r 2.28(2).
147 Ibid., r 2.28(3).
148 Ibid., r 2.28(4).
149 Ibid., r 2.31(1).
150 Ibid., r 2.31(2).
151 Ibid., r 2.31(3).
152 Ibid., r 2.25(6).

decision date (as the case may be).[153] If, at either a meeting of the company or the decision procedure of the creditors to consider the proposal, a resolution is moved for the appointment of a person other than the nominee to be supervisor, the person moving the resolution must produce to the chair or convener at or before the meeting or decision procedure respectively, confirmation that the person proposed as supervisor is qualified to act as an insolvency practitioner in relation to the company and that person's written consent to act (unless that person is present at the meeting and there signifies consent to act).[154]

2. The chair or convener

2.098 The chair of a meeting, whether acting as the chair of the meeting of members or as the convener of a decision procedure for creditors, must be the nominee or an appointed person.[155] A proxy-holder can be the chair, but they must not vote for a resolution which would directly or indirectly place the proxy-holder or any associate of the proxy-holder in a position to receive any remuneration, fees or expenses from the insolvent estate or fix or change the amount of, or the basis of, any remuneration, fees or expenses receivable by the proxy-holder or any associate of the proxy-holder out of the insolvent estate.[156] However, a proxy-holder may vote for such a resolution if the proxy specifically directs the proxy-holder to vote in that way.[157]

2.099 Rule 15.22 provides that the chair of a meeting may: allow any person who has given reasonable notice of wishing to attend to participate in a virtual meeting or to be admitted to a physical meeting; decide what intervention, if any, may be made at a meeting of creditors by any person attending who is not a creditor, or a meeting of contributories by any person attending who is not a contributory; and decide what questions may be put to any present or former officer of the company.

2.100 After the meeting or decision procedure which considered the proposal has been held, the convener or chair of the meeting is required by rule 2.38 to prepare a report, and the report must:

153 Ibid., r 2.33(1).
154 Ibid., r 2.33(2).
155 Ibid., r 2.34; r 15.21(1).
156 Ibid., r 16.7(1).
157 Ibid., r 16.7(2).

(a) state whether the proposal was approved or rejected and whether by the creditors alone or by both the creditors and members and, in either case, whether any approval was with any modifications;
(b) list the creditors and members who voted or attended or who were represented at the meeting or decision procedure (as applicable) used to consider the proposal, setting out (with their respective values) how they voted on each resolution or whether they abstained;
(c) identify which of those creditors were considered to be connected with the company;
(d) if the proposal was approved, state with reasons whether the proceedings are COMI proceedings, establishment proceedings or proceedings to which the EU Regulation, as it has effect in the law of the United Kingdom, does not apply; and
(e) include such further information as the nominee or the chair thinks it appropriate to make known to the court.[158]

The report must be filed at court within four business days of the company meeting being held[159] and the court must endorse the copy of the report with the date of filing.[160] 2.101

The chair (in the case of a company meeting) or otherwise the convener must give notice of the result of the consideration of the proposal to everyone who was invited to consider the proposal or to whom notice of a decision procedure or meeting was delivered as soon as reasonably practicable after a copy of the report is filed with the court.[161] 2.102

3. Proxies

Where there is a meeting, a person entitled to vote may grant a proxy to another.[162] A proxy-holder must not vote for a resolution which would directly or indirectly place the proxy-holder or any associate of the proxy-holder in a position to receive any remuneration, fees or expenses from the insolvent estate or fix or change the amount of, or the basis of, any remuneration, fees or expenses receivable by the proxy-holder or any associate of the proxy-holder out of the insolvent estate.[163] The upshot is that if a chair is the nominee and is granted a proxy, the proxy cannot be voted for resolutions relating to remuneration of the nominee. However, a proxy-holder may vote for such a resolution if the 2.103

158 Ibid., r 2.38(2).
159 Ibid., r 2.38(3). See s 4(6).
160 Ibid., r 2.38(4).
161 Ibid., r 2.38(5).
162 See Part 16 of the Insolvency Rules 2016.
163 Insolvency Rules 2016, r 16.7(1).

proxy specifically directs the proxy-holder to vote in that way.[164] Where an office-holder is appointed as proxy-holder and that proxy is used under rule 16.5(2) by another person acting as chair, the office-holder is deemed to be an associate of the person acting as chair.[165]

2.104 In the case of a meeting, a proxy-holder is not entitled to vote on behalf of a creditor unless the convener or chair has received the proxy intended to be used on behalf of that creditor.[166]

4. Quorums

2.105 Rule 15.20(1) provides that a meeting is not competent to act unless there is a quorum. Rule 15.20(2) explains that a quorum is, in the case of a meeting of creditors, at least one creditor entitled to vote.

2.106 Where the provisions of this rule as to quorum are satisfied by the attendance of the chair alone or the chair and one additional person, but the chair is aware, either by virtue of proofs and proxies received or otherwise, that one or more additional persons would, if attending, be entitled to vote, the chair must delay the start of the meeting by at least 15 minutes after the appointed time.[167]

5. Adjournments

2.107 The chair may (and must if it is so resolved) adjourn a meeting for not more than 14 days, but this is subject to any direction of the court.[168] Any further adjournment must not be to a day later than 14 days after the date on which the meeting was originally held (subject to any direction by the court).[169]

2.108 The chair of a meeting may, without an adjournment, declare the meeting suspended for one or more periods not exceeding one hour in total (or, in exceptional circumstances, such longer total period during the same day at the chair's discretion).[170]

164 Ibid., r 16.7(2).
165 Ibid., r 16.7(3).
166 Ibid., r 15.28(2).
167 Ibid., r 15.20(3).
168 Ibid., r 15.23(1).
169 Ibid., r 15.23(2).
170 Ibid., r 15.27.

In the case of *Re Symes (a Debtor)*,[171] a creditors' meeting was convened to vote on a proposal for an IVA. The necessary majority for approval of the proposal was not attained. The chairman filed a report with the court indicating that the proposal was rejected. It also stated that a number of creditors had, after the meeting, indicated that they would be in favour of a modified proposal. The judge made an order directing the holding of a further creditors' meeting. It was held, on appeal, that the judge had no jurisdiction to make such an order and that, therefore, the second meeting was invalid. It was stated that the meeting could not be regarded as an adjournment of the first meeting. The statutory provisions provided a process where there was only one creditors' meeting, and one report made to the court. The provisions did not provide any machinery and left no scope for calling a second meeting or for the making of a further report. **2.109**

6. Modifications

It might be appropriate for a proposal to be modified. Section 4(1A) of the Act provides that the company and its creditors may approve the proposal with or without modifications. It would seem that nothing prevents modifications from being proposed at the meeting or decision procedure stage. There is no requirement in the legislation that a company or its directors must agree to modifications to a proposal as submitted by creditors.[172] Modifications may include one conferring the functions proposed to be conferred on the nominee on another person qualified to act as an insolvency practitioner in relation to the voluntary arrangement.[173] No modification is permitted by virtue of the proposal ceasing to be one to which section 1(1) applies.[174] Also, any modification cannot be approved where it affects the rights of a secured creditor of the company to enforce their security.[175] The same goes for any preferential debt of the company which is to be paid otherwise than in priority to such of its debts as are not preferential debts; any ordinary preferential debt of the company is to be paid otherwise than in priority to any secondary preferential debts that it may have; a preferential creditor of the company is to be paid an amount in respect of that debt bearing to that debt a smaller proportion than is borne to preferential debt by the amount that is to be paid in respect of that other **2.110**

171 [1996] BCC 137.
172 L Doyle KC, A Keay and J Curl KC (eds), *Doyle, Keay and Curl: Annotated Insolvency Legislation 2025*, 13th ed, LexisNexis, [1.62].
173 Insolvency Act 1986, s 4(2).
174 Ibid., s 4(2).
175 Ibid., s 4(3).

debt; a preferential creditor of the company is to be paid an amount in respect of a secondary preferential debt that bears to that debt a smaller proportion than is borne to another secondary preferential debt by the amount that is to be paid in respect of that other debt; or in the case of a company which is a relevant financial institution (see section 387A), any non-preferential debt is to be paid otherwise than in accordance with the rules in section 176AZA(2) or (3).[176] The only exception is, in respect of secured or preferential debts, where the concurrence of the secured or preferential creditor is obtained.[177]

2.111 In *Young v Nero Holdings Ltd*[178] Michael Green J said that it was possible for a modification to be introduced during the course of an electronic voting procedure after creditors had begun voting and, if the proposal was ultimately approved, the modification should be treated as having been approved, provided that the company had also consented. He went on to say that that must especially be the case where the modification was solely for the benefit of creditors.[179]

7. Voting

(a) Introduction

2.112 The critical point comes at meetings and decision procedures when the members and creditors vote on the proposal put before them. Voting may take place at a physical meeting or pursuant to another form of decision procedure. If an electronic voting procedure is implemented (and provided for under r 15.4), and it is in fact the norm with the CVA process, it cannot be postponed or adjourned by directors or nominees without a court order. Michael Green J said in *Young v Nero Holdings Ltd*[180] that he accepted that an application could be made to the court, but he found it difficult to see what the application would seek and what relief the court could grant that would be consistent with the statutory framework and processes.[181] The judge said that it was not obvious to him that the court could bypass the Rules by permitting those creditors who had already voted to change their votes.[182] He observed that there would be no point postponing the process unless creditors could change their votes.[183] His

176 Ibid., s 4(4).
177 Ibid., s 4(3)(4).
178 [2021] EWHC 2600 (Ch), [2022] BPIR 189.
179 Ibid., [291].
180 Ibid.
181 Ibid., [172].
182 Ibid.
183 Ibid.

Lordship doubted whether section 246ZE(5) of the Act was intended to apply in this kind of situation, which would, effectively, terminate an almost complete electronic decision procedure and replace it with a new decision process where creditors could vote again.[184] Michael Green J went on to say that any application would certainly be novel and would carry risks and 'the difficulties highlighted above have to be taken into account in assessing the practicalities and reasonableness of both the directors' and nominees' decision not to make such an application'.[185] It has been said by one leading source that:

> If a modification benefitting creditors is supported by the company, where such a modification is proposed following the launch, but prior to the conclusion, of the electronic voting process, votes already received in favour of the unmodified CVA proposal may still be counted in favour of the proposal as modified. Modifications that are beneficial, or, at worst, neutral, to creditors can be made to the CVA proposal during the voting window.[186]

Where creditors are dissatisfied with the inclusion of a modification, they may seek to challenge it pursuant to section 6.[187] **2.113**

It will be quite common that the view of the proposal taken by His Majesty's Revenue and Customs ('HMRC') will be decisive as far as voting goes for the approval of creditors. HMRC is frequently a sizeable creditor and will usually have more information concerning the debtor's affairs compared to other creditors. Given the fact that HMRC now has been restored as a preferential creditor for some of its claims, it might be difficult to convince it that it is better that a CVA be implemented than the company going into liquidation. **2.114**

(b) The voting process

Where a vote is cast in a decision procedure that is not a meeting, it may not be changed.[188] For the decision to be made in relation to a decision procedure, the convener must receive at least one valid vote on or before the decision date.[189] **2.115**

(c) Voting rights of members

A member is entitled to vote according to the rights attaching to the member's shares, in accordance with the articles of the company.[190] A member's shares, **2.116**

184 Ibid.
185 Ibid., [173].
186 Mark Mullen (ed), *Tolley's Insolvency Law*, LexisNexis, [V4018.2].
187 *Young v Nero Holdings Ltd* [2021] EWHC 2600 (Ch), [2022] BPIR 189.
188 Insolvency Rules 2016, r 15.31(8).
189 Ibid., r 15.9(3).
190 Ibid., r 2.35(1).

for the purposes of voting, include any other interest that person may have as a member of the company.[191] The value of a member, for the purposes of voting, is determined by reference to the number of votes conferred on that member by the company's articles.[192]

(d) Voting rights of creditors

2.117 Under rule 15.9(1), a creditor's vote is taken into account in relation to a decision procedure, other than where votes are cast at a meeting, in the following circumstances: it was received by the convener on or before the decision date and it was accompanied by a proof in respect of the creditor's claim unless it has already been given to the convener. Rule 15.28(5) provides that every creditor who has notice of the decision procedure relating to the proposal is entitled to vote in respect of that creditor's debt.

2.118 Before considering the rights of creditors to vote, it must be noted that creditors owe each other duties of good faith,[193] and they are under an obligation to act and vote according to the interests of their class and not for some improper, collateral benefit.[194]

2.119 The meaning of 'creditor' is not always clear. It was considered by David Richards J (as he then was) in *Re T&N Ltd*,[195] a case that involved consideration of the position of the employees and former employees of the company as well as members of the families of employees who had been exposed to asbestos. At the relevant date, the date the CVA was approved, employees had not yet developed any asbestos-related diseases. His Lordship said that what was required for a person to be a creditor was the existence of 'a contingent liability', that is, a liability which, by reason of something done by the person bound, will necessarily arise or come into being if one or more certain events occur or do not occur, and it did not matter that such claimants did not have provable debts.[196] It was held that, considering the overall aims of a CVA in restructuring a company's affairs, a 'creditor' was not to be limited to persons who would have a provable claim in a winding up; the word ought to be given its widest possible meaning.[197] In light of *Re T&N*, an amendment was made

191 Ibid., r 2.35(2).

192 Ibid., r 2.35(3).

193 *Moorgate Industries UK Ltd v Mittal* [2022] EWHC 3009 (Ch), [2023] BPIR 476, [62].

194 *National Westminster Bank plc v Kapoor* [2011] EWHC 255 (Ch), [2011] BPIR 836, [81]; *Gertner v CFL Finance Ltd and another* [2018] EWCA Civ 1781, [80].

195 [2005] EWHC 2870 (Ch), [2006] 3 All ER 697, [2006] BPIR 532.

196 Ibid., [60], [142].

197 Ibid., [35].

to rule 13.12 of the Insolvency Rules 1986, defining 'debt' for the purposes of liquidation and administration, and this amendment was incorporated in the 2016 Rules (see rule 14.1). The amended 1986 Rules were considered by the Supreme Court in *Re Nortel, Re Lehman*,[198] which also examined the concept of contingent liability.

His Honour Judge Pelling QC (sitting as a High Court judge) held in *Re Beloit Walmsley Ltd*[199] that under the terms of the CVA before him, creditors with contingent claims in tort that had not accrued at the date of the meeting would not be included in the CVA. The arrangement established a trust of moneys for the benefit of creditors included in the arrangement and the court was unable to authorise a course of action which would see the supervisor of the arrangement engaging in a breach of the trust.[200] **2.120**

More recently, in *Discovery (Northampton) Ltd v Debenhams Retail Ltd*[201] Norris J said that the Act does not contain a definition of 'creditor' for the purposes of CVAs. Nevertheless, section 5(2) of the Act explains that the CVA will bind every person who was entitled to vote in the procedure by which the CVA was approved.[202] Entitlement to vote at a CVA is determined by rule 15.28(5). The provision states that every 'creditor' who has notice is entitled to vote 'in respect of that creditor's debt.' According to Norris J, the concepts of 'creditor' and 'debt' were therefore intertwined.[203] **2.121**

'Debt' is also not defined for the purposes of CVAs. Norris J in *Discovery (Northampton) Ltd* noted that it was defined for the purposes of administration and winding up under rule 14.1(3) and this definition could be applied equally to CVAs.[204] The judge went on to say that rule 14.1 contained further explanation of the terms 'debt or liability', and that 'liability' must therefore be a pecuniary one even if it cannot be characterised as a 'debt', present, future or contingent.[205] Consequently, his Lordship drew the conclusion that a 'creditor' included someone towards whom the company had a present pecuniary liability which would in the future, or may on a contingency, become payable as a debt.[206] **2.122**

198 [2013] UKSC 52, [2014] AC 209, [2013] 3 WLR 504, [2013] 4 All ER 887, [2013] BPIR 866.
199 [2008] EWHC 1888 (Ch), [2009] 1 BCLC 584.
200 Ibid., [21].
201 [2019] EWHC 2441 (Ch), [2020] BCC 9.
202 Ibid., [25].
203 Ibid.
204 Ibid., [26].
205 Ibid., [27].
206 Ibid., [28].

2.123 Votes are calculated according to the amount of the creditor's debt as of the decision date, or where the company is being wound up or in administration, the date of its going into liquidation or administration respectively.[207] In some cases, there may be creditors who do not appear to have a claim, but the claims might constitute future, prospective or contingent liabilities which could be bound by any arrangement approved and in respect of which they could vote. In *Re Millwall Football Club & Athletic Co (1985) plc*[208] employees were dismissed by an administrator. One of the employees claimed that his claim for compensation was covered by the CVA. The CVA stated that debts covered by the CVA included:

> all present, future, actual, prospective and contingent liabilities... incurred before the Record Date whether or not such debts arise out of circumstances which are actually known to the Group and whether or not such claims have yet to arise or are capable of being ascertained other than [six classes of debts, being those which were to be paid in full].

2.124 The Record Date was the date when the administration order was made. Rimer J held that the employee's claim was based on an obligation whose source was the employee's employment contract. That obligation was in existence on the Record Date and the liability of the company to the employee which arose after the termination of employment, could, as at the Record Date, properly be characterised as a future, prospective or contingent liability incurred before the Record Date within the meaning of the definition in the CVA terms.[209] Thus, the employee's claim was bound by the subsequently proposed voluntary arrangement.

2.125 Far more recently, in *Snoozebox Ltd v Health and Safety Executive*,[210] a case involving a CVA that was approved when the company was in administration, it was said that for the incurring of an obligation leading to a liability for a company in administration, the obligation had to have incurred, or been subject to, some step or combination of steps which (a) had some legal effect (such as putting it under some legal duty or into some legal relationship), and which (b) resulted in it being vulnerable to the specific liability in question, such that there would be a real prospect of that liability being incurred.[211] In this decision, the court said that where there is a claim for a fine or costs by the

---

207 Insolvency Rules 2016, r 15.31(1)(d).

208 [1998] 2 BCLC 272.

209 Ibid., 279.

210 [2023] EWHC 851 (Ch), [2023] BPIR 994.

211 Ibid., [62].

Crown, the Crown must establish that the claim constituted a contingent debt or liability to which the company was subject at the time of the CVA being voted for.[212]

Rule 15.33(1) provides that the convener or chair in respect of a decision procedure must ascertain entitlement to vote and admit or reject claims accordingly, and rule 15.33(2) states that the convener or chair may admit or reject a claim in whole or in part. If the convener or chair is in any doubt whether a claim should be admitted or rejected, the convener or chair must mark it as objected to and allow votes to be cast in respect of it, subject to such votes being subsequently declared invalid if the objection to the claim is sustained.[213] The chair or convener should take this action where a creditor's claim is made pursuant to a guarantee given by the company and the company disputes the liability. The claim is neither one for an unliquidated amount nor one whose value is not ascertained.[214] In the case of *Sea Voyager Maritime Inc v Bielecki*[215] a creditor with a contingent claim, which was disputed, had received a notice of the creditors' meeting and was held to have been entitled to vote, but with the proviso that the chair could have put an estimated minimum value on the claim and marked it as objected to. **2.126**

Rule 15.31(2) provides that a creditor may vote in respect of a debt of an unliquidated or unascertained amount if the convener or chair decides to put upon it an estimated minimum value for the purpose of entitlement to vote and admits the claim for that purpose. As far as placing a value on a debt, some older decisions seemed to indicate that there had to be some element of bilateral concurrence between the chair and the creditor who had made the claim.[216] This view was taken on the basis that rule 1.17(3) of the 1986 Rules said that the amount was to be £1 unless the chair *agrees* to put a higher value on it (our emphasis). **2.127**

In *Re Cranley Mansions Ltd: Saigol v Goldstein*[217] a creditor sought an order revoking the approval of a voluntary arrangement given at a creditor's meeting, on the grounds that her claim for £900,000 had only been valued at £1 for voting purposes by the chair. In fact, the judge ended up not allowing the application, even though of the view that there had to be bilateral concurrence **2.128**

212 Ibid., [51].
213 Insolvency Rules 2016, r 15.33(3).
214 *Re A Debtor (No 222 of 1990), ex parte the Bank of Ireland and others* [1992] BCLC 137, 144.
215 [1999] 1 All ER 628, [1999] 1 BCLC 133.
216 See, *Re Cranley Mansions Ltd: Saigol v Goldstein* [1994] BCC 576, 592.
217 [1994] BCC 576.

concerning the value of the vote, and there was not; the chair made a unilateral determination.[218] However, the later cases have taken the view that 'agrees' in the Rules did not mean that the chair had to come to an agreement with the creditor, but it was in fact intended to give the chair unilateral discretion which, however, was to be exercised fairly and be challengeable in the court. In *Doorbar v Alltime Securities Ltd*, decided shortly after *Cranley Mansions*, Knox J accepted the fact that the chair of the meeting was entitled to put a value of £1 on a debt, as the only agreement that was required was an expressed willingness by the chair to put an estimated minimum value on the debt in question.[219] This was approved on appeal before the Court of Appeal.[220] In the later case of *Re Newlands (Seaford) Educational Trust*,[221] the court applied a similar approach even though the relevant rule was different.[222] The Rules we have now plainly provide that this later approach is correct. In fact, the relevant provision, rule 15.31(3), makes no reference to 'agrees'. It provides that in a vote for a CVA, a debt of an unliquidated or unascertained amount is to be valued at £1 for the purposes of voting unless the convener, chair or an appointed person decides to put a higher value on it. Thus, this indicates that it is the unilateral decision of the chair that is crucial.

2.129 When considering what value to ascribe to a claim, Sir Andrew Morritt C said in *Re Newlands (Seaford) Educational Trust*, to which reference was made above, that:

> The chairman should not speculate. Nor is he obliged to investigate the creditor's claim. But he must examine such evidence, and I do not use that word in any technical sense, as the creditor puts forward and any relevant evidence provided by any other creditor or the debtor. If the totality of that evidence leads him to the conclusion that he can safely attribute to the claim a minimum value higher than £1 then he should do so.[223]

2.130 The judge went on to say that if a court is not provided with any evidence that would have led the chairman to believe, with any degree of confidence, that the value was greater than £1, then it is not able to do so.[224] Reference might be had to rule 15.33(3), which is discussed above.

---

218 Ibid., 592.
219 [1994] BCC 994, 1002.
220 [1996] 1 WLR 456, [1995] BCC 1149.
221 [2006] EWHC 1511 (Ch), [2006] BPIR 1230, [2007] BCC 195.
222 Ibid., [27].
223 Ibid., [28].
224 Ibid., [30].

In his judgment in *Re Rossi*,[225] ICCJ Mullen summarised the position as follows: 2.131

> the chair of a meeting must consider the claims presented to him or her. If the chair is satisfied that the claim is good at the time, it is admitted. If the chair is satisfied that the claim is bad, it is rejected. If there is doubt, it is admitted and marked that it is objected to and the creditor will be allowed to vote. Where the claim admitted is for an unascertained or unliquidated amount it will be valued at £1 unless the chair can safely place a higher minimum value on it. He or she does not need to investigate the claim but must consider the evidence provided to determine whether it is established. It is clear from the wording of the rules that it is for the creditor to make a claim and substantiate it to the chair's satisfaction.[226]

In *Leighton Contracting (Qatar) WLL v Simms*[227] a case dealing with, among other things, the precursor of rule 15.31(3), namely rule 1.17(3) of the 1986 Rules, the chairman at an approval meeting made the decision to attribute a value of £1 to a creditor's vote on the basis that it was unliquidated. The creditor argued that to the extent that the claim was unliquidated it should nevertheless have been valued at more than £1. Judge Simon Barker QC (sitting as a High Court judge) held that on the basis that it was liquidated, there was a real prospect of success for an argument to the effect that the chairman, even if he had considered, as he did, that it was unliquidated, should have gone on to consider the valuation of an unliquidated demand in excess of £1.[228] The judge was of the opinion that this would not have compromised the chairman's neutrality, which did not require abstention from discussion or passivity of approach.[229] 2.132

Where there are debts that are wholly secured, they will have, for voting purposes, a value of nil,[230] while the value for voting purposes of debts that are partly secured will be that of the value of the unsecured part.[231] Rule 15.31(7) provides that no vote may be cast in respect of a claim more than once on any resolution put to a meeting. However, this does not prevent a creditor from voting in respect of less than the full value of an entitlement to vote or casting a vote one way in respect of part of the value of an entitlement and another way in respect of some or all of the balance of that value.[232] As mentioned 2.133

225 [2022] EWHC 1053 (Ch), [2022] BPIR 1241.
226 Ibid., [28].
227 [2011] EWHC 1735, [2011] BPIR 1395.
228 Ibid., [37].
229 Ibid., [36].
230 Insolvency Rules 2016, r 15.31(4).
231 Ibid., r 15.31(5).
232 Ibid., r 15.31(9).

earlier, a vote cast in a decision procedure, which is not a meeting, may not be changed.[233]

2.134 In respect of a decision by a convener or chair, if that decision is reversed or varied, or votes are declared invalid, the court may order another decision procedure to be initiated or make such order as it thinks just, but the court may only make an order if it considers that the circumstances which led to the appeal give rise to unfair prejudice or material irregularity.[234]

2.135 A debt is claimed if it is claimed as due from the company to the person seeking to be entitled to vote.[235] The convener or chair may call for any document or other evidence to be produced if the convener or chair thinks it necessary for the purpose of substantiating the whole or any part of a claim of a creditor.[236] In a decision relating to a proposed CVA, every creditor, secured or unsecured, who has notice of the decision procedure is entitled to vote in respect of that creditor's debt.[237]

(e) Appeals

2.136 Rule 15.35(1)(2) provides that the chair or convener's decision on a creditor's entitlement to vote is subject to appeal to the court by any creditor or member of the company. The court's power to act on that appeal is, however, subject to the proviso to rule 15.35(3), namely that the matter must be such as to give rise to unfair prejudice or material irregularity. An appeal may not be made later than 21 days after the decision date,[238] except in relation to a proposed CVA, where an appeal may not be made after the end of the period of 28 days beginning with the day on which the first of the reports required by section 4(6) was filed with the court.[239] The date on which the nominee files the report is counted in calculating the time.[240] Section 6(3) also provides that in the case of a person who was not given notice, 28 days after they became aware that the meeting had taken place, such creditors can even apply after the arrangement

233 Ibid., r 15.31(8).
234 Ibid., r 15.35(3).
235 Ibid., r 15.28(3).
236 Ibid., r 15.28(4).
237 Ibid., r 15.28(5).
238 Ibid., r 15.35(4).
239 Insolvency Act 1986, s 6(3); ibid., r 15.35(5)(a).
240 *Re Bournemouth & Boscombe Athletic Football Club Company Ltd* [1998] BPIR 183, 184; *Re Beloit Walmsley Ltd* [2008] EWHC 1888 (Ch), [2009] 1 BCLC 584, [2008] BPIR 1445, [29]; *Snoozebox Ltd v Health and Safety Executive* [2023] EWHC 851 (Ch), [2023] BPIR 994.

has come to an end, provided it did not do so prematurely. Unlike with an IVA, the court has no jurisdiction to extend this period.[241]

If appeals are instituted by creditors, they have the burden of proof where they are seeking to vote in a creditors' decision procedure or to demonstrate they have a right to vote. The burden of proof falls on the creditor to make out their debt on the balance of probabilities.[242] If creditors challenge the proof of a creditor, the burden of proof in respect of a proof of debt submitted by a creditor, which is challenged by another creditor, is on the creditor whose proof is challenged.[243] **2.137**

Appeals are not appeals proper,[244] as the court is not reviewing the decision of the convener or chair, but rather, the court must determine anew, on the evidence before it, whether a claim should be admitted.[245] The nature of the exercise which the court conducts on an appeal is simply to examine the evidence before it and arrive at a conclusion whether, on balance, the claim was established and, if so, in what amount. In making its determination, the court is not confined to the evidence that was before the chair at the time that he or she made the decision but is entitled to consider whatever admissible evidence on the issue the parties to the appeal choose to place before the court.[246] **2.138**

The chair or convener is not personally liable for any costs incurred by any party in relation to an appeal, unless the court so orders.[247] It has been made clear that the starting point in any consideration of costs is that the chair or convener is not liable.[248] In *Re a Debtor (No 222 of 1990) (No 2)*[249] Harman J made an order for costs against the chairman of a meeting in respect of his exercise of his discretion under the Rules of the Supreme Court on the ground that the chairman, as nominee of the arrangement, had fallen far short of **2.139**

241 *Bournemouth & Boscombe*, ibid., 186; *Beloit Walmsley*, ibid; *Tucker and Spratt (Joint Supervisors of Energy Holdings (No 3) (In Liquidation) v Gold Fields Mining LLC* [2009] EWCA Civ 173, [2009] BPIR 704, [20].

242 *McCarthy v Tann* [2015] EWHC 2049 (Ch), [2015] BPIR 1224; *Lynch v Cadwallader* [2021] EWHC 328 (Ch), [2021] BPIR 854, [82]; *Re Rossi* [2022] EWHC 1053 (Ch), [2022] BPIR 1241, [28].

243 *Farrar Construction Limited, Levi Solicitors LLP v Wilson and JKR Property Development Limited* [2022] EWHC 24 (Ch).

244 *Lynch v Cadwallader* [2021] EWHC 328 (Ch), [2021] BPIR 854, [82]. The case dealt with an appeal against an officeholder's decision in relation to a proof of debt.

245 *Elser v Sands* [2022] EWHC 32 (Ch).

246 *Re A Company (No 004539 of 1993)* [1995] 1 BCLC 459, 466; *National Westminster Bank plc v Kapoor* [2011] EWHC 255 (Ch), [2011] BPIR 836, [87].

247 Insolvency Rules 2016, r 15.35(6).

248 *Nimat Halal Food v Patel* [2020] EWHC 734 (Ch), [2020] BPIR 976, [7].

249 [1993] BCLC 233.

the professional standard expected of him. Later, in *Smurthwaite v Simpson-Smith*,[250] the Court of Appeal upheld the costs order made by the trial judge against the chairman of a meeting. The judge had criticised the conduct of the chair of a creditors' meeting that was considering an IVA proposal. Nevertheless, it is clear that a convener or chair will only be held personally liable for costs in special circumstances.[251] Chief ICC Judge Briggs in *Nimat Halal Food v Patel*[252] said that:

> An order should not ordinarily be made against an office holder personally. Something more is required. Something more relates to the conduct of the office holder. The degree of conduct deserving of a personal costs order will depend on the circumstances of each case. A mere mistake is unlikely to be sufficient. Acting in a neutral manner, on an appeal from a rejection of proof, is unlikely to be sufficient. Acting for a personal advantage in resisting an appeal is very likely to lead to a personal costs order. Such conduct would present a 'special case' and a 'good reason', and may be characterised as 'irrational conduct', or 'unreasonable conduct'.[253]

2.140 Later, the judge said, in *Burke v Peabody Construction Ltd*,[254] that for a nominee to be held liable personally for costs, he or she must be guilty of some element of personal misconduct.

(f) Majority of votes required

2.141 As far as the creditors are concerned, according to rule 15.34(3), it is only when three-quarters or more (in value) of those creditors responding to a proposal vote in favour of a decision supporting the proposal that a CVA or a modification is approved. A decision is not made if more than half of the total value of the unconnected creditors vote against it.[255] For these purposes, a creditor is unconnected unless the convener or chair decides that the creditor is connected with the company, and in deciding whether a creditor is connected, reliance may be placed on the information provided by the company's statement of affairs or otherwise in accordance with the Rules, and the total value of the unconnected creditors is the total value of those unconnected creditors whose claims have been admitted for voting.[256]

250 [2006] EWCA Civ 1183, [2006] BPIR 1504.
251 *Nimat Halal Food v Patel* (n 248), [7].
252 Ibid.
253 Ibid., [13].
254 [2024] EWHC 392 (Ch).
255 Insolvency Rules 2016, r 15.34(4).
256 Ibid., r 15.34(5).

Resolutions other than ones relating to approval of the proposal can be passed by a simple majority in value.[257] 2.142

For the decision to be made in relation to a decision procedure, the convener must receive at least one valid vote on or before the decision date.[258] 2.143

If the chair of a meeting applies a proxy contrary to the Rules (in relation to voting in respect of the nominee or supervisor's remuneration), his or her vote using that proxy does not count towards the majority.[259] 2.144

A decision of the chair which is made pursuant to Chapter 8 of Part 12 of the Rules, which deals with creditor voting and majorities, is subject to appeal. Appeals are covered by rule 15.35, and discussed above.[260] 2.145

For the company to approve the CVA there must be an ordinary resolution passed by the members.[261] 2.146

A resolution is passed by members by correspondence or at a meeting of the company when a majority (in value) of those voting has voted in favour of it.[262] This is subject to any express provision to the contrary in the articles.[263] A resolution is not passed by correspondence unless at least one member has voted in favour of it.[264] The value of members' voting is determined by reference to the number of votes conferred on each member by the company's articles. As with voting by the creditors, if the chair's application of a proxy is used contrary to Rules on voting in respect of the nominee or supervisor's remuneration, then it does not count. 2.147

F. PROTECTING CREDITORS

There are certain protective measures in place in the legislation. First, under section 4(3), neither the company nor the creditors can approve a proposal or modification of a proposal for a CVA if it affects the right of a secured creditor to enforce its security, save where the creditor concerned agrees. An execution creditor who has proceeded under a writ of control, pursuant to which a 2.148

257 Ibid., r 15.34.
258 Ibid., r 15.9(3).
259 Ibid., r 16.7(1).
260 See [2.136]–[2.140].
261 Insolvency Rules 2016, r 2.36.
262 Ibid., r 2.36(1).
263 Ibid., r 2.36(2).
264 Ibid., r 2.36(3).

High Court Enforcement Officer has taken walking possession of chattels, is a secured creditor for this purpose.[265] A landlord's right of re-entry is not a security for the purposes of these provisions.[266]

2.149 The Court of Appeal in *Khan v Permayer*,[267] a case dealing with an IVA, said that a secured creditor can be held by the court to have waived their right to enforce their security if they claim the full amount owed to them without deducting the value of their security and they participate in the arrangement by exercising their vote and receiving a dividend on the debt.[268] Later, a differently constituted Court of Appeal in *Whitehead v Household Corporation*,[269] also a case addressing an IVA, distinguished *Khan* on the basis that in the earlier case it was clear from the terms of the arrangement itself that the creditor intended to abandon his security and had agreed to be treated as an unsecured creditor in respect of the whole of the debt.[270] In the case before the Court in *Whitehead*, Chadwick LJ (with whom Sedley and Scott Baker LJJ concurred) said there was nothing in the terms of the arrangement itself which suggested that the creditor concerned intended to abandon any part of its security.[271] Thus, resolution of the issue as to whether a creditor had surrendered its security very much relies on the terms of the arrangement, including whether those terms recognised the security and its holder's right to enforce it.

2.150 In the same fashion as section 4(3), section 4(4) provides that neither the company nor the creditors can approve a proposal or modification of a proposal for a CVA if: any preferential debt of the company is to be paid otherwise than in priority to such of its debts as are not preferential debts; any ordinary preferential debt of the company is to be paid otherwise than in priority to any secondary preferential debts that it may have; a preferential creditor of the company is to be paid an amount in respect of an ordinary preferential debt that bears to that debt a smaller proportion than is borne to another ordinary preferential debt by the amount that is to be paid in respect of that other debt; a preferential creditor of the company is to be paid an amount in respect of a secondary preferential debt that bears to that debt a smaller proportion than is borne to another secondary preferential debt by the amount that is to be paid in respect of that other debt; in the case of a company which is a

265 *Peck v Craighead* [1995] BCC 525.
266 *Razzaq v Pala* [1998] BCC 66.
267 [2001] BPIR 95.
268 Ibid., [26]–[27].
269 [2002] EWCA Civ 1647, [2003] 1 WLR 1173, [2003] 1 All ER 319, [2003] BPIR 1482.
270 Ibid., [22].
271 Ibid.

relevant financial institution (see section 387A), any non-preferential debt is to be paid otherwise than in accordance with the rules in section 176AZA(2) or (3), without the agreement of the creditor concerned.

The agreement of a secured or preferential creditor cannot be constituted by passive acquiescence, as there must be positive consent or agreement.[272] **2.151**

G. APPROVAL

1. General

The decision to approve takes effect if, in accordance with the Rules, it has been taken by the meeting of the company summoned under section 3 and by the company's creditors pursuant to that section, or (subject to any order made under section 4A(6)) it has been taken by the company's creditors pursuant to that section.[273] **2.152**

Section 4(1A) provides that the company and its creditors may approve the proposed voluntary arrangement with or without modifications. The modifications may include one conferring the functions proposed to be conferred on the nominee on another person qualified to act as an insolvency practitioner in relation to the voluntary arrangement.[274] But no modification is permitted by virtue of the proposal ceasing to be one to which section 1 applies. Section 4A(2) provides that a decision concerning the proposal has effect if, in accordance with the rules, it has been taken by the meeting of the company summoned under section 3 and by the company's creditors pursuant to that section, or (subject to any order made under s 4A(6)) it has been taken by the company's creditors pursuant to section 3. **2.153**

If the decision of the creditors differs from that taken by the company meeting, a member of the company may apply to the court under section 4A(3). What this means is that, absent an application by a member under section 4A(3), an arrangement could be imposed by the creditors without the members' approval. However, to the extent that the court could rule in favour of a member who votes in favour of the proposal and the creditors do not, the legislation, theoretically, provides for a quasi-cram down as far as the creditors are concerned, but it is most unlikely that a court would rule in favour of the **2.154**

---

272 *Peck v Craighead* (n 265).

273 Insolvency Act 1986, s 4A(2).

274 Ibid., s 4(2).

member unless there was some impropriety. Any application by a member must be made within 28 days beginning with the day on which the decision was taken by the company's creditors, or where the decision of the company meeting was taken on a later day, that day.[275] On an application by a member under section 4A(3) the court may order the decision of the company meeting to have effect instead of the decision of the company's creditors, or make such other order as it thinks fit.[276]

2.155 Where the company makes an order pursuant to section 4A(6), the member who applied for the order must serve sealed copies of it on the proposer and the supervisor. The member who applied for the order must also, within five business days of the order, deliver an office copy of the order to the registrar of companies.[277] If the directors are the proposer a single copy may be delivered to the company at its registered office.[278] The proposer or the supervisor must, as soon as reasonably practicable, deliver a notice of the order to all persons who had received a notice to vote on the matter or who are affected by the order.[279]

2.156 A CVA, when approved, operates as a statutory contract between the debtor and its creditors[280] In *Davis v Martin-Sklan*[281] Blackburne J explained that the approval of the arrangement gave rise to 'a species of statutory contract' binding the debtor and the creditors. The CVA takes effect as if it were a consensual agreement. In *Johnson v Davies*[282] Chadwick LJ (with whom Ward and Kennedy LJJ agreed) referred to the terms of the IVA as a 'statutory hypothesis'.[283] His Lordship said that a creditor of the debtor company is bound by the arrangement as the result of a statutory hypothesis that requires him or her to be treated as if he or she had consented to the arrangement.[284] Chadwick LJ went on to say that a creditor who is in some way prejudiced by the decision of the majority to approve proposals which have the effect of releasing a co-debtor (of the company) against whom the creditor would otherwise have

275 Ibid., s 4A(4).
276 Ibid., s 4A(6).
277 Insolvency Rules 2016, r 2.37(5).
278 Ibid., r 2.37(3).
279 Ibid., r. 2.37(4).
280 *Re Arthur Rathbone Kitchens Ltd* [1998] BPIR 1, 14; *Narandas-Girdhar v Bradstock* [2016] EWCA Civ 88, [2016] 1 WLR 2366, [2016] BPIR 428, [35].
281 [1995] BCC 1122.
282 [1999] Ch 117.
283 Ibid., 129, 138.
284 Ibid., 129, 138.

recourse can apply to the court, under section 262 (section 6 for a CVA), for the approval of the meeting to be revoked.[285]

Mann J characterised the terms of an IVA as a deeming provision in *Tanner v Everitt*.[286] Christopher Pymont QC (sitting as a Deputy High Court judge) in *In re SHB Realisations Ltd (formerly BHS Ltd) (in liquidation)*[287] said that while there is a contractual analysis of a CVA, the Act makes it unnecessary and inappropriate to consider any of the usual principles of contract formation (offer, acceptance, consideration, intention to create legal relations), all of which are irrelevant.[288] Later HHJ Simon Barker QC (sitting as a High Court judge) in *Re Rhino Enterprises Holdings Ltd*[289] rejected the argument that the effect of a CVA being regarded as a statutory hypothesis did not mean that a CVA is a contract.[290] **2.157**

For the most part, approval will not affect third parties. An exception to this might be where a party is a co-debtor of the company. The prime example is a guarantor of a company's debt. In *Johnson v Davies*[291] Chadwick LJ stated: **2.158**

> It is up to the debtor to propose, and for the creditors to accept or reject, proposals which either do or do not have the effect of releasing co-debtors and sureties. A creditor who is prejudiced by the decision of the majority to approve proposals which have the effect of releasing a co-debtor against whom he could otherwise have recourse can apply to the court, under section 262 of the Act of 1986, for the approval of the meeting to be revoked.[292]

It is not possible to imply a restriction on the right of a third party to bring proceedings separately against a co-debtor,[293] as it would be unfair if solvent debtors escaped liability.[294] **2.159**

2. Report of results

Rule 2.38(1) provides that a report concerning the meeting or decision procedure that was held to consider the proposal must be prepared by the chair or the convener. Rule 2.38(2) then details the contents of the report. It must: **2.160**

---

285 Ibid., 138.
286 [2004] EWHC 1130 (Ch), [2004] BPIR 1026.
287 [2018] EWHC 402 (Ch), [2018] 2 BCLC 654, [2018] BPIR 818, [2018] Bus LR 1173.
288 Ibid., [28].
289 [2020] EWHC 2370 (Ch), [2021] BPIR 144.
290 Ibid., [77].
291 [1999] Ch 117, [1998] BPIR 607.
292 Ibid., 138; 624.
293 Ibid., 128–129 (Ch); *March Estates plc v Gunmark* [1996] 2 BCLC 1, 5.
294 *RA Securities Ltd v Mercantile Credit Co Ltd* [1994] 2 BCLC 721.

set out a statement as to whether the proposal was approved or rejected and whether by the creditors alone or by both the creditors and members and, in either case, whether any approval was with any modifications; list the creditors and members who voted or attended or who were represented at the meeting or decision procedure (as applicable) used to consider the proposal, setting out (with their respective values) how they voted on each resolution; identify which of those creditors were considered to be connected with the company; if the proposal was approved, state with reasons whether the proceedings are proceedings, establishment proceedings or proceedings to which the EU Regulation as it has effect in the law of the United Kingdom does not apply; any such further information as the nominee or the chair thinks it appropriate to make known to the court.

2.161 After the conclusion of the company meeting and within four days, the chair of the meeting is to report the result of the meeting to the court and, immediately after reporting to the court, is to give notice of the result of the meeting to such persons as may be prescribed.[295] The court must endorse the copy of the report when it is filed with the date of filing.[296] Section 4(6A) provides that after the company's creditors have decided whether to approve the proposed voluntary arrangement, the person who sought the decision must report the creditors' decision to the court and, immediately after reporting to the court, give notice of the creditors' decision to such persons as may be prescribed.

2.162 The chair (in the case of a company meeting) or otherwise the convener must give notice of the result of the consideration of the proposal to everyone who was invited to consider the proposal or to whom notice of a decision procedure or meeting was delivered as soon as reasonably practicable after a copy of the report is filed with the court.[297] Where the decision approving the CVA has effect under section 4A with or without modifications, the supervisor must as soon as reasonably practicable deliver a copy of the convener's report or, in the case of a meeting, the chair's report to the registrar of companies.[298]

2.163 The filing of the chair or convener's report with the court is nothing more than a reporting requirement. The upshot of the approval under section 4A is that the arrangement has effect and the court is not involved in the arrangement unless any application is made to it under section 6. The court must accept the

---

295 Insolvency Act 1986, s 4(6).
296 Insolvency Rules 2016, r 2.38(4).
297 Ibid., r 2.38(5).
298 Ibid., r 2.38(6).

outcome of the company meeting, the creditors' decision procedure and the report.[299]

3. Who is bound?

Whether a creditor is bound will depend on whether their debts or claims are included within the CVA. Whether or not the particular debt or claim of a creditor is included within a CVA depends on the construction of its terms. In determining the claims covered, it is necessary to undertake a construction of the CVA's terms. According to section 5(2), the voluntary arrangement takes effect as if made by the company at the time the creditors decided to approve the voluntary arrangement, and it binds every person who in accordance with the Rules was entitled to vote in the qualifying decision procedure by which the creditors' decision to approve the voluntary arrangement was made, or would have been so entitled if he or she had had notice of it. It is obviously binding on the creditors voting in favour of it. **2.164**

The following relates to an application challenging the approval of the proposal under section 6 of the Act. Under section 6(4), if the court is satisfied as to either of the grounds mentioned in section 6(1) (unfair prejudice or material irregularity), the court may do either of the following.[300] First, it may give a direction to any person for the summoning of a further company meeting to consider any revised proposal the person who made the original proposal may make, or in the case falling within section 6(1)(b) and relating to the company meeting, a further company meeting to reconsider the original proposal. Secondly, the court may direct any person to seek a decision from the company's creditors (using a qualifying decision procedure) as to whether they approve any revised proposal the person who made the original proposal may make. Thirdly, the court may direct any person or in a case falling within section 6(1)(b) and relating to the relevant qualifying decision procedure, to seek a decision from the company's creditors (using a qualifying decision procedure) as to whether they approve the original proposal. The effect of section 5(2) applies to the creditors as at the date of the summoning of the later meeting or decision procedure, not merely those who were entitled to vote at the time of the original meeting or procedure.[301] The same applies if the application was made under section 6(2A). In relation to section 6(4)(b), which provides that if the **2.165**

299 *Smith-Evans v Smailes* [2013] EWHC 3199 (Ch), [2014] BPIR 306, [29], [30]. In this case, HHJ Purle QC (sitting as a High Court judge) said that if it were otherwise, it would be unworkable.

300 Insolvency Act 1986, s 6(4)(a) is not considered here.

301 Ibid., s 6(4)(b)(c). See, *Price v Davis* [2014] EWCA Civ 26, [2014] BPIR 494, [25].

court gives a direction to any person for the summoning of a further company meeting to consider any revised proposal the person who made the original proposal may make, this would cover both creditors who are not known to the nominee who institutes the creditors' decision procedure and also creditors who are known but to whom notice is deliberately not provided or notice is not given due to oversight.

2.166 If, when the arrangement ceases to have effect, any amount payable under it to a person bound by it, because of section 5(2)(b)(ii) (a person who would have been so entitled to vote if he or she had had notice of it), has not been paid, and the arrangement did not come to an end prematurely, the company will at that time become liable to pay that amount to that person.[302] This issue is discussed in more detail in Chapter 5.

2.167 As far as who is a creditor for the purposes of a CVA, there is nothing in the legislation which gives us a definition of 'creditor'. There is every indication for saying that those owed unliquidated debts are covered by the term 'creditor'.'[303]

2.168 Whilst a present debt will be covered by a CVA's terms, there has been some debate concerning future and contingent debts. In *Re Cancol Ltd*,[304] the issue before the court was whether as a matter of law a CVA could bind persons entitled to future or contingently payable debts or whether it could only bind persons entitled to the benefit of presently enforceable claims. In this case landlords of the company's premises argued that they were not bound by the CVA. The landlords asserted that they could claim against the company. They averred that the word 'creditor' had to be given its 'ordinary meaning' and that meant that a person entitled to the benefit of a liability presently due, whether or not quantified by judgment, where there is a liability to pay damages, is bound. According to the landlords, that did not cover rent due in the future under an existing lease because that is a liability which is both future and contingent.[305] Knox J rejected these arguments and held that future and contingent creditors were included in the category of creditors for the purposes of section 5 and who were bound by a CVA.[306] The judge said that a narrow construction of 'creditor' within section 5, which would include only those with a present right to payment, would produce anomalous results.[307] His Lordship

302 Insolvency Act 1986, s 5(2A).
303 Insolvency Rules 2016, r 15.31(3).
304 [1996] 1 All ER 37.
305 Ibid., 41.
306 Ibid., 45, 46.
307 Ibid., 44, 45.

had, earlier in *Doorbar v Alltime Securities Ltd*,[308] rejected the argument that the landlords put to him in *Cancol* in relation to an IVA, and this view was upheld by the Court of Appeal.[309] The judge made the point that there was no difference between an IVA and a CVA in this respect.[310]

In *Discovery (Northampton) Ltd v Debenhams Retail Ltd*[311] Sir Alastair Norris (sitting as a judge of the High Court) described a claim for future rent as a pecuniary claim under an existing legal relationship, which qualified as a 'debt' for the purposes of a CVA. Therefore, the judge concluded that a landlord who has a claim to future rent may be categorised as a creditor regarding the rent falling due under a continuing lease and so would be bound by a CVA. **2.169**

In *Re Wisepark Ltd*[312] it was held that a claim for costs of legal proceedings, which had not yet been awarded to the claimant by an order of the court, was not a contingent liability within section 382. It was a claim that only came into existence when the court made an order for costs. Accordingly, a person with such a claim was not bound by the voluntary arrangement. Consequently, the claimant could pursue the claim against the company outside of the voluntary arrangement if there was a court order relating to the claim. **2.170**

In *Re Millwall Football Club & Athletic Co (1985) plc*[313] it might be recalled that employees were dismissed by the administrator of the company concerned. One of the employees claimed that his claim for compensation was not bound pursuant to the CVA. The CVA stated that debts covered by the CVA included: **2.171**

> all present, future, actual, prospective and contingent liabilities... incurred before the Record Date whether or not such debts arise out of circumstances which are actually known to the Group and whether or not such claims have yet to arise or are capable of being ascertained other than [six classes of debts, being those which were to be paid in full].

The Record Date was the date when the administration order was made. Rimer J held that the claim was based on an obligation whose source was the employee's employment contract. That obligation was in existence on the Record Date and the liability of the company to the employee which arose after the termination of his employment, could, as at the Record Date, properly be **2.172**

308 [1995] 1 BCLC 316.
309 *Doorbar v Alltime Securities Ltd* [1995] BCC 1149.
310 [1996] 1 All ER 37, 42.
311 [2019] EWHC 2441 (Ch), [2020] BCC 9.
312 [1994] BCC 221.
313 [1998] 2 BCLC 272.

characterised as a future, prospective or contingent liability incurred before the Record Date within the meaning of the definition in the CVA terms.[314] It was clear from the definition in the CVA that it made no difference that, as of the Record Date, the claim had not arisen or was not capable of being ascertained. Thus, the employee's claim was bound by the subsequently proposed voluntary arrangement.

2.173 A liquidator with a preference claim against the company that had entered a CVA was held to be a creditor for the purposes of the CVA where the liquidator had been appointed under a winding up that occurred after the approval of the CVA.[315] A preference claim is a contingent liability.[316]

2.174 The terms of a CVA might exclude contingent liabilities from being within the CVA. Consequently, if a CVA does exclude such claims, whether a liability is contingent or not could be critical. In *County Bookshops Ltd v Grove*,[317] where contingent liabilities were excluded, a debt that was owed pursuant to an agreement was payable by three instalments, each to be due at the expiry of 30 days after submission of an invoice in respect of each debt. As at the relevant date for the purposes of the arrangement, the dates for invoicing two of the instalments had passed, but no invoices had been issued. Neuberger J held that while the liability to pay was contingent upon the issue of invoices, since the right to issue the two invoices had already arisen, in commercial terms the liability in respect of the two instalments was not a contingent liability within the terms of the CVA.

2.175 If a creditor has two claims against the debtor company and the creditor can only vote in respect of one of them, he or she is not bound by the CVA in relation to the other claim.[318]

2.176 Creditors who are aware that they will, or may, have claims against the debtor company at some point in the future, are entitled to agree to be bound by a CVA in respect of those claims if and when they become liquidated debts. If creditors in fact lodge a proof, they will be deemed to have agreed and will be bound by the CVA when the debts are liquidated.[319]

---

314 Ibid., 279.

315 *Re North Point Global Limited; Brittain v Chamberlain* [2020] EWHC 1648 (Ch), [2020] 2 BCLC 676.

316 Ibid.

317 [2002] BPIR 772.

318 *Doorbar v Alltime Securities Ltd* [1994] BCC 994, 1000. An appeal to the Court of Appeal was dismissed ([1995] BCC 1149).

319 *Re Goldspan Ltd* [2003] BPIR 93.

If an arrangement is approved at a further meeting which is held pursuant to a direction of the court made under section 6, where there has been a challenge to what occurred at the original meeting, section 5(2) applies to the creditors as at the date of the summoning of the later meeting, not merely those who were entitled to vote at the time of the original meeting. This was held to be the case by the Court of Appeal in *Price v Davis*.[320] The Court also said that creditors whose claims arise after the date of the original meeting can be creditors entitled to vote at a further meeting summoned under section 6.[321] **2.177**

Finally, in *Snoozebox Ltd v Health and Safety Executive*[322] Richard Farnhill (sitting as a Deputy High Court judge) said that the Crown is bound by a CVA under section 434.[323] **2.178**

H. THE AFTERMATH OF THE APPROVAL

1. General

A CVA which has been approved operates by analogy with a contract between the debtor and all creditors,[324] thus a CVA has contractual effect, but it does not mean that it has every attribute of a contract or that every principle of the law of contract applies to it.[325] **2.179**

One of the most important things that eventuates following the approval of a CVA is that a supervisor is appointed to oversee the CVA's implementation. Much of the discussion concerning the supervisor and their role is left to Chapters 4 and 6, as we feel that it is best located there. **2.180**

The nominee, or their replacement, becomes known as the supervisor of the voluntary arrangement automatically by force of section 7(2) on the arrangement coming into effect under section 4A. **2.181**

The circumstances when the nominee does not become supervisor are set out in sections 2(4) and 4(2). The former is where the court has appointed a **2.182**

---

320 [2014] EWCA Civ 26, [2014] BPIR 494. This was a case dealing with an IVA, but it applies equally to CVAs.

321 Ibid., [40].

322 [2023] EWHC 851 (Ch), [2023] BPIR 994.

323 Ibid., [47].

324 *Lloyds Bank plc v Ellicott* [2003] BPIR 632, [51]; *Narandas-Girdhar v Bradstock* [2016] EWCA Civ 88, [2016] BPIR 428, [34].

325 *In re SHB Realisations Ltd (formerly BHS Ltd) (in liquidation)* [2018] EWHC 402 (Ch), [2018] 2 BCLC 654, [2018] BPIR 818, [2018] Bus LR 1173, [28].

replacement nominee because the original nominee failed to submit a report to the court in accordance with section 2(2). The latter applies where the proposal has been modified so as to confer the functions of the nominee on another appropriately qualified person.

2.183 Where a CVA has effect under section 4A, if the supervisor is not the same person as the proposer, the proposer must, as soon as reasonably practicable, do all that is required to put the supervisor in possession of the assets included in the CVA.[326]

2. What happens with an existing liquidation or administration?

2.184 As we explained earlier, it is possible for a CVA to be approved while a company is being wound up or is in administration. It is rare for the former to occur, but it is possible. It is more likely that a CVA will be approved in an administration. This might well not be as frequent as in the past now that the Part A1 Moratorium procedure has been introduced by the Corporate Insolvency and Governance Act 2020.

2.185 If the company was in liquidation or administration at the time of the approval of a CVA, the court may, according to section 5(3), do one or both of the following:

(a) stay or sist all proceedings in the winding up or provide for the appointment of the administrator to cease to have effect;
(b) give such directions with respect to the conduct of the winding up or the administration as it thinks appropriate for facilitating the implementation of the voluntary arrangement.

2.186 The first of these options (section 5(3)(a)) is subject to section 5(4), which provides that if at any time before the end of the period of 28 days beginning with the first day on which each of the reports required by section 4(6) and section 4(6A) has been made to the court, or at any time when an application under section 6 or an appeal in respect of such an application is pending, or at any time in the period within which such an appeal may be brought, an order under section 5(3)(a) cannot be made.

2.187 The provisions do not indicate who qualifies as an applicant under section 5(3), but it has been submitted 'that such an application may be made by any party with an interest in the CVA, which would include the company itself, the

326 Insolvency Rules 2016, r 2.39(1).

nominee or supervisor, a liquidator or administrator, a member of the company or a creditor, whether or not an arrangement creditor'.[327]

If the supervisor is not the same person as the administrator or liquidator, the supervisor must, before taking possession of the assets included in the CVA, deliver to the administrator or liquidator an undertaking to discharge the balance referred to in rule 2.39(3) out of the first realisation of assets or, upon taking possession of the assets included in the CVA, discharge such balance.[328] **2.188**

The balance due to the liquidator or administrator (or, where the liquidation is a compulsory one, the Official Receiver, whether or not in their capacity as liquidator – any sums due to the Official Receiver take priority over those due to the liquidator) is any balance owed in respect of remuneration or on account of fees, costs, charges and expenses properly incurred and payable under the Act or the Rules and any advances made in respect of the company, together with interest at the rate specified in section 17 of the Judgments Act 1838 at the date when the company went into liquidation or administration.[329] **2.189**

The administrator or liquidator, or the Official Receiver not acting as liquidator, has a charge on the assets included in the CVA in respect of any sums comprising such balance, subject only to the deduction from realisations by the supervisor of the proper costs and expenses of such realisations.[330] **2.190**

The supervisor must from time to time, out of the realisation of assets, discharge all guarantees properly given by the liquidator or administrator for the benefit of the company and shall pay all the administrator's or liquidator's expenses.[331] Sums due to the Official Receiver take priority over those due to any other person under rule 2.39.[332] **2.191**

3. Claims arising between proposal being proposed and approval

Where the company, in relation to which a proposal is being made, is not already in liquidation or has entered administration, it is not altogether clear whether those who have supplied goods or performed work between the time of the proposal being put forward and the time when it is approved will be entitled to be paid in priority to existing creditors. There might be specific **2.192**

327 Doyle KC et al., *Doyle, Keay and Curl: Annotated Insolvency Legislation 2025* (n 172), [1.64].
328 Insolvency Rules 2016, r 2.39(2).
329 Insolvency Act 1986, s 2.39(3).
330 Insolvency Rules 2016, r 2.39(4).
331 Ibid., r 2.39(5).
332 Ibid., r 2.39(6).

provision made in the proposal for the discharge of such claims before all other claims. If not, then it might be argued that the creditors would be able to claim against the company.

2.193 Where the above occurs and where the company was in liquidation or administration, the creditors will be paid as part of the expenses of the liquidation or administration.

I. CHALLENGING THE ARRANGEMENT

1. Introduction

2.194 The Act and the Rules provide two routes that a person might employ to challenge the decisions of the company meeting or creditors' decision procedure relating to the approval of the proposal. Section 6(1) sets out the routes. The first is that a voluntary arrangement which has effect under section 4A may be challenged if it unfairly prejudices the interests of a creditor, member or contributory of the company.[333] The second is that there has been some material irregularity at or in relation to the meeting of the company, or in relation to the relevant qualifying decision procedure.[334] In *Richmondshire District Council v Dealmaster Ltd*[335] HHJ Davis White QC (sitting as a High Court judge) said that unfair prejudice was directed at the effect of the scheme on the relevant creditors, whereas material irregularity was directed at some problem in the procedure by which the voluntary arrangement came into force, usually connected with the processes related to the creditors' meeting.[336] There is no express right to challenge the proposal on the ground that it is ultra vires the ambit of the relevant statutory provisions.

2.195 The CVA takes effect upon approval and it is effective (and not suspended) even if a challenge is mounted under section 6 of the Act.[337]

2.196 It is to be emphasised that the power in section 6 and the two routes provided are an exhaustive remedy that precludes other forms of challenge.

2.197 Section 6(2) explains who may challenge the decisions. It provides that any of the following might apply to challenge a decision, namely: a person entitled, in

333 Insolvency Act 1986, s 6(1)(a).

334 Ibid., s 6(1)(b).

335 [2021] EWHC 2892 (Ch), [2022] BPIR 31, [2022] BCC 252.

336 Ibid., [5]. This was approved of in *Re Rossi* [2022] EWHC 1053 (Ch), [2022] BPIR 1241, [26].

337 *Paramount Licensing Inc v Batty* [2024] EWHC 3287 (Ch), [38].

accordance with the rules, to vote at the meeting of the company or in the relevant qualifying decision procedure; a person who would have been entitled, in accordance with the rules, to vote in the relevant qualifying decision procedure if the person had had notice of it; the nominee or any person who has replaced the person under sections 2(4) or 4(2); if the company is being wound up or is in administration, the liquidator or administrator. Besides establishing that they come within one of the above categories of people who may instigate a challenge, the applicant also must establish 'a legitimate interest in the relief sought'.[338] According to Michael Green J in *Nero Holdings Ltd v Young*[339] this was not a matter of jurisdiction, but a matter of judicial restraint.

In undertaking the balancing exercise in deciding whether to exercise discretion, the court would take into account the strength and legitimacy of the applicant's interest in the relief being sought.[340] It was stated in *Re SHB Realisations Ltd (Formerly BHS Ltd (In Liquidation))*[341] by Christopher Pymont QC (sitting as a Deputy High Court judge) that the company has no voice in this process, save insofar as matters which could be said to affect its interests are taken up by the persons who are entitled to apply – persons either whose financial interests are affected by the CVA or who are otherwise interested in implementation of the CVA, such as the nominee, liquidator or administrator.[342] **2.198**

Any application under section 6(1) cannot be made: **2.199**

(a) after the end of 28 days beginning with the first day on which each of the reports required by section 4(6) and (6A) has been made to the court; or
(b) in the case of the person who was not given notice of the qualifying decision procedure, after the end of 28 days beginning with the day on which they became aware that the qualifying decision procedure had taken place,

but (subject to that) an application made by a person within section 6(2)(aa) on the ground that the voluntary arrangement prejudices their interests may be made after the arrangement has ceased to have effect, unless it came to an end prematurely.[343] Unlike with an IVA, the court has no jurisdiction to extend **2.200**

338 *Nero Holdings Ltd v Young* [2021] EWHC 1453 (Ch), [2021] BPIR 1324, [73] per Michael Green J.
339 [2021] EWHC 1453 (Ch), [2021] BPIR 1324.
340 Ibid., [73(6)].
341 [2018] EWHC 402 (Ch), [2018] BPIR 818.
342 Ibid., [30].
343 Insolvency Act 1986, s 6(3).

the 28-day period in section 6(1)(a), whether before or after the expiration of the period.[344]

2.201 Applications under section 6 are final and not interim for the purposes of rule 25 of the CPR, which deals with, amongst other things, interim remedies. The consequence is that evidence which is wholly based on information and belief is not admissible.[345]

2.202 As would be expected, the burden of proof is on the one challenging the CVA.[346]

2.203 As the nominee or supervisor acts as an agent for the debtor, the costs of a successful application will be paid out of the debtor's estate, and it is rare for an order to be made against the nominee or supervisor.[347] This is unless there has been some personal conduct on the part of the nominee that would justify an order for costs against him or her.[348] An order might be made against a nominee or supervisor if their position had plainly shifted from neutrality to one of litigation aggression.[349]

2. On grounds of unfair prejudice

2.204 A voluntary arrangement which has effect under section 4A may be challenged, under section 6(1)(a), if it unfairly prejudices the interests of a creditor, member or contributory of the company. The Act does not define 'unfair prejudice' and no previous insolvency legislation has employed the term. The context of the term is somewhat different from section 994 of the Companies Act 2006, in that creditors' rights are concerned with a CVA whereas it is members' rights with section 994 and it is in relation to the management of the company; thus, the voluminous case law under section 994 of the Companies Act 2006 (and its predecessors) appears to be of little or no assistance in

---

344 *Re Bournemouth and Boscombe AFC Co Ltd* (n 240); *Snoozebox Ltd v Health and Safety Executive* (n 240); and this appears to have been accepted by the Court of Appeal in *Tucker and Spratt (Joint Supervisors of Energy Holdings (No 3) (In Liquidation) v Gold Fields Mining LLC* [2009] EWCA Civ 173, [2009] BPIR 704.

345 *Re A Debtor (No 87 of 1993)* [1996] BCC 74.

346 *Newlon Housing Trust v Mizen Design/Build Ltd* [2023] EWHC 127 (Ch), [2023] BPIR 932, [10], [13]. An appeal from the decision was dismissed by Sir Anthony Mann.

347 *Re Naeem (a Bankrupt) (No 18 of 1988)* [1990] 1 WLR 48, 51; *Burke v Peabody Construction Ltd* [2024] EWHC 392 (Ch), [2024] BPIR 460, [13].

348 Ibid.

349 *Burke v Peabody Construction Ltd* [2024] EWHC 392 (Ch), [2024] BPIR 460, [15].

relation to section 6.[350] The prejudice must affect the creditor in their capacity as a creditor of the debtor, and not in some other capacity.[351]

It must be noted that to fall within section 6(1)(a), the action impugned by the applicant challenging the CVA must be both unfair and prejudicial. In *Lazari Properties 2 Ltd v New Look Retailers Ltd*[352] Zacaroli J (as he then was) said that prejudice to a creditor was likely to be readily identifiable and readily established, such as if the amount owing to creditors is reduced (without them receiving payment) or if they lose a benefit relating to the debt, such as if their security is impaired. It was, according to the judge, more difficult to say what are the circumstances that render the prejudice 'unfair'.[353] **2.205**

Whether the interests of a creditor are unfairly prejudiced is a matter to be determined by consideration of the facts at the time that the CVA was approved;[354] it is not for the courts to speculate whether the terms of a proposed CVA which were put forward were the best that could have been obtained, or whether it would have been better if it had not contained all of the terms which it did contain.[355] **2.206**

Each case has to be considered on its merits and so determining what is unfair prejudice is fact-sensitive. In *Prudential Assurance Co Ltd v PRG Powerhouse Ltd*[356] Etherton J said that there was no single and universal test for judging unfairness in this context, and the question must depend on all the circumstances of the case, including in particular the alternatives available and the practical consequences of a decision to confirm or reject the arrangement,[357] and the alternatives might include not only liquidation but also the possibility of a different and fairer scheme.[358] Nevertheless, his Lordship did say that, depending on the circumstances, a comparison with what the position would have been on a scheme of arrangement under section 425 of the Companies Act 1985 (now Part 26 of the Companies Act 2006) may be of assistance in **2.207**

350 *Doorbar v Alltime Securities Ltd* [1995] BCC 1149, 1159 (CA).

351 *Sea Voyager Maritime Inc v Bielecki* [1999] 1 All ER 628, [1999] 1 BCLC 133.

352 [2021] EWHC 1209 (Ch), [2022] 1 BCLC 557, [2021] BPIR 920.

353 Ibid., [108].

354 *Prudential Assurance Company Ltd v PRG Powerhouse Limited* [2007] EWHC 1002 (Ch), [2008] 1 BCLC 289, [2007] BPIR 839, [71].

355 Ibid., [73].

356 [2007] EWHC 1002 (Ch), [2008] 1 BCLC 289, [2007] BPIR 839, [2007] BCC 500.

357 Ibid., [74]. Also, see *Commissioners of the Inland Revenue v The Wimbledon Football Club Ltd* [2004] EWHC 1020 (Ch), [18] (an appeal to the Court of Appeal was dismissed (*Commissioners of Inland Revenue v The Wimbledon Football Club Ltd* [2004] EWHC 655 (Ch), [2004] BPIR 700); *Richmondshire DC v Dealmaster Ltd* [2021] EWHC 2892 (Ch), [2022] BPIR 31, [2022] BCC 252, [96].

358 *Commissioners of the Inland Revenue v The Wimbledon Football Club Ltd* [2004] EWHC 1020 (Ch), [18].

considering the issue of unfair prejudice in a CVA.[359] However, the judge said that caution must be exercised when carrying out such a comparative exercise. The fact that a particular class of creditors could and might have prevented the approval of a scheme of arrangement did not necessarily mean that they had been unfairly prejudiced within the meaning of section 6. According to *Young v Nero Holdings Ltd*[360] the assessment of what is a relevant alternative to a CVA is largely one of commercial judgment and as such the courts tend to defer to the directors' views, coupled with those of the nominee, as to what would be likely to happen if the restructuring did not go ahead.[361]

2.208 A CVA which has the effect of leaving a creditor in a less advantageous position than before the CVA would be prejudicial to the creditor.[362] Usually, as alluded to above, the critical issue will be whether the prejudice was 'unfair'.[363] In determining whether the interests of an applicant are unfair, the court must consider all the circumstances of the case as there is no single and universal test for judging unfairness. In particular, a court should consider the alternatives available and the practical consequences of a decision to confirm or reject the arrangement.[364] Also, on occasions, a differential approach to creditors, while prejudicial, may be necessary to ensure fairness[365] so an applicant might be able to claim prejudice but not a lack of fairness, and so they will not succeed in their application as prejudice must be unfair in itself.[366]

2.209 Three matters of importance in establishing a claim under section 6(1)(a) are as follows. First, in *Commissioners of the Inland Revenue v The Wimbledon Football Club Ltd*[367] Lightman J said that the unfair prejudice that is alleged must have been caused by the terms of the CVA itself.[368] Secondly, the matters which form the basis of an unfair prejudice claim must be sufficiently conclusive and

359 [2007] EWHC 1002 (Ch), [2008] 1 BCLC 289, [2007] BPIR 839, [2007] BCC 500, [95].

360 [2021] EWHC 2600 (Ch), [2022] BPIR 189.

361 Ibid., [142].

362 *Prudential Assurance Company Ltd v PRG Powerhouse Limited* (n 354), [71]; *Richmondshire DC v Dealmaster Ltd* [2021] EWHC 2892 (Ch), [2022] BPIR 31, [2022] BCC 252.

363 *Mourant & Co Trustees Ltd v Sixty UK Limited (in administration)*, [67]. *HMRC v Portsmouth City Football Club* [2010] EWHC 2013 (Ch), [2011] BCC 149, [2010] BPIR 1123, [41].

364 *SISU Capital Fund Ltd v Tucker* (n 90), [71]; *Prudential Assurance Company Ltd v PRG Powerhouse Limited* (n 354), [74]; *Mourant & Co Trustees Ltd and others v Sixty UK Limited (in administration) and others* (n 23), [67].

365 *Prudential Assurance*, ibid, [88]; *Lazari Properties 2 Ltd v New Look Retailers Ltd* [2021] EWHC 1209 (Ch), [2022] 1 BCLC 557, [2021] BPIR 920.

366 *IRC v Wimbledon Football Club Ltd* [2004] EWCA Civ 655, [2005] 1 BCLC 66, [2004] BPIR 700, [2004] BCC 638 [18].

367 [2004] EWHC 1020 (Ch).

368 *Re A Debtor (No 259 of 1990)* [1992] 1 WLR 226, 228, *Commissioners of the Inland Revenue v The Wimbledon Football Club Ltd* [2004] EWHC 1020 (Ch), [18]. Also, see *SISU Capital Fund Ltd v Tucker* (n 90), [69].

not merely issues of conjecture.[369] Thirdly, it has been stated that the prejudice that is claimed must be experienced in the complainant's capacity as a creditor and not in any other capacity.[370] A plain instance of prejudice is where the terms of the CVA produced discriminatory treatment amongst creditors of the company. Nevertheless, as mentioned above, in *Lazari Properties 2 Ltd v New Look Retailers Ltd*[371] Zacaroli J said that differential or preferential treatment of creditors in the terms set out in a CVA does not in itself establish unfair prejudice.[372] It was necessary to ask whether the imbalance in treatment was disproportionate, and also whether the differential treatment might be justified, for example by the need to secure the continuation of the company's business by paying essential suppliers or service providers. Zacaroli J went on to say that whether unfair prejudice existed depended on all the circumstances,[373] and:

> an important consideration was whether there was a fair allocation of the assets available within the CVA between the compromised creditors and other sub-groups of creditors. That would include considering the source of the assets from which the treatment of the different sub-groups derived, and whether they would or could have been made available to all creditors in the relevant alternative.[374]

Earlier, in *Commissioners of the Inland Revenue v The Wimbledon Football Club Ltd*[375] Lightman J likewise said that merely being treated differently to another class of creditor was not, of itself, unfairly prejudicial to the creditor so treated, although it may give cause to enquire and require an explanation. Lightman J went on to say that depending on the circumstances, differential treatment may be necessary to ensure fairness and may be necessary to secure the continuation of the company's business which underlies the arrangement.[376] Where there is provision for differential treatment of different creditor classes, then, according to Zacaroli J in *Lazari Properties 2 Ltd v New Look Retailers Ltd*,[377] the CVA may be unfairly prejudicial even if that differential treatment can be objectively justified.[378] **2.210**

---

369 *National Westminster Bank plc v Scher* [1998] BPIR 224, 230.
370 *Sisu Capital Fund Ltd v Tucker* (n 90), [70].
371 [2021] EWHC 1209 (Ch), [2022] 1 BCLC 557, [2021] BPIR 920.
372 Ibid., [111].
373 Ibid., [191].
374 Ibid., [193].
375 [2004] EWHC 1020 (Ch), [18].
376 Ibid.
377 [2021] EWHC 1209 (Ch), [2022] 1 BCLC 557, [2021] BPIR 920.
378 Ibid., [190]. This was applied by ICCJ Prentis in *Newlon Housing Trust v Mizen Design/Build Ltd* [2023] EWHC 127 (Ch), [2023] BPIR 932. An appeal from the decision was dismissed by Sir Anthony Mann.

2.211 One must compare the complainant creditor's position with that of the other creditors and not consider matters that arise due to the position of the former. Unfairness must be considered in relation to what would happen to the complainant creditor in a winding up or scheme of arrangement and the comparative position of other creditors. Knox J in *Doorbar v Alltime Securities Ltd (No 2)*[379] said:

> Unfair prejudice ... is a reference to the degree of prejudice to one creditor or class of creditors as compared with other creditors or class of creditors. It involves an assessment of any imbalance between possible prejudices to one or the other ... The concept of unfair prejudice is aimed at disproportionate prejudice on one side or the other.[380]

2.212 In *Prudential Assurance Co Ltd v PRG Powerhouse Ltd*[381] the debtor company's business involved retailing products at several places. It was experiencing financial difficulties and thus proposed a CVA. The company was looking to close several stores which were not successful, and so the landlords of the premises where these stores operated were offered a reduced dividend in the CVA. The dividend payable to landlords would be paid out of funds provided by the company's parent, which also acted as guarantor under each of the company's leases. The proposals included a term that having received the right to be paid the amount provided for in the CVA, the landlords of the closed stores would be prevented from pursuing the parent company for sums due under the guarantees. All other creditors were to be paid in full, and these creditors voted in favour of the CVA, which was approved. The landlords challenged the CVA. Etherton J accepted that the landlords had been unfairly prejudiced. Nevertheless, Etherton J held that a CVA could prevent a creditor from enforcing rights against third parties if enforcing those rights would then mean action being taken against the debtor, as it would in the case of a guarantee. So, while a CVA in itself did not release a guarantor, there was nothing to prevent the CVA from providing that the creditor could not pursue it. Etherton J said that in a case where landlords were not being paid in full whereas other creditors were, and the former were being prevented from taking proceedings against guarantors, this would involve unfair prejudice. If the company was taken into liquidation, landlords would be paid on a pari

379 [1996] BPIR 128.

380 Ibid., 132.

381 [2007] EWHC 1002 (Ch), [2008] 1 BCLC 289, [2007] BCC 500.

passu basis and have the benefit of pursuing guarantors, a loss that was disproportionate; in a scheme of arrangement, they could have vetoed the intended plan.[382]

In his decision, Etherton J said, in relation to guarantees, that there was no doubt that it is legally possible for a CVA to provide that a creditor cannot take steps to enforce an obligation of a third party to the creditor, which would give rise to a right of recourse by the third party against the debtor company, such as payment by a guarantor who could then claim repayment from the debtor pursuant to a right of indemnity, as this would fall within the broad term 'scheme of arrangement of its affairs' in section 1(1).[383] There is no difference in substance between an obligation of that nature and an obligation of the creditor to deal with the third party as if the creditor's contract with the third party did not exist.[384] If the former obligation is enforceable by the debtor company against the creditor, there is no legitimate policy reason, and nothing in the relevant legislation, which prevents the latter obligation from being likewise enforced by the debtor company.[385] **2.213**

In *Newlon Housing Trust v Mizen Design/Build Ltd*[386] ICCJ Prentis indicated that companies proposing CVAs must ensure that if proposals seek to compromise guarantee liabilities, they must contain sufficient information regarding the guarantors' position to enable guarantee creditors to reach an informed decision. **2.214**

What the last couple of paragraphs tell us is that if creditors wish to retain their rights against a guarantor (or some other third party), it is necessary that they ensure that the provision in the CVA which provides for the release of the company from the debt that is guaranteed, on the condition that the company complies with the terms of the CVA, makes it clear that this provision will not release the guarantor, or else the guarantor will be released. In *Greene King plc v Stanley*[387] a creditor made it plain, prior to the approval of a CVA, that it wished to continue to rely on third-party security in addition to a claim in the CVA as a creditor, and in the Court of Appeal, Jonathan Parker LJ (with whom Crane and Tuckey LJJ concurred) held that the one giving the charge **2.215**

382 Ibid., [108].
383 Ibid., [60].
384 Ibid., [61].
385 Ibid.
386 [2023] EWHC 127 (Ch), [2023] BPIR 932. An appeal from the decision was dismissed by Sir Anthony Mann.
387 [2002] BPIR 491.

under the security had not been released. In coming to such a view, the court will examine all the circumstances, including the dealings between the parties leading up to the arrangement.

2.216 In relation to a guarantor who has guaranteed the company's debt, the guarantor is able to claim an indemnity from the company once he or she has paid the creditor who relies on the guarantee.[388] The guarantor will be a party to the CVA as a contingent creditor at the time of the CVA being approved. Consequently, the guarantor will be bound under section 5 by the CVA whether or not he or she had notice of the creditors' decision procedure. Ordinarily, the terms of the CVA should deal with such potential liabilities.

2.217 As discussed earlier in the chapter, in *Johnson v Davies*[389] Chadwick LJ (with whom Ward and Kennedy LJJ agreed) said that a creditor who is in some way prejudiced by the decision of the majority to approve proposals which have the effect of releasing a co-debtor (of the company) against whom he or she would otherwise have recourse, can apply to the court, under section 262 (section 6 for a CVA), on the basis that the action constitutes unfair prejudice.[390]

2.218 It would seem from what Warren J said in *SISU Capital Fund Ltd v Tucker*[391] that even the fact that an office-holder was in a position of conflict, even serious conflict, and that they were in breach of their professional rules, this was not sufficient, by itself, to establish unfair prejudice.[392]

2.219 In determining whether an arrangement was unfairly prejudicial, the courts have developed and employed two tests, which have been called the 'vertical' and 'horizontal' comparators.[393] The former was the irreducible minimum below which the return in a CVA could not go and was to be compared with what the creditors' position would have been in the event that the CVA was not approved, typically their position in a winding up.[394] But it is not enough, in order to preclude a finding of unfair prejudice, that the vertical comparator test is satisfied in respect of objecting creditors, for consideration has to be given to the horizontal comparator, namely determining what was the position

388 *Johnson v Davies* [1998] 2 BCLC 252 (CA).
389 [1999] Ch 117.
390 Ibid., 138.
391 [2005] EWHC 2170 (Ch), [2006] BPIR 154, [2006] BCC 623.
392 Ibid., [122].
393 *Prudential Assurance Co Ltd v PRG Powerhouse Ltd* (n 354), [75].
394 *Lazari Properties 2 Ltd v New Look Retailers Ltd* (n 365), [108].

as between the creditor challenging the CVA and other creditors or classes of creditors.[395]

In *Mourant & Co Trustees Ltd v Sixty UK Limited (in administration)*[396] landlords brought proceedings to challenge a CVA. A company, S, had taken leases over several premises and it was intending to close stores operating at the premises owned by the landlords who were objecting to the CVA. S's parent had guaranteed payment of the rent to these landlords when the leases were first entered into. S went into administration after suffering trading problems, and the administrators proposed a CVA. The effect of the CVA was to release S's parent from all liability under the guarantees upon payment of a sum of £300,000 to the complainant landlords. This amount purported to represent 100 per cent of S's estimated liability to the landlords on a surrender of the leases and to be calculated on the basis of advice received and certain specified assumptions. The landlords were to be deprived of taking action against the parent as guarantor during the remainder of the leases, which still had over seven years to run. All other creditors under the CVA would continue to be paid in full, subject to normal terms and conditions, while the parent had agreed to defer repayment of a sum of just under £15m due to it from S. Henderson J said that on a vertical comparison, in a liquidation the landlords would still have had the benefit of the guarantees for the remainder of the term of the leases. Also, they would have had the option, if the liquidator disclaimed the leases, to require the parent company to take equivalent leases in its own name. It was not permissible for either S or the parent to take unilateral action so as to amend any of those contractual provisions, and, absent the terms of the CVA, the landlords could have continued to enforce the guarantees against the parent.[397] The judge said that on a horizontal comparison, some creditors were to be paid in full under the CVA, while the present and future claims of the guaranteed landlords were to be discharged at a fraction of their value.[398] The conclusion of Henderson J was that there was no justification for this difference in treatment. 2.220

If a reasonable and honest person in the same position as the creditor who is challenging the CVA might reasonably have approved the CVA, that would 2.221

395 Ibid., [109].
396 [2010] EWHC 1890 (Ch), [2010] BPIR 1264, [2011] 1 BCLC 383.
397 Ibid., [75].
398 Ibid., [69].

be powerful and probably conclusive evidence against a finding of unfair prejudice.[399]

2.222 At various points in time, but particularly in the past 15 years, there have been many CVAs, of which *Prudential Assurance Co Ltd v PRG Powerhouse Ltd* (discussed above) was one, which have been challenged by landlords on the basis of unfair prejudice. For instance, in *Thomas v Ken Thomas Ltd*[400] the Court of Appeal considered the rights of landlords in a CVA and, in particular, the effect of a CVA on a landlord's right to forfeit. The Court opined that a landlord could not forfeit a lease to a company subject to a CVA, based on non-payment of rent owed prior to the approval of the CVA. Neuberger LJ (with whom Mummery and Jacobs LJJ concurred) said that the obligation of the tenant to pay the pre-CVA rent had been replaced by the payment obligations under the CVA proposal and the landlord lost not only the right to demand the full amount of the rent due, but also the right to pursue the proprietary remedy of forfeiture for failure to pay.[401] However, when it came to rent that became due post-CVA, the Court stated that a company should not trade on at the expense of its present or future creditors in order to benefit its past creditors, and so the company should be expected to pay the full rent to which the landlord was contractually entitled. Neuberger LJ said that a CVA should provide that post-CVA rent was able to be claimed, or if it did not provide, then, in the absence of special circumstances, the landlord might well be entitled to object to the proposals as unreasonable.[402]

2.223 Challenges to CVAs, on the basis of unfair prejudice, in respect of football clubs that have implemented the so-called 'football creditors' rule' have failed. The rule is essentially that sums due to other clubs and players must be paid in full as a condition of the club being permitted to continue to play in the English Premier League or the English Football League. So, if a CVA provides for the full payment to football creditors under the rule, it cannot be regarded as unfairly prejudiced. HMRC failed in two challenges, made on the basis of unfair prejudice, because of the rule. First, in *HMRC v Portsmouth City Football Club*,[403] HMRC challenged the approval of a CVA and Mann J dismissed it. Amongst other things, he said that the commercial realities

399 See, e.g., *Prudential Assurance Company Ltd v PRG Powerhouse Limited* (n 365), [2007] BCC 500 at [96]; *SISU Capital Fund Ltd v Tucker* (n 18), [81].
400 [2006] EWCA Civ 1504, [2007] BPIR 959.
401 Ibid., [39].
402 Ibid., [34].
403 [2010] EWHC 2013 (Ch), [2011] BCC 149, [2010] BPIR 1123.

behind the CVA required football creditors to be paid in full, for if they were not, the club, Portsmouth City FC (the debtor company), could not continue in the League and that would mean that the company was finished.[404] As Mann J explained:

> If the club goes into winding up the golden share [the share football clubs have in the League] is cancelled and the right to play in the Premier or Football League is lost. Player registrations are cancelled, so the liquidator has no players to sell. The leagues' rules provide that moneys owing to the club by the league are to be applied to pay football creditors. The result is likely to be a financial disaster. The means of earning further money are lost, the assets are seriously devalued and moneys formerly due are not paid. Moneys from the league are a very significant part of a club's income.[405]

HMRC was not actually challenging the football creditor rule as such, and in the absence of such a general ruling, Mann J said that there was no apparent unfair prejudice. Subsequently, in *HMRC v Football League Ltd*[406] HMRC challenged the articles in the articles of association of the English Football League, which incorporated the football creditors' rule, on the basis that they were void and unenforceable under insolvency law, but the challenge failed. **2.224**

It has been established that where a creditor has voted against a CVA and applies to challenge it on the basis that he or she had been unfairly prejudiced, due to the fact that there had been no proper investigation of, among other things, the debtor's assets, such failure to investigate was not, and was not capable of constituting, unfair prejudice.[407] **2.225**

In concluding this section of the chapter, it might be prudent to remind ourselves of what was said in both *SISU Capital Fund Ltd v Tucker*[408] and *Mourant & Co Trustees Ltd v Sixty UK Limited (in administration).*[409] In the former, Warren J said that nominees must seek to ensure that a proposal is capable of securing the necessary statutory majorities and would not be unfairly prejudicial to any creditor, and this might be done by arranging for there to be consensus between all creditors or by establishing a consensus between the majority.[410] In the case of no consensus being reached, nominees should, if possible, present a proposal for approval which they considered did not **2.226**

404 Ibid., [71].
405 Ibid., [10].
406 [2012] EWHC 1372 (Ch), [2013] 1 BCLC 285.
407 *Re a Debtor (No 259 of 1990)* (n 368), 228; *National Westminster Bank plc v Scher* (n 369), 229.
408 [2005] EWHC 2170 (Ch), [2006] BPIR 154.
409 [2010] EWCA 1890 (Ch), [2010] BPIR 1264, [2011] 1 BCLC 383.
410 [2005] EWHC 2170 (Ch), [2006] BPIR 154, [118].

unfairly prejudice any creditor constituency. Indeed, they should not present proposals unless they know that there was a reasonable prospect of their being adopted.[411] In *Mourant*, Henderson J said that when a CVA proposal is being constructed, nominees should:

> maintain an independent stance, to act in good faith, and only to propose a CVA if they are satisfied that it will not unfairly prejudice the interests of any creditor, member or contributory of the company. The need for a responsible and professional attitude is even more pronounced where the CVA is structured in such a way that it is bound to be passed by the votes of creditors whose position is either unaffected or improved, and where another much smaller class of creditors is to be deprived of valuable contractual rights.[412]

3. On grounds of material irregularity

2.227 Section 6(1)(b) provides the second ground which may be relied on to challenge a CVA. This ground is that there was a material irregularity in relation to the meeting of the company or the relevant qualifying decision procedure that applies to the voting by creditors.

2.228 In *Re A Debtor (No 87 of 1993) (no 2)*[413] Rimer J said that 'on the true construction of section 262(1)(b) [equivalent to s 6(1)(b) for CVAs], a material irregularity in a debtor's proposal or statement of affairs is a material irregularity for the purposes of that subparagraph, and that upon being satisfied as to the existence of such an irregularity the court is entitled to exercise its jurisdiction under section 262(4) [equivalent to section 6(4) for CVAs] in whatever may be the most appropriate manner'.[414]

2.229 Section 6(7) indicates that some irregularities will not fall within section 6(1)(b). It states that:

> Except in pursuance of the preceding provisions of this section, (a) a decision taken at a company meeting summoned under section 3 is not invalidated by any irregularity at or in relation to the meeting, and (b) a decision of the company's creditors made in the relevant qualifying decision procedure is not invalidated by any irregularity in relation to the relevant qualifying decision procedure.

2.230 It is not sufficient to establish that there has been an irregularity, the irregularity must be material.[415] The test of 'materiality' is objective; the subjective

411 Ibid., [119].
412 [2010] EWCA 1890 (Ch), [2010] BPIR 1264, [2011] 1 BCLC 383, [88].
413 [1996] BCC 80.
414 Ibid., [108].
415 *Re Sweatfield Ltd* [1997] BCC 744, 750 (HHJ Weeks QC, sitting as a High Court judge).

approach of actual creditors was not appropriate for determining materiality, and the question was whether an objective creditor would have considered and assessed the terms of the CVA differently.[416]

If a creditor was not given notice of the qualifying decision procedure even though the creditor's existence was known, this would be an irregularity in relation to the decision procedure.[417] **2.231**

If there is an irregularity found at a meeting or in a decision procedure, a court might not find that it was material. Robert Walker LJ (as he then was) in the Court of Appeal in *Cadbury Schweppes plc v Somji*[418] said that the test for materiality of an irregularity was whether, objectively assessed, an error or omission 'would be likely to have made a material difference to the way in which creditors would have considered and assessed the terms of the proposed IVA'.[419] A similar approach was adopted in both the later cases of *Golstein v Bishop*[420] and *Discovery (Northampton) Ltd v Debenhams Retail Ltd*.[421] **2.232**

In *Re Trident Fashions plc*[422] the administrators, in the course of proposing a CVA, failed to disclose that there had been alternative, and in fact higher, offers made for the debtor company's business. The court considered this to have been an irregularity, but it was not material because, on the evidence, there was doubt as to whether full disclosure would have had any effect on the decision whether or not to approve the CVA. Similarly, the failure to give notice of the qualifying decision procedure to a creditor is not a 'material irregularity' unless their vote would have affected the decision made.[423] **2.233**

Lord Briggs LJ (as he was then) (with whom Black and Ryder LJJ concurred) supported a broad view of the IVA equivalent of section 6(1)(b) in the Court of Appeal decision of *Narandas-Girdhar v Bradstock*.[424] His Lordship opined that section 262 (the IVA equivalent of section 6) applied to regulate the validity or otherwise of an IVA wherever the allegedly invalidating event (or non-event) occurs at, or in connection with, a creditors' meeting.[425] The judge said that **2.234**

416 *Young v Nero Holdings Ltd* [2021] EWHC 2600 (Ch), [2022] BPIR 189, [145].
417 See, e.g., *Re A Debtor (No 259 of 1990)* [1992] 1 All ER 641.
418 [2001] 1 WLR 615, CA, 626.
419 Ibid., [25].
420 [2016] EWHC 2187 (Ch), [2017] BPIR 51, [66]–[68].
421 [2019] EWHC 2441 (Ch), [2020] BCC 9, [128]–[130].
422 [2004] EWHC 293 (Ch), [2004] 2 BCLC 35.
423 *Re A Debtor (No 259 of 1990)* (n 368); *Doorbar v Alltime Securities Ltd* [1995] BCC 1149 (CA).
424 [2016] EWCA Civ 88, [2016] BPIR 428.
425 Ibid., [36], [50].

he preferred this approach to the narrower approach favoured in some first instance decisions that the phrase 'material irregularity' in section 262(1)(b) means some irregularity which does not of itself render the approval of the IVA a nullity.[426] Briggs LJ said that, amongst other things, against accepting this narrower approach was that it would deprive the court of the flexible jurisdiction under section 262(4) (section 6(4) for CVAs):

> to make sensible provision in an appropriate case for suspending approval, or summoning a further meeting to consider a revised proposal. It would also remove the discretion given to the court as to how if at all to respond to the challenge, in every case where the irregularity was of the invalidating kind. All that the court could do would be to strike down the IVA as void, leaving the debtor and creditor to start all over again. This would be so even if (as here) the invalidity was raised by someone who had supported the approval of the IVA from start to finish, and adhered to it for many years, where the invalidating event has caused him no prejudice at all. This seems to me so greatly to emasculate the obvious purpose of section 262 in its context as to conflict with Parliament's intention, purposively viewed.[427]

2.235 The judge went on to say (and putting it in terms relevant to a CVA and under the 2016 Rules) that to come within section 6(1)(b) the irregularity should be material (which means more than de minimis or irrelevant) and that it should have occurred at or in connection with a decision procedure instigated to consider a proposal for a CVA.[428]

2.236 There may be a material irregularity where there are errors in relation to the voting at a meeting or on a decision procedure, such as the convener of a decision procedure preventing someone from voting on a decision procedure. In *Richmondshire District Council v Dealmaster Ltd*[429] HHJ Davis-White QC (sitting as a High Court judge) said that an example of material irregularity: 'might include misleading or incomplete information to those voting at the meeting, and other defects in procedure at or about the meeting (such as a person being admitted to vote who should not have been or in the correct amount).'[430] In a much earlier case, *Re A Debtor (No 222 of 1990), ex parte the Bank of Ireland*,[431] at a meeting convened to consider whether to approve a voluntary arrangement proposed by C, the chairman, S, ruled that five creditors who had been given notice of and were present at the meeting were not

426 Ibid.
427 Ibid., [51].
428 Ibid., [36], [53].
429 [2021] EWHC 2892 (Ch), [2022] BPIR 31, [2022] BCC 252.
430 Ibid., [5].
431 [1992] BCLC 137.

entitled to vote on the ground that their claims were for unliquidated amounts or their value was not ascertained within the then Insolvency Rules. The debts of the five creditors were a result of guarantees given to them by C. The voluntary arrangement was approved at the meeting.

The five creditors sought orders against C and S under section 262 (the IVA equivalent of section 6). Harman J held that the claims of the five creditors were not for unliquidated amounts or claims whose value was unascertained within the Rules but were disputed debts. The judge stated that where the chairman of the meeting was in doubt about whether to admit or reject a creditor's claim for the purpose of an entitlement to vote, the chairman was required by the Rules to mark the claim as objected to and allow the creditor to vote, subject to the creditor's vote being subsequently declared invalid if the objection to the claim was sustained. Where debts are disputed this was the only proper process for the chairman to follow. Therefore, S's failure to admit the votes of the five creditors was a material irregularity. The same result will occur where a convener or a chair allows someone who is not entitled to vote to do so.[432] If a challenge relates either to allowing or disallowing someone's right to vote, then the court must examine the evidence before the chair or convener in order to determine whether, on balance, a claim was established and, if so, in what amount.[433] In considering the matter, the court is not confined to the evidence that was before the chair at the time that he or she made a decision but is entitled to consider whatever evidence on the issue the parties chose to place before the court.[434] **2.237**

It has been held to be a material irregularity where the chairman of the creditors' meeting wrongly prevented the debtor's largest creditor from lodging a proxy form for the purposes of a re-convened meeting.[435] **2.238**

In dealing with the issue of voting, the way that a convener or chair treats proxies could result in a material irregularity. In *Rowbury v Official Receiver*,[436] the chair of the creditors' meeting declined to suspend the meeting to enable a proxy to be corrected, and so it could not be voted. This was deemed to be a material irregularity and thus the court ordered the revocation of the arrangement. **2.239**

---

432 *National Westminster Bank plc v Scher* (n 369), 227.
433 *Re a Company (No 004539 of 1993)* [1995] BCC 116, 120.
434 Ibid., 120.
435 See, e.g., *Re Cardona* [1997] BCC 697.
436 [2015] EWHC 2276 (Ch), [2016] BPIR 477.

2.240 A successful material irregularity claim was made in *Re Gatnom Capital and Finance Ltd*,[437] where the court considered that two claims which amounted to in excess of 80 per cent of the value being voted at the meeting, and which had been marked as objected to but allowed to vote, were in fact shams. Roth J held that a decision at the creditors' meeting to approve a CVA that was carried only because of the votes based on alleged liabilities that did not in truth exist constituted a material irregularity.[438]

2.241 In *CFL Finance Ltd v Gertner*[439] a proposal for an IVA was approved with one creditor, K, having 90 per cent of the value, voting in favour. Dissenting creditors challenged the IVA on the basis that K had entered into an agreement with the debtor (and others) before the creditors' meeting which provided for full and final settlement of liabilities owed by the debtor (and others) to K. The fact that the agreement had been made was not disclosed to the creditors' meeting. HHJ Keyser QC (sitting as a High Court judge) held that this demonstrated a breach of the good faith principle and if a debtor failed to act in good faith in relation to their creditors, when proposing a CVA, this constituted a material irregularity.[440] The good faith principle was referred to by Malins V-C in *McKewan v Sanderson*[441] in the following way:

> Now I take it to be thoroughly settled, both in Courts of Law and Equity, that where there is a bankruptcy, or an arrangement with creditors by composition or insolvency, when insolvency exists as contradistinguished from bankruptcy, it is the duty of all creditors who have once taken part in the proceedings of bankruptcy or composition to stand to share and share alike. Equality is the only principle that can be applied, and if one creditor, unknown to the other creditors – not unknown to one or two, but to the general body – enters into an arrangement by which he gets for himself from the debtor, or from any one on behalf of the debtor, any collateral advantage whatever, that is a fraud upon the other creditors …

2.242 The decision of Judge Keyser was appealed, but the Court of Appeal[442] approved of what the judge had said, and the appellate court opined that the good faith principle was to be applied strictly.[443]

2.243 A material irregularity may occur not only because of something happening in relation to the convening and conduct of the meeting or the decision

---

437 [2010] EWHC 3353, [2011] BPIR 1013.
438 Ibid., [41].
439 [2017] EWHC 111 (Ch), [2017] BPIR 336.
440 Ibid., [81], [84].
441 (1875) LR 20 Eq 65.
442 *Gertner v CFL Finance Ltd and another* [2018] EWCA Civ 1781.
443 Ibid., [80].

procedure, but also if there have been defects in compliance with the statutory scheme antecedent or extraneous to the instigation or conduct of the decision procedure,[444] such as something stated in the statement of affairs.

In *Peck v Craighead*[445] P obtained a consent judgment against Mr and Mrs C and also by way of execution a writ of fieri facias. The sheriff took possession of chattels which formed part of the business of Mr and Mrs C. Later the creditors of Mr and Mrs C approved an IVA. The issue that had to be considered by the court was whether or not P was a secured creditor. If P was, then the approval meeting could not, without P's consent, affect or modify his rights with respect to the goods in the possession of the sheriff. Mr M Mann QC (sitting as a Deputy High Court judge) (as he then was) held that P was a secured creditor and the refusal to recognise this fact at the meeting was a material irregularity. **2.244**

A court might well find that a material irregularity had occurred where there was a failure to make appropriate disclosures. Nevertheless, the court would only interfere if a judgment about the material to be placed before the creditors was a judgment to which no reasonable insolvency practitioner could come. That judgment was to be made on the basis of the material available at the time and not with the benefit of hindsight.[446] The non-disclosure of information to creditors voting on a CVA only constituted a material irregularity if there was a substantial chance that the non-disclosed material would have made a difference to the way in which the creditors voted.[447] What constitutes sufficient detail to enable creditors to reach an informed decision is very much dependent on the facts and, therefore, will differ from case to case.[448] **2.245**

Just as a failure to disclose may constitute a material irregularity, so might the inclusion of false or misleading information in a proposal.[449] If there is false or misleading information contained in a proposal, such as misrepresentations, that may constitute a material irregularity.[450] In *Inland Revenue* **2.246**

---

444 *Fletcher v Vooght* [2000] BPIR 435, *Vlieland-Boddy v Dexter Ltd* [2004] BPIR 235; *Inland Revenue Comrs v Bland* [2003] BPIR 1274; *Narandas-Girdhar v Bradstock* [2016] EWCA Civ 88, [2016] BPIR 428, [36], [53].

445 [1995] 1 BCLC 337.

446 *Re Trident Fashions (No.2)* [2004] EWHC 293 (Ch), [2004] 2 BCLC 35; *Young v Nero Holdings Ltd* (n 187).

447 *Somji v Cadbury Schweppes plc* [2001] 1 BCLC 498, [35]; *Carraway Guildford (Nominee A) Ltd v Regis UK Ltd* [2021] EWHC 1294 (Ch), [2022] 1 BCLC 709, [59].

448 *Lazari Properties 2 Ltd v New Look Retailers Ltd* (n 365), [301].

449 *Re A Debtor (No 87 of 1993) (No 2)* [1996] BCC 80, [1996] 1 BCLC 63, [1996] BPIR 6.

450 Ibid., 108; *Inland Revenue Commissioners v Duce* [1999] BPIR 189, 194.

Commissioners v Duce[451] the county court judge at first instance held that there had been material irregularity as the debtor had failed to disclose the correct identity of creditors and the identity of the creditor who would purchase one of the debtor's assets. The judge revoked the approval of the IVA. On appeal by the debtor, Hazel Williamson QC (sitting as a Deputy High Court judge) dismissed the appeal and held that there had been material misrepresentations or wrong disclosures in the proposal capable of amounting to a material irregularity.

2.247 It has been suggested that normally it will be appropriate to join the nominee, and possibly one or more creditors, to an application alleging material irregularity at or in relation to a meeting at which the nominee and/or such creditors have been involved.[452]

2.248 Finally, if a creditor did not receive notice of the vote for the proposal and his or her vote could have made a difference to the final vote, the creditor would be entitled to make a challenge on the basis of a material irregularity.

4. The powers of the court

2.249 The courts are granted wide powers on hearing a challenge to a CVA under either or both of the two routes discussed above, and the powers are provided for in section 6(4)–(6). Section 6(4) provides that the court may do one or both of the following:

> (a) revoke or suspend any decision approving the voluntary arrangement which has effect under section 4A, or in a case falling within section 6(1)(b), any decision taken by the meeting in question which has effect under that section;
> (b) give a direction to any person for the summoning of further meetings to consider any revised proposal the person who made the original proposal may make, or, in a case falling within section 6(1)(b) [material irregularity], a further company or (as the case may be) creditors' meeting to reconsider the original proposal;
> (c) direct any person–
>   (i) to seek a decision from the company's creditors (using a qualifying decision procedure) as to whether they approve any revised proposal the person who made the original proposal may make, or
>   (ii) in a case falling within section 6(1)(b) and relating to the relevant qualifying decision procedure, to seek a decision from the company's creditors (using a qualifying decision procedure) as to whether they approve the original proposal.

451 [1999] BPIR 189.

452 Doyle KC et al., *Doyle, Keay and Curl: Annotated Insolvency Legislation 2025* (n 172), [1.65].

If an arrangement is suspended by court order, the arrangement is of no effect while that order remains on foot.[453] **2.250**

In a challenge brought under section 6(1)(b), Lord Briggs LJ in the Court of Appeal in *Narandas-Girdhar v Bradstock*[454] approved (with the concurrence of Black and Ryder LJJ) a broad view of the section, giving the court the power to act in any case where the irregularity is material.[455] **2.251**

It was made plain in *Mourant & Co Trustees Ltd v Sixty UK Limited (in administration)*[456] that the power in section 6(4)(b) is only exercisable where the court is satisfied as to either of the grounds contained in section 6(1).[457] Thus, a case on unfair prejudice and/or material irregularity has to be made out to the court's satisfaction before such an order can be made.[458] **2.252**

According to section 6(5), where at any time after giving a direction under section 6(4)(b), the court is satisfied that the person who made the original proposal does not intend to submit a revised proposal, the court is to revoke the direction and revoke or suspend any decision which took effect under section 4A. Section 6(6) provides that where the court, on an application under section 6 with respect to any meeting or relevant qualifying decision procedure, gives a direction under section 6(4)(b) or (c), or revokes or suspends an approval under section 6(4)(a) or (5), the court may give such supplemental directions as it thinks fit and, in particular, directions with respect to things done under the voluntary arrangement since it took effect. **2.253**

In *Inland Revenue Commissioners v Duce*[459] Hazel Williamson QC (sitting as a Deputy High Court judge), hearing an appeal from the county court, said that if a debtor has lied in a material way in respect of a proposal which he or she is putting forward, this: **2.254**

> can be sufficiently serious that the court can decline to exercise any discretion to order another meeting. If the untruths are 'sufficiently heinous' that the debtor is shown to be unfit to have an opportunity to put forward a further arrangement at all, or if they show that no serious and viable proposal can be put forward, or that plainly the matter ought to be investigated, then the court can decline to order a further meeting and should do so.

453 *Price v Davis* [2014] EWCA Civ 26, [2014] BPIR 494, [30]–[31].
454 [2016] EWCA Civ 88, [2016] BPIR 428.
455 Ibid., [36]. This was a case dealing with an IVA, and the Court addressed s 262(4), the equivalent of s 6(4).
456 [2010] EWHC 1890 (Ch), [2010] BPIR 1264, [2011] 1 BCLC 383.
457 Ibid., [13].
458 Ibid.
459 [1999] BPIR 189.

> The question in each case must be whether the inaccuracies or lies, or whatever they are, are shown to have gone that far.[460]

2.255 The deputy judge went on to say that:

> in my judgment, there is a balancing exercise to be performed between the seriousness and the heinousness of the irregularity and the likely attitude of the other creditors. In this case, the judge did not conduct such an exercise and in my judgment he erred in principle in not doing so. Therefore, the decision whether or not to order a further meeting was an exercise of discretion on a wrong principle and I can, and do, proceed to substitute my own discretion.[461]

2.256 While the court had broad discretion, it has a duty to act in setting aside an arrangement where the arrangement is in clear conflict with a statutory provision. The courts have made it clear, as mentioned in earlier parts of the chapter, that they can decline to make an order if the making of an order would damage the interests of the creditors. The court's discretion to revoke remains, even following the termination of an arrangement.[462]

2.257 The court has the role of watchdog as far as the interests of creditors who do not challenge any decision to approve the proposal are concerned. One commentary has stated that:

> [t]hose creditors would be justifiably unhappy if the proposal were revoked, and they were left to prove in more expensive bankruptcy proceedings in circumstances where they would not have taken a sufficiently dim view of the debtor's conduct to vote down the proposal.[463]

2.258 Rule 2.40 governs any court order of revocation or suspension under section 6. According to rule 2.40(2) the person who applied for the order under section 6 must deliver a sealed copy of it to the proposer and the supervisor (if different). If the directors are the proposer a single copy of the order may be delivered to the company at its registered office.[464] If the order includes a direction by the court under section 6(4)(b), the applicant for the order must deliver a notice that the order has been made to the person who is directed to take such action.[465] Under rule 2.40(5), the proposer must, as soon as reasonably practicable, deliver a notice that the order has been made to all of those

---

460 Ibid., 197.
461 Ibid., 201.
462 *Regis UK Limited (in administration)* [2019] EWHC 3073 (Ch), [26].
463 Mullen (ed), *Tolley's Insolvency Law* (n 186).
464 Insolvency Rules 2016, r 2.40(3).
465 Ibid., r 2.40(4).

persons to whom a notice to consider the matter was delivered or who appear to be affected by the order, and within five business days of delivery of a copy of the order (or within such longer period as the court may allow), deliver (if applicable) a notice to the court advising that it is intended to make a revised proposal to the company and its creditors, or to invite reconsideration of the original proposal. The applicant for the order then must deliver a copy of the order to the registrar of companies within five business days of the making of the order with a notice which must contain the date on which the voluntary arrangement took effect.[466]

Section 6(5) provides that where any direction for the summoning of the company meeting and qualifying decision procedure is given for the purposes of the consideration of a revised proposal, and the court is subsequently satisfied that the person concerned does not intend to submit a revised proposal, the court must revoke the direction and revoke or suspend any approval given at the previous meeting. **2.259**

As with any appropriate case, the court may order costs against non-parties where there is a challenge under section 6, and where the circumstances are exceptional. This occurred in *Re Gatnom Capital and Finance Ltd*.[467] **2.260**

466 Ibid., r 2.40(6).
467 [2010] EWHC 3353 (Ch), [2011] BPIR 1013.

3

THE MORATORIUM

A. INTRODUCTION

3.001 The Cork Committee[1] was set up in 1977 and published its report in June 1982. As explained in Chapter 1, among the proposals considered by the Cork Committee were two new procedures, administration and company voluntary arrangements ('CVAs'), both aimed at encouraging, wherever possible, company or business rescue, rather than liquidation. Both procedures were introduced and remain in force under the Insolvency Act 1986 ('the Act').

3.002 One of the problems that has always faced attempts by a company to reach a negotiated settlement with its creditors is that, by the time the company realises it needs to do something, time may be in very short supply. The CVA regime has not proven as popular as had been hoped when the Cork Committee recommended its creation back in 1982. There are arguably a number of reasons for this. One reason appears to be that there was no provision within the CVA regime, as originally drafted, for a moratorium (or temporary stay) on creditor action while the proposal was drawn up and considered. The Cork Committee recognised this weakness in relation to schemes of arrangement and suggested that the moratorium in administration might fill this gap. In

1 *Report of the Insolvency Law Review Committee, Insolvency Law and Practice*) Cmnd 8558 (1982).

giving effect to Cork's recommendations, the law has since 1986 provided for a company to enter administration and, as a consequence, obtain the benefit of the administration moratorium,[2] before putting together a proposal for a CVA. This was certainly a suggestion made by the Cork Committee when formulating the rescue culture introduced by the Act.[3] It has not proven to be a successful route. The problem, under the old administration regime which was in force between 1986 and 2003, was that the only way to put a company into administration was by going to court. The time and expense of obtaining an administration order were often prohibitive.[4] Even when placing a company into administration became simpler and cheaper following the Enterprise Act 2002, this avenue to promulgate a CVA has remained relatively rare.[5]

As will be explained below, the need for a separate form of moratorium to support a company looking to propose a CVA, which is reasonably straightforward and economical, was recognised in the early 1990s. There have been numerous attempts at identifying how this goal might be achieved. We have seen two statutory procedures introduced, and the results remain, to some extent, inconclusive. In this chapter, we will consider the reform debate which went on between 1986 and 2000. We will then look at the moratorium introduced by the Insolvency Act 2000. Finally, we will consider the Moratorium now available, which in 2020 replaced the 2000 version. **3.003**

B. 1986–2000 NO MORATORIUM

In November 1992, a working party was set up by the Insolvency Service to examine why company rescue provisions had not been used more frequently. The working party identified, amongst other weaknesses, the lack of a moratorium in the CVA process.[6] **3.004**

In 1993, a consultation document, *Company Voluntary Arrangements and Administration Orders*,[7] was published by the Insolvency Service. Among the proposals considered was the introduction of a short moratorium on creditors' **3.005**

2 Insolvency Act 1986, Sch B1, paras 42 and 43.

3 Cork Report at [424].

4 For an account of the original administration procedure, see, e.g., A Keay and P Walton, *Insolvency Law Corporate and Personal*, 1st ed (Pearson, 2004).

5 P Walton, C Umfreville and L Jacobs, *Company Voluntary Arrangements: Evaluating Success and Failure* (May 2018).

6 See The Government, *Research Paper (00/79)* dated 17 October 2000, supporting the Insolvency Bill (Bill 173 of 1999–2000) ('2000 Bill Research Paper') at p 9.

7 Insolvency Service, *Company Voluntary Arrangements and Administration Orders*, October 1993.

actions to give time for a CVA to be put together. This short moratorium would be brought into effect following a statement by an insolvency practitioner that there was a reasonable prospect of a successful CVA. It would last initially for no more than 28 days, but it could be extended by the agreement of the creditors for a maximum of another two months.

3.006 In April 1995, the Insolvency Service published a summary of responses to its October 1993 consultation document.[8] It also published for further consultation revised proposals for a new CVA procedure.[9]

3.007 In November 1995, the then government announced its intention (when parliamentary time allowed) to add the option of a moratorium to the existing CVA procedure. [10] At the time of the General Election in May 1997, the consultation on this proposal was still in progress.[11]

3.008 Despite the change of government in 1997, the proposal was retained by the incoming administration. A White Paper[12] in 1998 specifically identified, amongst a more wide-ranging review of insolvency law, the intention to legislate for a moratorium on creditors' actions to allow a business in financial difficulties up to three months to come to an agreement with its creditors.

3.009 That review led to a consultation document in September 1999, entitled *A Review of Company Rescue and Business Reconstruction Mechanisms*.[13] This work ultimately led to the major changes introduced to the insolvency regime by the Enterprise Act 2002.[14] Rather than wait for the wider review to be completed, the government pressed ahead with the plan for a moratorium, which was the main subject of an Insolvency Bill and was subject to a short technical consultation, also in September 1999.[15]

3.010 Interestingly, the DTI Select Committee that examined the Bill concluded at the time: 'In an ideal world we would prefer that the legislation be deferred

---

8 Insolvency Service, *Company Voluntary Arrangements and Administration Orders: Summary of Responses,* April 1995.

9 Insolvency Service, *Revised Proposals for a new Company Voluntary Arrangement Procedure: A Consultative Document*, April 1995.

10 DTI press notice P/95/839, *Company Voluntary Arrangements*, 27 November 1995.

11 2000 Bill Research Paper at p 10.

12 Department of Trade and Industry, *Our Competitive Future: Building The Knowledge Driven Economy: Government's Competitiveness White Paper*, Cm 4176, December 1998.

13 Insolvency Service, *A Review of Company Rescue and Business Reconstruction Mechanisms*, September 1999.

14 See the White Paper Insolvency Service, *Insolvency – A Second Chance,* Cm 5234 July 2001.

15 2000 Bill Research Paper at pp 12–13.

until it can be merged with the results of the wider review; but the world is not ideal and opportunities for such legislation are not frequent.'[16]

The Association of Business Recovery Professionals (known as 'R3') made a number of observations highlighting some of the shortcomings of the Bill's moratorium.[17] The proposed moratorium procedure's availability to only small companies was seen as arbitrary as larger companies were usually more capable of being rescued and might benefit from its use. R3 also pointed out some gaps in the effect of the moratorium and some rather ambiguous drafting around, for example, the ability of secured creditors to take action during the moratorium. Importantly, one weakness identified by R3 was that the CVA proposal needed to be already formulated before a moratorium could come into effect. R3 commented that the earlier consultation in 1995 had suggested a moratorium could be put into place so as to allow time to formulate the proposal which it thought might have been more useful. The requirement for the insolvency practitioner nominee to express their opinion that the proposal had a reasonable prospect of being approved and implemented was criticised. This was seen as problematic for any insolvency practitioner in that it required them to predict the voting intentions of creditors. R3 also considered that the monitoring responsibilities of the insolvency practitioner during the moratorium were unnecessary and would not encourage use. Although there was no power for the insolvency practitioner to apply to the court for directions, their actions could still be the subject of creditor or member action in court if there was dissatisfaction with their actions. The duties appeared onerous. R3 also complained that the new, separate rules for a CVA commenced using a moratorium were unnecessary. R3's view was that once the moratorium had come to an end, any approved CVA should be treated as an ordinary CVA thereafter. The divergence in procedure was an unwelcome complication. **3.011**

Despite criticism, the CVA-specific moratorium provisions of the Insolvency Act 2000 introduced a new Schedule A1 to the Act. **3.012**

C. 2000–2020 SCHEDULE A1 MORATORIUM

The expense of acquiring an administration order, under the pre-Enterprise Act ('EA') 2002 regime and the costs incurred in having an administrator **3.013**

16 Trade and Industry Select Committee (HC) Draft Insolvency Bill, HC 112, 1999–2000, 14 December 1999 at [8].

17 B Jones, 'The Moratorium Provisions for the Company Voluntary Arrangement Procedure in the Insolvency Bill 2000' (2000) 16 *Insolvency Law and Practice* 77.

running the company were frequently prohibitive, at least for small companies. The prospects of a successful CVA being implemented without the benefit of a moratorium are limited to circumstances where the creditors are willing to be supportive. The lack of popularity of CVAs in the pre-EA period was believed to be due in part at least to the original 1986 regime's assumption that administration (and its moratorium) would be available to all companies, when in fact, as mentioned above, in practice, it was not. The problem encountered, namely, the way in which the courts dealt with administration petitions, meant that obtaining the order was in itself too expensive a process for many companies. The irony of the post-EA 2002 system is that it is far easier to put the company into administration nowadays and therefore the requirement for a separate moratorium procedure under Schedule A1 always looked as though it was going to be surplus to requirements. In practice, the Schedule A1 procedure was rarely, if ever, used, both for this reason and partly because its terms were, in places, somewhat more restrictive than if the company was placed into administration. Many of R3's observations about the potential problems with Schedule A1 proved accurate.

3.014 Research showed that in practice, when a company was considering a CVA, it was rare that either the Schedule A1 procedure or administration was used to create a temporary breathing space.[18] Although this suggests that companies considering a CVA do not necessarily need the protection of a moratorium, it is the case that a great many CVAs terminate prematurely. Such a high premature termination rate might be improved upon if companies more routinely bought themselves some more time, via a form of moratorium, to consider the details of their proposed CVA, and importantly, to make necessary changes which the company's business needs to make if it is to be a viable undertaking in the future.

3.015 We shall look at the repealed Schedule A1 procedure in outline.

3.016 Broadly speaking, the effect of the now repealed Schedule A1 (given effect by s 1A) was to allow directors of 'small companies' to obtain a short moratorium for their company during which a CVA proposal could be put to the creditors. The meaning of 'small companies' for this purpose was taken from the definition contained within section 382(3) of the Companies Act 2006, which, prior

18 Walton et al., *Company Voluntary Arrangements: Evaluating Success and Failure* (n 5).

to the repeal of Schedule A1,[19] stated that to be eligible, the company had to satisfy at least two of the following requirements:

(1) its annual turnover could not exceed £10.2 million;
(2) its balance sheet total did not exceed £5.1 million; and
(3) it had no more than 50 employees.

A company could not take advantage of this procedure if (among other things[20]): **3.017**

(1) the company was in administration, liquidation (including where a provisional liquidator was in post), administrative receivership or was already subject to a CVA; or
(2) in the previous 12 months a moratorium had been in force in relation to the company which did not result in a CVA being approved or did result in a CVA which had ended prematurely.[21]

If the company was eligible, the directors had to submit to a nominee (who had to be a licensed insolvency practitioner) a proposal for a CVA along with a statement of the company's affairs. The nominee had to reply to the directors stating whether or not, in their opinion: **3.018**

(1) the proposal had a reasonable prospect of being approved and implemented;
(2) the company was likely to have sufficient funds available during the moratorium period to enable it to carry on its business; and
(3) that the proposal should be considered by a meeting of the company's members and by the company's creditors.[22]

The nominee was entitled to rely on the information furnished by the directors unless they had reason to doubt its accuracy.[23] **3.019**

In order to obtain the moratorium, the directors had to file with the court a copy of the proposal, a statement of affairs of the company, a statement that the company was eligible and a statement from the nominee that they held the **3.020**

19 This definition was updated on a number of occasions during the 2000–2020 period; see, e.g., the Companies Act 1985 (Accounts of Small and Medium-Sized Enterprises and Audit Exemption) (Amendment) Regulations 2004 (SI 2004/16).

20 Banks and insurance companies were ineligible under para 2 of Sch A1 repealed, and various other types of companies such as those operating within the capital markets were ineligible under paras 4A–4K of Sch A1 of the Act, repealed. These provisions recognised the policy of excluding such businesses from mainstream insolvency procedures. Specialist insolvency regulations applied instead.

21 Insolvency Act 1986, Sch A1, para 4 repealed.

22 Ibid., para 6(2) repealed.

23 Ibid., para 6(3) repealed.

favourable opinions listed above and consented to act.[24] The moratorium came into effect upon these documents being filed. The moratorium ended after 28 days, or earlier upon decisions being taken by the members' meeting and the creditors.[25] The moratorium could be extended for a further two-month period by the agreement of both the members and the creditors.[26] Once in effect, the moratorium had to be advertised and notice of it given to:

- the company;
- any creditor who had petitioned for a winding-up order against the company; and
- the Registrar of Companies.[27]

3.021 The existence of the moratorium had to be stated on all business documents, whether hard copy or electronic, and on all of the company's websites[28] and the company could not obtain credit of £250 or more without disclosing the moratorium.[29]

3.022 The moratorium itself, not surprisingly, was in very similar terms to that imposed in administration.[30] It contained one very important addition which affected a floating charge holder's rights. Such a debenture holder was prevented from appointing an administrative receiver or an administrator. The powers that a debenture holder had in the administration regime, in relation to having its choice of administrator or administrative receiver appointed, were absent here. Furthermore, a floating charge was prevented from crystallising during the moratorium.[31]

3.023 Whilst the moratorium was in force, the company continued under the managerial control of the directors who were able to dispose of assets in the ordinary course of business. Any other disposal was only possible if there were reasonable grounds for believing that it would benefit the company and either the creditors' committee (if there was one) or the nominee (if there was not a committee) approved the disposal.[32]

24 Ibid., para 7 repealed.
25 Ibid., para 8 repealed.
26 Ibid., para 32 repealed.
27 Ibid., para 10 repealed.
28 Ibid., para 16 repealed.
29 Ibid., para 17 repealed.
30 Ibid., para 12 repealed.
31 Ibid., paras 13 and 43 repealed.
32 Ibid., para 18 repealed.

The company had similar powers, under paragraph 20 of Schedule A1, to dispose of assets subject to fixed charges or hire purchase agreements (defined to include conditional sale, chattel leasing and retention of title agreements) as an administrator has under paragraphs 71 and 72 of Schedule B1. A court order or the creditor's consent was similarly needed to exercise this power, and the proceeds from the sale had to go to pay off the creditor. If a reasonable price was not realised, the company had to make up the shortfall. The power under paragraph 20 to sell floating charge assets was also similar to the power an administrator has under paragraph 70 of Schedule B1. Once floating charge assets were sold, the charge in effect moved to the proceeds of sale or substituted property. The power to deal with floating charge assets was seen as being drafted in an ambiguous way and, on a purely literal interpretation, it seemed that the company could only deal with assets subject to a floating charge with the consent of the debenture holder or leave of the court. If this had been the case, as the floating charge would usually cover all the company's property both present and future, the company would be effectively paralysed. Although capable of a more purposive interpretation, such inherent uncertainty did not appear to encourage the use of the Schedule A1 regime. **3.024**

During the moratorium, the nominee was under a duty to monitor the company's affairs in order to form an opinion as to whether the CVA continued to have a reasonable prospect of being approved and implemented and that the company was likely to have enough money to continue to run the business.[33] Again, the nominee had the right to rely on information received from the directors unless they were put on enquiry. If the nominee believed that the CVA was no longer viable, they had to withdraw their consent to act and the moratorium was thereby terminated.[34] This duty on the nominee to continuously monitor the proposed CVA during the moratorium was peculiar to Schedule A1. It was seen by practitioners as potentially an onerous duty and was likely to be seen by a nominee as another factor vitiating against the use of Schedule A1. **3.025**

While the moratorium was in force, the nominee could be replaced by the court on an application by the directors who alleged a breach of duty by the nominee or that there were other circumstances whereby it was inappropriate for the nominee to continue.[35] A director, member, creditor or third party affected by the moratorium who was 'dissatisfied' by an act, omission or decision of the **3.026**

33 Ibid., para 24 repealed.
34 Ibid., para 25 repealed.
35 Ibid., para 28 repealed.

nominee could bring an action against the nominee.[36] This provision appeared to be extremely widely phrased and potentially opened up the nominee to unforeseeable types of claims. Also of concern to the nominee was the power of any creditor (where the company did not intend to bring an action itself) to apply to the court on the basis that an action or decision of the nominee had caused loss to the company.[37]

3.027 The members and creditors made decisions in much the same way as under the substantive provisions of the Act, as detailed above. The way in which the CVA was dealt with after the proposal had been approved was essentially the same.

D. 2020 ONWARDS – THE STANDALONE MORATORIUM

3.028 The Schedule A1 moratorium, which was specifically linked to a proposal for a company voluntary arrangement, was little used in practice.[38] The idea of an effective moratorium continued to be considered and consulted upon by the UK Government.[39]

3.029 The government's initial preference was for a form of pre-insolvency moratorium. The idea was that a company, which was not yet technically insolvent but was experiencing or might experience some form of financial distress, was likely to benefit from a short-term moratorium. The moratorium would provide a stay on creditor action while the company considered possible turnaround options. Crucially, the proposed moratorium was not to be available to companies that were already insolvent. Many practitioners feared that this restriction would make the pre-insolvency moratorium largely redundant in practice. If solvency needed to be shown, it was thought that few if any companies would wish to take advantage of the new procedure.

3.030 Partly as a reaction to the concerns of practitioners, partly as a reaction to international developments[40] and partly as an urgent reaction to the Coronavirus

36 Ibid., para 26 repealed.

37 Ibid., para 27 repealed.

38 See, e.g., Walton et al., *Company Voluntary Arrangements: Evaluating Success and Failure* (n 5) at para 4.1.2.

39 *A Review of the Corporate Insolvency Framework: a consultation on options for reform* (May 2016) was followed by a similar consultation in 2018. In its response to its consultations on insolvency law reform (*Insolvency and Corporate Governance – Government Response* 26 August 2018), the government stated an intention to introduce, amongst other things, a new restructuring procedure based partly on the US Ch.11 procedure, and a short-term moratorium available to virtually all companies.

40 See: the World Bank's Principles for Effective Insolvency and Creditor/Debtor Regimes, Principle C5.3, which recommends that 'a stay of actions by secured creditors should be imposed ... in reorganisation

pandemic, the government changed its moratorium plans and, as part of a suite of insolvency-related measures in the Corporate Insolvency and Governance Act 2020 ('CIGA'),[41] introduced a new form of standalone Moratorium which is found in Part A1 to the Act.[42] It is intended for use by companies that are insolvent or are likely to become insolvent. Significantly, the Moratorium is designed to lead to the rescue of the company, not merely to a beneficial realisation of its assets.[43]

CIGA repealed Schedule A1. Although it is still too early to judge the likely long-term popularity of the Moratorium, there are a number of concerns as to how it operates in practice and it may require amendment in order for it to become more popular.[44] **3.031**

The Moratorium is a standalone procedure and not linked to any other procedure. The Moratorium is a debtor-in-possession procedure whereby the directors remain in control of the company and the intention and purpose behind entering the Moratorium is to rescue the company. It may be used on its own to provide a temporary breathing space for the company to turn its fortunes around or used in conjunction with a proposal for a CVA, scheme of arrangement or restructuring plan. As will be seen below, the legislation is different from, but bears some comparison in terms of complexity with, its predecessor under the repealed Schedule A1. **3.032**

proceedings where the collateral is needed for the reorganisation. The stay should be of limited, specific duration, strike a proper balance between creditor protection and insolvency proceeding objectives and provide for relief from the stay by application to the court'; the 2019 EU Restructuring Directive [Directive (EU) 2019/1023 of the European Parliament and of the Council of 20 June 2019 on preventive restructuring frameworks, on discharge of debt and disqualifications, and on measures to increase the efficiency of procedures concerning restructuring, insolvency and discharge of debt, and amending Directive (EU) 2017/1132 (Directive on restructuring and insolvency); and the UNCITRAL Legislative Guide on Insolvency Law, which sets out provisions that are now seen as core components of a modern insolvency regime, including a stay of enforcement action.

41 CIGA made provision for both temporary and permanent changes to the insolvency regime in light of the Coronavirus pandemic and its anticipated economic aftermath.

42 Part A1 of the Act is supplemented by Part A1 to the Insolvency (England and Wales) Rules 2016 (SI 2016/1024) ('the Rules'). Most applications to court in relation to a Moratorium will be governed by the requirements of rr 1A.28–1A.32.

43 For an explanation of the reasons behind the CIGA reforms, see the CIGA Impact Assessment dated 21 April 2020, available on the UK Government website.

44 See the Regulatory Policy Committee's *Post-Implementation Review of Corporate Insolvency and Governance Act 2020* dated 22 June 2023, which accepts recommendations to amend the legislation on Moratoriums.

1. Eligible companies

3.033 The Act does not list which companies are eligible but rather lists those which are not. Companies are not eligible to apply for a Moratorium if:

- they are subject to an insolvency procedure (such as a CVA, administration or liquidation);[45]
- a winding-up petition is outstanding (unless the court orders otherwise);[46]
- the company is already subject to a Moratorium, or at any time in the period of 12 months ending with the filing date, a Moratorium of the company was in force;[47] or
- at any time in the period of 12 months ending with the filing date, the company was subject to a CVA or was in administration.[48]

3.034 In a similar way to the Schedule A1 moratorium, certain specific types of company are also ineligible for a Moratorium (for example, insurance companies; banks; electronic money institutions; recognised investment exchanges and clearing houses; securitisation companies; parties to capital market arrangements; public-private partnership project companies; and overseas companies with corresponding functions).[49]

3.035 These exceptions appear to be consistent with standard HM Treasury restrictions and entirely reasonable. However, the exception found in paragraphs 13 and 14 of Schedule ZA1 to the Act prevents many medium or large companies from considering entering a Moratorium as they exclude any company which has raised at least £10 million under a capital market arrangement. This exception does limit the potential use of the Moratorium to mainly small and medium-sized entities ('SMEs') and is a matter which may be amended in time to open up the Moratorium to more companies.[50] Although the Moratorium was intended to be widely available to all sizes of company, this restriction is a weakness reminiscent of its predecessor.

---

45 Insolvency Act 1986, Sch ZA1, para 2(2)(a) and s A4.

46 Ibid., A4.

47 Ibid., Sch ZA1, para 2(1)1 subject to s A42(6).

48 Ibid., Sch ZA1, para 2(b).

49 See the list in Insolvency Act 1986, Sch ZA1. Under s A5 of the Act, an overseas company that is otherwise eligible may apply to the court for a Moratorium.

50 See P Walton and L Jacobs, *Insolvency Service Corporate Insolvency and Governance Act 2020 – Final Evaluation Report* November 2022 at [4.3].

2. Procedure to obtain a Moratorium

A Moratorium may be obtained by a company's directors either by filing certain documents with the court,[51] or, where certain conditions exist,[52] by applying to the court for an order. 3.036

(a) Filing at court

Directors may obtain a Moratorium by filing relevant documents in court.[53] No court hearing is required, and no court order needs to be made. The filing of the requisite documents brings into force the Moratorium.[54] The documents which must be filed are: 3.037

(a) a notice that the directors wish to obtain a Moratorium;
(b) a statement from a qualified person (who will become the Monitor) that the person:
  (i) is a qualified person (a licensed insolvency practitioner[55]); and
  (ii) consents to act as the Monitor in relation to the proposed Moratorium;
(c) a statement from the proposed Monitor that the company is an eligible company;
(d) a statement from the directors that, in their view, the company is, or is likely to become, unable to pay its debts (within the definition found in s 123 of the Act[56]); and
(e) a statement from the proposed Monitor that, in the proposed Monitor's view, it is likely that a Moratorium for the company would result in the rescue of the company as a going concern.[57]

At this stage, the directors are declaring that the company is or is likely to become insolvent. The Monitor must state that the company is eligible and also their belief that a going concern rescue is likely[58] if the company has 3.038

51 Insolvency Act 1986, s A3.

52 Ibid., ss A4 and A5.

53 Ibid., s A3(2)

54 Ibid., s A7(1)(a).

55 Ibid., s 390A.

56 See the leading case *BNY Corporate Trustee Services Ltd v Eurosail-UK 2007-3BL Plc* [2013] UKSC 28, [2013] 1 WLR 1408, [2013] BCC 397 in which the Supreme Court stressed that insolvency involves the application of both a cash-flow test under s 123(1)(e) and a balance sheet test under s 123(2) with contingent debts possibly payable in the distant future being more speculative to value.

57 Insolvency Act 1986, s A6. Under r 1A.3, the directors must also file a notice containing certain prescribed information with the court. Rules 1A.4 and 1A.5 provide for additional content that the filed documents must contain and, importantly, require the various statements being made under s A6 to be made within the period of five business days prior to the date of filing. Companies regulated under the Financial Services and Markets Act 2000 will also need to provide a reference to the written consent of the appropriate regulator under s A49.

58 For a consideration as to how decision-making by insolvency practitioners is assessed by the court, see generally A Keay, P Walton and J Curl, *Corporate Governance and Insolvency* (Edward Elgar Publishing 2022), Chapter 8.

the benefit of a Moratorium. This will usually require the Monitor to have knowledge of both the financial situation the company is in and the plan that the company has to turn around its fortunes. It is nevertheless possible for a Monitor to believe that a rescue is likely if they know, at least in general terms, what is planned. For example, it may be that the company has already secured the services of a reputable turnaround expert who will be charged with putting together a rescue package.

(b) Application to court

3.039 If there is an outstanding winding-up petition[59] against the company (or the company is an overseas company)[60] the directors will have to apply to court for an order for a Moratorium. The court will only make an order where the company is subject to a winding-up petition if it is satisfied that the Moratorium would achieve a better result for the company's creditors as a whole than would be likely if the company were wound up (without first being in a Moratorium).[61] This provision allows the court wide discretion to make a Moratorium order ostensibly even if it does not appear that it will lead to the rescue of the company as a going concern. The words used are based on the second of the statutory objectives for administration and are usually adopted by an administrator in cases where the company's business is sold on as a going concern even if there is no intention for the company itself to continue.[62] However, in *Re Grove Independent School Ltd*[63] the court explained that the requirement for a better result for the creditors had to be read alongside section A6, which refers to the documents and evidence that the court will have, including a statement from the proposed Monitor that in their view, a Moratorium for the company would likely result in the rescue of the company as a going concern.

3.040 The court in *Grove* explained that a comparison was needed between two alternative uncertain outcomes: first, the likely or probable outcome for the company's creditors if the Moratorium were made (taking into account the proposed Monitor's evidence that it would be likely to result in the company's rescue as a going concern); and second, the likely or probable outcome for

59 Insolvency Act 1986, s A4. Rules 1A.7–1A.10 specify the content of the application and accompanying documents which are required to be filed under ss A4 and A5.

60 Insolvency Act 1986, s A5.

61 Ibid., s A4(5).

62 See Sch B1, para 3(1)(b). For a consideration of how the court views the administrator's decision as to which statutory objective to follow, see, e.g., *Davey v Money* [2018] EWHC 766 (Ch), [2018] Bus LR 1903; *Re Zinc Hotels (Holdings) Ltd* [2018] EWHC 1936 (Ch), [2018] BCC 968; and *Brewer v Iqbal* [2019] EWHC 182 (Ch), [2019] BCC 746.

63 [2023] EWHC 2546 (Ch).

the company's creditors if the company entered liquidation without first being subject to a Moratorium. The court could only exercise its discretion to order a Moratorium if it was satisfied that the first possible outcome was likely to be better than the second. The court has to be satisfied of this on a balance of probabilities. It is not sufficient for the court to recognise merely a real prospect or possibility that it would be better.[64] The evidence of the proposed Monitor is likely to be a crucial factor in the court's deliberations. If the proposed Monitor's evidence is sufficiently convincing so that the court accepts it, the court is likely to accept that it has a discretion to order a Moratorium. The court will generally recognise that in most cases, a rescue as a going concern will lead to a better result for the creditors than an immediate insolvent liquidation. The comparison is not a 'profoundly technical exercise' but is to be conducted 'in a broad fashion, in accordance with commercial realities'.[65]

It may be that the court will still make a Moratorium order in cases where a sale of the business is one of the options being contemplated rather than solely a rescue as a going concern, as long as a rescue as a going concern is likely at the time of the order being made. Such a result will normally be easier to achieve by an out-of-court administrator appointment, but the benefit of the Moratorium is that the management team remains in control of the company and therefore in control of any sale process if the rescue as a going concern turns out not to be feasible. The problem with any attempt to use a Moratorium in this way is that the Monitor is under a duty to bring the Moratorium to an end under section A38 if they think that the Moratorium is no longer likely to result in the rescue of the company as a going concern. However, as long as rescue as a going concern remains a genuinely feasible option up to the time of any sale, this may still be a legitimate use of the process. **3.041**

The Moratorium will come into force when the court makes its order.[66] **3.042**

(c) Formalities pursuant to the Moratorium being entered

Once a Moratorium begins, the company must display a notice that the Moratorium is in force and the identity of the Monitor, on any business premises, on any websites and on every business document.[67] **3.043**

64 The court in *Grove* (ibid.) distinguished its approach under Part A1 of the Act from its approach to applications for administration orders under Sch B1 to the Act, where the court had to be satisfied that administration would be 'reasonably likely to achieve the purpose of the administration' which had been interpreted as requiring a 'real prospect' of its achievement, not a greater than 50 per cent chance.

65 [2023] EWHC 2546 (Ch) at [14].

66 Insolvency Act 1986, s A7(1)(b) and (c).

67 Ibid., s A19.

3.044 Under section A8, as soon as reasonably practicable after a Moratorium commences, the directors must notify the Monitor of that fact. Subsequently, as soon as reasonably practicable after receiving such a notice, the Monitor must notify the following that a Moratorium for the company has come into force:

(a) the registrar of companies;[68]
(b) every creditor of the company of whose claim the Monitor is aware;
(c) in a case where the company is or has been an employer in respect of an occupational pension scheme that is not a money purchase scheme, the Pensions Regulator; and
(d) in a case where the company is an employer in respect of such a pension scheme that is an eligible scheme within the meaning given by section 126 of the Pensions Act 2004, the Board of the Pension Protection Fund.

3.045 If either the directors or the Monitor fails to comply with these notice requirements, they commit an offence under section A8.

3. The role of the Monitor

3.046 As explained above, a Moratorium is only possible if it is supported by the agreement to act and continued supervision of a Monitor. The Monitor must be a licensed insolvency practitioner and is an officer of the court.[69] Joint Monitors are permitted. The Insolvency Service has provided specific guidance to Monitors.[70] On the application of the directors or the Monitor, the court may order the removal of a Monitor or the appointment of an additional or replacement Monitor.[71] The dynamic between the Monitor and the directors is important. The Monitor has various powers to bring a Moratorium to

68 See generally rr 1A.11–1A.12 and Form MT01 available on the Companies House website. Other forms must be filed in the event, e.g., that the Moratorium is extended, ends for whatever reason (see Forms MT02–MT09). See also para 10 of the Practice Direction relating to the Corporate Insolvency and Governance Act 2020 issued by the Chancellor on 2 July 2020 for an explanation of when Moratorium documents are to be treated for filing purposes. See also Dear IP Issues 105 and 106.

69 Insolvency Act 1986, s A34. In the New South Wales Supreme Court decision in *Re Hydrodec Group plc* [2021] NSWSC 755, a UK company which had entered into a Moratorium in the UK, applied for recognition in Australia under the Australian version of the UNCITRAL Model Law on Cross-Border Insolvency. The Australian Court decided that the Moratorium was a 'foreign proceeding' for Model Law purposes and that its Monitors were the foreign representatives (rather than the company as debtor in possession). However, the recognition sought was refused as the Court found that the company's centre of main interests was in the USA, not the UK, and so the Moratorium did not prevent the Court from making a winding-up order.

70 See *Insolvency Act 1986 part A1: moratorium – guidance to monitors* available on the Insolvency Service website. In addition, both the Pensions Regulator and HMRC have provided specific guidance from their respective viewpoints on how they will consider a company in Moratorium. Both are available on those organisations' respective websites.

71 Insolvency Act 1986, s A39 (see also rr 1A.25–1A.26).

an end and so the directors must be careful to keep the Monitor informed as to how the company's business is operating. If the Monitor is not kept sufficiently well-informed, they may have to take steps to terminate the Moratorium.

4. How long does the Moratorium last?

Whether it begins by filing documents at court or by court order, the Moratorium lasts for an initial period of 20 business days.[72] This is not dissimilar to the initial period under the Schedule A1 moratorium. The directors may act to extend or request an extension of the initial period but only after the first 15 business days of the Moratorium have elapsed. 3.047

The Moratorium may be extended by the directors themselves for a further period of 20 business days by a repeat filing of relevant papers in court.[73] This type of extension can only be made once. If the directors acquire the consent of the pre-Moratorium creditors[74] (by a qualifying creditors' decision procedure) to an extension, it may be extended for up to one year from the date it began.[75] An extension with the consent of the creditors may be sought more than once. 3.048

Directors may also apply to the court for an extension. The court has wide discretion to order an extension for whatever period it thinks fit.[76] A Moratorium may be extended by the court more than once. 3.049

A Moratorium is also extended where consideration of a proposal for a CVA is pending until the CVA proposal has been considered (or withdrawn).[77] 3.050

72 Ibid., s A9(1) and (2).

73 Ibid., s A10. The documents which must be filed at court to extend the Moratorium include: a statement that all Moratorium debts (and pre-Moratorium debts for which the company does not have a payment holiday) have been paid or otherwise discharged; a statement from the directors that, in their view, the company is, or is likely to become, unable to pay its pre-Moratorium debts; and a statement from the Monitor that, in the Monitor's view, it is likely that the Moratorium will result in the rescue of the company as a going concern. The documents filed must comply with the requirements of rr 1A.14–1A.15.

74 See Insolvency Act 1986, s A12, the creditors for these purposes are only those who are owed debts for which the company has a payment holiday during the Moratorium (see s A18).

75 Insolvency Act 1986, ss A11 and A12.

76 See Insolvency Act 1986, s A13 which requires such an application to include a statement by the directors that all debts which have arisen during the Moratorium have been discharged, that the company remains unable to pay its pre-Moratorium debts, and a statement from the Monitor that, in the Monitor's view, it remains likely that the Moratorium will result in the rescue of the company as a going concern. The detailed content of these documents is further provided for under rr 1A.18–1A.19.

77 Insolvency Act 1986, s A14.

3.051 The court may also extend a Moratorium in the course of proceedings to consider either a scheme of arrangement or restructuring plan (under, respectively, Parts 26 and 26A of the Companies Act 2006).[78]

3.052 Whenever a Moratorium is extended or comes to an end, the directors must notify the Monitor (and provide a copy of any court order).[79]

5. The stay on actions

3.053 The stay on creditor action under the Moratorium[80] is very similar to the moratorium imposed when a company enters administration under Schedule B1 to the Act.[81] During the Moratorium, the company cannot generally enter liquidation or administration without the permission of the court; no landlord can exercise a right of forfeiture; most security rights cannot be enforced; no repossession of hire purchase goods is possible; and generally no legal process may be instituted or continued against the company (except for employment claims by workers). Applications for permission to allow enforcement action by creditors are likely to be subject to the same criteria the court uses in administration cases.[82] Such applications are only open to creditors whose debts are incurred during the Moratorium or whose debts are incurred before the Moratorium but are not part of the 'payment holiday'. There is a total ban on such applications by creditors whose debts are pre-Moratorium debts that fall within the 'payment holiday'.[83]

3.054 Floating charges will not crystallise during the Moratorium.[84] This restriction allows the company, and therefore its directors, to continue to run the company in the ordinary course of business. An event that occurs during the Moratorium, which would otherwise have permitted a floating charge holder to give notice that the charge has crystallised, may be used by the floating charge holder to give notice as soon as practicable once the Moratorium has come to an end.

3.055 Major decisions are subject to the consent of the Monitor or the court.[85] A company with the benefit of a Moratorium may apply to the court for permission

78 Ibid., s A15.
79 Ibid., s A17 and rr 1A.20–1A.21.
80 Ibid., ss A20 and A21.
81 See Insolvency Act 1986, Sch B1, paras 42 and 43.
82 See, e.g., *Re Atlantic Computer Systems plc* [1992] Ch 505.
83 Insolvency Act 1986, s A21(2).
84 Ibid., s A22.
85 Ibid., ss A25 to A32.

to sell hire purchase goods or assets subject to fixed charges.[86] The court may grant permission if it thinks that the sale will support the rescue of the company as a going concern. The power is similar to that found in administration and subject to similar safeguards.[87]

6. Payment holiday

The Moratorium provides for a 'payment holiday', that is a break from paying debts owed by the company which were incurred prior to entering the Moratorium. It is a characteristic of the Moratorium that the company has to be able to pay debts incurred during the Moratorium but that it does not have to pay its pre-Moratorium debts during the Moratorium.[88] Indeed, there are restrictions in general on the company preventing it from paying pre-Moratorium debts.[89] **3.056**

As the Moratorium is built on the foundation that the company will be able to pay its debts arising during the Moratorium, it does not prevent creditors from demanding payment in relation to debts incurred during the Moratorium. The restrictions imposed are on the pre-Moratorium creditors who are owed pre-Moratorium debts[90] for which a company has a 'payment holiday' during the Moratorium.[91] **3.057**

The 'payment holiday' does have important exceptions. It does not apply to pre-Moratorium debts payable in respect of:[92] **3.058**

(a) the Monitor's remuneration or expenses;
(b) goods or services supplied during the Moratorium;
(c) rent in respect of a period during the Moratorium;
(d) wages or salary arising under a contract of employment;
(e) redundancy payments; or
(f) debts or other liabilities arising under a contract or other instrument involving financial services.[93]

---

86 Ibid., ss A31 and A32.

87 See Insolvency Act 1986, Sch B1, paras 71 and 72.

88 Under the Insolvency Act 1986, s A25, a company in Moratorium may not obtain credit to the extent of £500 or more from a person unless the person has been informed that a Moratorium is in force in relation to the company.

89 Insolvency Act 1986, s A28.

90 Pre-Moratorium debts are generally those debts falling due before the Moratorium and include debts that fall due during the Moratorium by reason of a pre-Moratorium obligation.

91 Insolvency Act 1986, s A18(2). See also s A53.

92 Ibid., s A18(3).

93 Debts that are not included in the payment holiday are given priority in any liquidation that follows on from a failed rescue attempt that used the Moratorium. However, s 174A in a subsequent liquidation

3.059 The importance of this is that such debts must be paid during the Moratorium if the creditors owed those debts require payment. Although the Moratorium prevents enforcement action without the court's permission for such debts, importantly, they must be paid during the Moratorium as if they are debts incurred during the Moratorium. The consequence of not being able to pay such debts is that the Monitor must bring the Moratorium to an end.[94]

3.060 The requirement to meet debts for which the company does not have a 'payment holiday' may lead to strategic decisions. For example, where rent is a significant expense, if the company's quarterly rent payment is due during the proposed Moratorium period, the company must pay, and if it cannot, the Monitor will need to terminate the Moratorium. It may therefore be decided to wait for the rent payment date to lapse without payment, prior to the company entering into the Moratorium. Waiting will mean the outstanding rent falls within the 'payment holiday'.

7. Disgruntled creditors

3.061 The actions of directors and the actions and remuneration of Monitors may be challenged in court by, among others, the creditors or a subsequent administrator or liquidator.[95] Various offences may be committed by the officers of the company in relation to the Moratorium, for example, concealing company property whose value is at least £500 or fraudulently removing company property whose value is at least £500.[96]

8. Termination

3.062 The role of the Monitor is to monitor the company's affairs for the purpose of forming a view as to whether it remains likely that the Moratorium will result in the rescue of the company as a going concern.[97] If such a rescue is no longer likely, the Monitor must bring the Moratorium to an end by filing a notice at court. Similarly, the Monitor must terminate the Moratorium if they

(and Sch B1, para 64A in a subsequent administration) commenced within 12 weeks after the end of the Moratorium prevents banks from obtaining such a priority for pre-Moratorium debt by accelerating payment of that pre-Moratorium debt during the Moratorium in an attempt to re-categorise the whole capital debt as Moratorium debt. For some concerns regarding the exact meaning of financial services in this context, see Walton and Jacobs, *Insolvency Service Corporate Insolvency and Governance Act 2020 – Final Evaluation Report* (n 50), [4.3].

94 Insolvency Act 1986, s A38.

95 Ibid., ss A42–A44. An application by an administrator or liquidator must be brought within two years of the end of the Moratorium (r 1A.28).

96 Ibid., s A46.

97 Ibid., s A35.

think that the company is unable to pay any of its Moratorium debts (or pre-Moratorium debts for which the Moratorium does not provide the company a payment holiday).[98]

Under rule 1A.24 in deciding whether to bring a Moratorium to an end due to inability to pay debts, the Monitor must disregard: (a) any debts that the Monitor has reasonable grounds for thinking are likely to be: (i) paid, or (ii) compounded to the satisfaction of the creditor, within five business days of the decision; and (b) any debts in respect of which the creditor has agreed to defer payment until a time that is later than the decision. **3.063**

In *Re Corbin & King Holdings Ltd*,[99] a secured creditor made an application to court on the ground that an act, omission or decision of the Monitor during the Moratorium had unfairly harmed its interests.[100] The case involved a group of companies where Topco was the majority shareholder in a number of operational companies ('Opcos') which ran restaurants. The case appears to have involved a battle for control of the restaurants. Topco was financed by MHG. MHG's loan to Topco was guaranteed by the Opcos. Topco defaulted on the loan. MHG demanded payment. At this point, K offered to purchase all of the applicant's interests in Topco and the Opcos for a sum equivalent to the value of the loan. This offer was not accepted. MHG appointed administrators to Topco. The Opcos entered into Moratoriums. MHG then called in the Opcos' guarantees. K made an improved offer. MHG applied to the court to terminate the Moratoriums on the ground that the Monitors should have terminated the Moratoriums when it was clear that the Opcos could not pay the guarantee. Guarantees are excepted from the 'payment holiday' as contracts involving 'financial services'. As soon as it was clear the guarantee could not be paid, the applicant argued the Moratoriums should have been terminated. By not doing so, the applicant therefore argued that Monitors had unfairly harmed their interests. **3.064**

In considering the actions and motivations of the Monitors, the court explained that the duty to terminate the Moratorium arose once the Monitor 'thinks' a particular circumstance exists. The court adopted the interpretation of 'thinks' which applied in the context of administration.[101] The standard of review was one of good faith and rationality. There was no suggestion of bad faith on the **3.065**

98 Ibid., s A38. The requirements for the notice to be filed at court under s A38 are found in r 1A.23.
99 [2022] EWHC 340 (Ch).
100 Insolvency Act 1986, s A42.
101 *Davey v Money* [2018] Bus LR 1903 at [255] per Snowden J.

facts. The issue was whether the Monitors had acted in a manner which was perverse in the sense that no reasonable Monitor could have so acted, making their decision irrational.

3.066 The court held that when the Monitors were considering whether the Opcos were able to pay the debt demanded, they were entitled to take a flexible and commercially realistic approach, taking into account the circumstances as a whole (including K's improved offer). It had been permissible for the Monitors to take into account the likelihood of the improved offer leading to the discharge of the loan, which would have relieved the Opcos under the guarantee.

3.067 On the facts, the court decided that the offer to purchase did offer the prospect of the immediate receipt by Topco of funds sufficient to discharge the loan (and wipe away the guarantee liability of the Opcos). The court declined to terminate the Moratoriums as the Opcos were trading successfully, and there was the immediate prospect of the loan being repaid and the guarantee liabilities evaporating.

3.068 The case suggests that if financial creditors are not supportive of a Moratorium, Monitors need to be extremely careful in deciding not to bring a Moratorium to an end if those financial creditors call in their debt. Although the facts were unusual in this case, it is far more likely that the calling in of such a financial debt will necessitate the termination of the Moratorium.

3.069 Although a Moratorium may terminate prematurely without success, it will also be terminated where it has led to a successful outcome, where the objective of rescuing the company as a going concern has been achieved. This could occur when the company enters into a court-sanctioned scheme of arrangement or restructuring plan (under Parts 26 or 26A of the Companies Act 2006, respectively) or enters into a relevant insolvency procedure, such as a CVA, administration or liquidation.[102]

9. The future of the Moratorium

3.070 The government[103] itself has recognised certain problems exist with the Moratorium legislation. Eligibility criteria often limit the use of the Moratorium to SMEs even though larger companies might find it a useful measure. In relation to SME companies, the Moratorium might be more frequently used

102 Insolvency Act 1986, s A38.

103 See the Regulatory Policy Committee's *Post-Implementation Review of Corporate Insolvency and Governance Act 2020* dated 22 June 2023.

in cases where a financial restructure is needed if the Moratorium's payment holiday was extended to financial creditors. Regardless of company size, there are significant concerns that the Moratorium alters pre-existing priorities in any subsequent insolvency. The alteration of creditor priorities may have unintended consequences and creates uncertainty for some creditors. There are also concerns within the insolvency practitioner profession that there are reputational risks to those who act as Monitor of a Moratorium.

4

DURING THE CVA

A. INTRODUCTION

4.001 This chapter proceeds on the assumption that a CVA has been approved by the members and creditors and therefore, the regime is set in motion. The chapter deals with those issues which are pertinent to the company operating while subject to a CVA.

4.002 The person who implements the CVA is known as the supervisor. Some aspects of the office of the supervisor and his or her role and powers are discussed in this chapter and the balance in Chapter 6.

4.003 The terms of the CVA are carried out in much the same way as any other commercial contract. If all creditors are paid according to what the company promised pursuant to the CVA, the CVA will complete. If the company does not satisfy the terms of the CVA, for example, if it is unable to keep up with any payments that it has promised to make, the CVA's terms will often make provision for how to deal with its termination. A CVA which terminates will often lead to the company entering a subsequent insolvency procedure such as a liquidation. These last issues just mentioned are discussed in depth in Chapter 5. The primary elements of the chapter are: consideration of accounts, reports, fees and expenses that are pertinent to CVAs; general implementation issues and challenges that may be made to the implementation of CVAs; what involvement courts might have in the life of a CVA; issues pertinent to a construction of CVAs; consideration of variations to extant CVAs; issues surrounding the provision of essential supplies; and an examination of the remuneration and powers of supervisors.

B. EARLY ACTIONS

Where the decision approving a CVA has effect under section 4A, and the supervisor is not the same person as the proposer, the proposer must, as soon as reasonably practicable, do all that is required to put the supervisor in possession of the assets included in the CVA.[1] **4.004**

In the case where the company is in administration or liquidation and the supervisor is not the same person as the administrator or liquidator, the supervisor must, before taking possession of the assets included in the CVA, deliver to the administrator or liquidator an undertaking to discharge the balance mentioned in the next sentence out of the first realisation of assets, or upon taking possession of the assets included in the CVA, discharge such balance.[2] The balance is any balance due to the administrator or liquidator, or to the Official Receiver not acting as liquidator by way of fees or expenses properly incurred and payable under the Insolvency Act 1986 ('the Act') or the Insolvency Rules 2016 ('the Rules'), and on account of any advances made in respect of the company together with interest on such advances at the rate specified in section 17 of the Judgments Act 1838 at the date on which the company entered administration or went into liquidation.[3] The administrator or liquidator, or the Official Receiver not acting as liquidator, has a charge on the assets included in the CVA in respect of any sums comprising such balance, subject only to the deduction from realisations by the supervisor of the proper costs and expenses of such realisations.[4] **4.005**

The supervisor must, from time to time out of the realisation of assets, discharge all guarantees properly given by the administrator or liquidator for the benefit of the company and pay all the expenses of the administrator or liquidator or of the Official Receiver not acting as liquidator.[5] Any sums due to the Official Receiver take priority over those due to any other person.[6] According to paragraph 18 of Statement of Insolvency Practice ('SIP') 3.2, when acting as **4.006**

1 Insolvency Rules 2016, r 2.39(1).
2 Ibid., r 2.39(2).
3 Ibid., r 2.39(3).
4 Ibid., r 2.39(4).
5 Ibid., r 2.39(5).
6 Ibid., r 2.39(6).

supervisor, the insolvency practitioner should have certain procedures in place to ensure that:

(a) where a proposal is modified, creditors have been made aware of the final form of the accepted CVA;
(b) the CVA is supervised in accordance with its terms;
(c) the progress of the CVA is monitored;
(d) any departures from the terms of the CVA are identified at an early stage and appropriate action is taken promptly by the supervisor;
(e) any discretions conferred on the supervisor are exercised where necessary, on a timely basis and that exercise is reported at the next available opportunity;
(f) any variation to the terms of the CVA has been appropriately approved before it is implemented;
(g) enquiries by creditors and shareholders are dealt with promptly;
(h) full disclosure is made of the costs of the CVA and of any other sources of income of the insolvency practitioner, associates of the insolvency practitioner or their firm, in relation to the case, in reports; and
(i) if the costs of the CVA have increased beyond previously reported estimates, this increase should be reported at the next available opportunity and an explanation of the increase provided.

C. ACCOUNTS AND REPORTS

4.007 The Rules require the supervisor to keep accounts and records where the CVA authorises or requires the supervisor: (a) to carry on the business of the company; (b) to realise assets of the company; or (c) otherwise to administer or dispose of any of its funds.[7] The accounts and records which must be kept are of the supervisor's acts and dealings in, and in connection with, the CVA, including in particular records of all receipts and payments of money.[8] The supervisor must preserve any such accounts and records which were kept by any other person who has acted as supervisor of the CVA and are in the supervisor's possession.[9] The supervisor is obliged to deliver reports on the progress and prospects for the full implementation of the CVA to the registrar of companies, the company, the creditors bound by the CVA, the members, and if the company is not in liquidation, the company's auditors (if any) for the time being.[10] The reports do not have to be delivered to members if the court, in its discretion and on application by the supervisor, dispenses with the delivery of

7 Ibid., r 2.41(1).
8 Ibid., r 2.41(2).
9 Ibid., r 2.41(3).
10 Ibid., r 2.41(4).

such reports or summaries to members, either altogether or on the basis that the availability of the report to members is to be advertised by the supervisor in a specified manner.[11]

The notice which accompanies the report when delivered to the registrar of companies must contain the date on which the voluntary arrangement took effect.[12] **4.008**

The first report referred to above must cover the period of 12 months commencing on the date on which the CVA was approved and a further report must be made for each subsequent period of 12 months.[13] Each report must be delivered within the period of two months after the end of the 12-month period.[14] However, a report is not required if the obligation to deliver a final report because the CVA has been fully implemented or terminated (and under r 2.44) arises in the two-month period.[15] **4.009**

Where the supervisor is authorised or required to do any of those actions referred to in r 2.41(1) (see [4.007] above), the report must include or be accompanied by a summary of receipts and payments required to be recorded or state that there have been no such receipts and payments.[16] **4.010**

Statement of Practice 7[17] sets out the presentation of financial information in insolvency proceedings and this aims to render transparency and fairness of primary importance in all the dealings of office-holders.[18] The SIP includes the following requirements for the supervisor: **4.011**

- receipts and payments accounts should provide figures both for the period under review and on a cumulative basis;[19]
- receipts and payments accounts should show categories of items under headings appropriate for the insolvency appointment, where practicable, following headings used in prior statements of affairs or estimated outcome statements. An analysis should be provided to enable comparison with the 'estimated to realise' figures in any previously issued document;[20]

---

11 Ibid., r 2.41(4)(d) and r 2.41(10).
12 Ibid., r 2.41(5).
13 Ibid., r 2.41(6).
14 Ibid., r 2.41(7).
15 Ibid., r 2.41(8).
16 Ibid., r 2.41(9).
17 1 April 2021 and available at: https://www.r3.org.uk/technical-library/england-wales/sips/more/29123/page/1/sip-7-presentation-of-financial-information-in-insolvency-proceedings/
18 Paragraph 2.
19 Paragraph 7.
20 Paragraph 9.

- the following should be disclosed, either separately in the receipts and payments account or by way of note: Office-holder's remuneration, showing the amounts paid on each basis; amounts paid to the office-holder in respect of the supervision of trading; all other amounts required to be approved in the same manner as remuneration; amounts paid to the office-holder from the estate in respect of pre-appointment costs; any amounts paid to the office-holder or their associates or firm other than out of the estate, giving the amounts paid, the name of the payor, their relationship to the insolvent estate and the nature of the payment; amounts paid to subcontractors for work that would otherwise have to be carried out by the office-holder or their staff;[21]
- realisations by or on behalf of the office-holder should be shown gross, with the costs of realisation shown separately as payments;[22]
- payments should be stated by category, distinguishing payments made under duress, in settlement of reservation of title claims, to secured creditors, and to preferential creditors and unsecured creditors as dividends. The dates and amounts of dividends (pence in the pound) should also be stated;[23]
- where any moneys are held which do not form part of the estate and are due to be paid to third parties, the amount should be disclosed, together with any agreed fee charged to the person entitled to the moneys.[24]

4.012 Not more than 28 days after the final completion or termination of the CVA, the supervisor must notify all the creditors and members who are bound by it that the arrangement has been fully implemented or (as the case may be) has terminated.[25] The notice must state the date the CVA took effect and must be accompanied by the supervisor's report summarising all receipts and payments. It must include (if applicable) a statement as to the amount paid to any unsecured creditors by virtue of section 176A (prescribed part) and explain any difference in the actual implementation as compared with the proposal as approved or (in the case of termination) explain why the arrangement has terminated.[26] Within the same period, the supervisor must send to the registrar of companies and to the court a copy of the notice and a copy of the report, and they must not vacate office until such copies have been sent.[27] The supervisor must not vacate office until after the copies of the notice and report have been delivered to the registrar of companies and filed with the court.[28]

---

21 Paragraph 15.
22 Paragraph 21.
23 Paragraph 24.
24 Paragraph 28.
25 Insolvency Rules 2016, r 2.44(1).
26 Ibid., r 2.44(2).
27 Ibid., r 2.44(3).
28 Ibid., r 2.44(5).

The above time limit of 28 days may be extended by the court. **4.013**

The Secretary of State may, during the CVA, or after its full implementation or termination, require the supervisor to produce for inspection (either at the premises of the supervisor or elsewhere) both the supervisor's accounts and records in relation to the CVA and copies of reports and summaries prepared in compliance with rule 2.41.[29] The Secretary of State is entitled to require the supervisor's accounts and records to be audited and, if so, the supervisor must provide such further information and assistance as the Secretary of State requires for the purposes of audit.[30] **4.014**

If a supervisor fails to provide to the registrar of companies any returns or reports that he or she should make, then the supervisor may be disqualified, as section 3 of the Company Directors Disqualification Act 1986 provides that: **4.015**

> The court may make a disqualification order against a person where it appears to it that he has been persistently in default in relation to provisions of the companies legislation requiring any return, account or other document to be filed with, delivered or sent, or notice of any matter to be given, to the registrar of companies.

This includes persons other than directors. **4.016**

It is always possible that the supervisor comes across evidence of illegality on the part of the directors and he or she is then under an obligation to send a report to the relevant authority (the Director of Public Prosecutions in England and Wales and the Lord Advocate in Scotland). **4.017**

D. FEES AND EXPENSES

Rule 2.43(a) provides that fees for the nominee's services agreed with the company (or, as the case may be, the administrator or liquidator) and disbursements made by the nominee before the decision approving the CVA takes effect under section 4A. The supervisor will be responsible for paying fees or expenses which are sanctioned by the terms of the CVA, or where they are not sanctioned by the terms of the CVA, would be payable, or correspond to those which would be payable, in an administration or winding up.[31] **4.018**

---

29 Ibid., r 2.42(1).
30 Ibid., r 2.42(2).
31 Ibid., r.2.43(b).

E. IMPLEMENTATION

4.019 Once approved, the person who oversees a CVA and actually implements it is usually the person who was the nominee of the proposal that was approved as a CVA, and he or she is known as the supervisor.[32] The role of supervisor may be undertaken by two or more practitioners. In such a case, the creditors may resolve whether acts to be done in connection with the arrangement may be done by any one of them or must be done by both or all the relevant practitioners.[33]

4.020 During the implementation of the CVA, the directors of the company are likely to be required, by the terms of the arrangement, to provide the supervisor with information regarding the company's assets, liabilities and other affairs. They may also be required to attend on the supervisor and his or her agents, representatives or nominees at specified times and do all such other tasks reasonably required by the supervisor to enable him or her to discharge their functions and duties under the arrangement.[34] Also, in some CVAs, the directors of the company will be obliged to provide the supervisor with accounts relating to the company's affairs as the supervisor may reasonably require.[35]

4.021 In implementing the arrangement, the supervisor will be required to accept creditors' claims and pay creditors in accordance with the terms of the arrangement. The job of the supervisor is not to force the debtor to make payments; however, he or she needs to advise the debtor of the consequences of failing to comply with the terms of the arrangement, one of which could well be liquidation. If it is necessary for variations to be made to the voluntary arrangement, then the supervisor will be involved in negotiations with the debtor and the creditors.

4.022 During the implementation process, it might be necessary for the supervisor to consult with the creditors. Provision will usually be made in the terms of the arrangement for how creditors can be involved in decisions concerning the arrangement. For instance, paragraph 60 of R3's Standard Conditions for CVAs[36] provides terms concerning how creditors may vote.

---

32 Insolvency Act 1986, s 7(2).

33 Insolvency Rules 2016, r 2.3(1)(i).

34 For instance, see para 24.1 of the *R3 Standard Conditions for CVAs*, September 2020 and available at: https://www.r3.org.uk/technical-library/england-wales/technical-guidance/r3-standard-form-covid-19-cva-proposal/

35 For instance, see, ibid., para 24.2.

36 Ibid.

Best practice guidance on the implementation of a voluntary arrangement appears at paragraph 23 of SIP 3.1, which deals with IVAs. In particular, paragraph 23(d) provides that 'Any departures from the terms of the IVA are identified at an early stage and appropriate action is then taken promptly by the supervisor'. **4.023**

Notwithstanding the fact that section 7 of the Act is headed 'Implementation of proposal', the provisions of the Act provide no specific guidance on the implementation of the proposal itself.[37] Nevertheless, the Rules in rules 2.41–2.44 provide detailed rules of procedure. Furthermore, the way that the arrangement is implemented will be determined by the terms of the arrangement itself. **4.024**

Creditors, or in fact other persons, may from time to time challenge, while the CVA is being implemented, what the supervisor is or is not doing. The court may, pursuant to section 7(3), confirm, reverse or modify any act or decision of the supervisor, give the supervisor directions or make such other order as it thinks fit on the application of a creditor or any other person. It has been argued that the words 'other person' will 'extend to any person capable of establishing to the court that he has a sufficient interest in the voluntary arrangement. This might include the directors of the company or, alternatively, a person with a beneficial interest in the arrangement assets.'[38] **4.025**

The supervisor may, under section 7(4), apply to the court for directions in relation to any particular matter arising under the voluntary arrangement. For instance, the supervisor might seek directions concerning the proper interpretation of the terms of a CVA.[39] Also, the supervisor is included among the persons who may apply to the court for the winding up of the company or for an administration order to be made in relation to it. It should be noted that the Court of Appeal has said, confirming the decision at first instance, in *Re Alpa Lighting Ltd*[40] that the court has no power to amend a CVA pursuant to section 7(4)(a). This matter is discussed later in more detail.[41] **4.026**

37 L Doyle KC, A Keay and J Curl KC (eds), *Doyle, Keay and Curl: Annotated Insolvency Legislation 2025*, 12th ed, LexisNexis, [1.67].

38 Ibid. and referring to *Port v Auger* [1994] 1 WLR 862, 873–874.

39 *Horrocks v Broome* [1999] BPIR 66.

40 [1997] BPIR 341.

41 Below at [4.063]–[4.072].

4.027 Paragraph 9.1 of R3's Standard Conditions for CVAs[42] provides that: 'Upon the full implementation of the Arrangement, the Supervisor shall, if the Company has complied with its obligations under the Arrangement, issue a notice … stating that the Arrangement has been fully implemented.' The effect of the implementation of the arrangement will usually be that the company shall be released from all debts which are subject to the arrangement.[43]

4.028 The terms of the arrangement may, as do R3's Standard Conditions, provide that the supervisor is empowered to issue a certificate of full implementation notwithstanding that the company has not complied with all of its obligations as per the terms of the arrangement, provided the company has done certain things. In R3's proforma, the conditions are: made all the payments required under the terms of the arrangement; provided a full explanation of any breach of the terms of the arrangement required by the supervisor; paid to the supervisor such sum (if any) as the supervisor shall reasonably have required to compensate the creditors for any reduction in dividend caused by the company's breach of the terms of the arrangement.[44]

4.029 The provisions of the CVA should not be ignored by either the company or the supervisor. Having said that, there is often some flexibility built into the arrangement. But as far as mandatory provisions are concerned, they should be put into effect.

4.030 Chadwick J (as he then was) made it plain in *Vadher v Weisgard*[45] that a CVA should not continue to be implemented:

> where the cost of supervising the voluntary arrangement represented by the insolvency practitioner's time and correspondence costs are absorbing whatever contributions are being made by the debtor. Voluntary arrangements are not approved for the purpose of providing an income to the supervisor. They are approved in order to enable the creditors to receive payment of, or a dividend in respect of, their debts. If the debtor is failing to co-operate to such an extent that the contributions are being absorbed in the supervisor's proper expenses, then the arrangements are not working and should be brought to an end.[46]

4.031 Lastly, it should be noted that a supervisor has no power to remove any of the directors of the debtor company during the implementation of the CVA.

---

42 *R3 Standard Conditions for CVAs* (n 34) and available at: https://www.r3.org.uk/technical-library/england-wales/technical-guidance/r3-standard-form-covid-19-cva-proposal/

43 Paragraph 9.2.

44 Paragraph 10.1.

45 [1998] BPIR 295.

46 Ibid., 298.

F. INVESTIGATIONS

Unlike other insolvency regimes, like liquidations for instance, neither the nominee nor the supervisor is bound to undertake any formal investigation into the conduct of company directors in a voluntary arrangement. Supervisors are not required to file any report for the purposes of disqualification. **4.032**

Section 7A provides that where the approval of a CVA has taken effect under section 4A, then if it appears to the supervisor that any past or present officer of the company has committed an offence in connection with the CVA, the supervisor must forthwith report the matter to the appropriate authority, which will be the Secretary of State in England and Wales and the Lord Advocate in Scotland, and provide the appropriate authority with such information and give the authority such access to and facilities for inspecting and taking copies of documents (being information or documents in the possession or under the control of the supervisor and relating to the matter in question) as the authority requires. **4.033**

G. COURT INVOLVEMENT

It is likely that court involvement in the operation phase of a CVA will not be common. As mentioned earlier, a supervisor may apply to the court for directions pursuant to section 7(4). The courts might also have some involvement in other situations. The court may appoint a person to act as supervisor by way of substitution of one already acting or where there is a vacancy, or appoint a further supervisor to assist in the implementation of the arrangement.[47] An application may be made to the court under section 7(3) to challenge any act, omission or decision of the supervisor by the debtor, any of the creditors, or any other person who is dissatisfied by the relevant act, omission or decision. On such an application, the court may: **4.034**

(a) confirm, reverse or modify any act or decision of the supervisor;
(b) give him directions; or
(c) make such other order as it thinks fit.

An example of an application of section 7(3) occurred in *County Bookshops Ltd v Grove*,[48] where X, a party who it was alleged was a creditor, applied to the court in relation to the supervisor's rejection of the proof X had submitted. **4.035**

47 Insolvency Act 1986, s 7(5).
48 [2002] EWHC 1160 (Ch), [2003] 1 BCLC 479, [2002] BPIR 770, [2002] BPIR 772.

The proof claimed that three instalments under a supply agreement were payable. X contended that the supervisors had been wrong to reject the proof and applied for a declaration that X should be admitted as a creditor in respect of the three instalments. Neuberger J (as he then was) found that X was entitled to prove in relation to the three instalments. It was held in *Alman v Approach Housing Ltd*[49] that a creditor who could not persuade the supervisor to agree to his or her debt could apply under section 7(3).

4.036 In *Re Hellard v Goldfarb*[50] the original supervisor had been replaced by new supervisors. The latter applied for a direction on how they should pay a sum that they recovered, as a result of investigations into the original supervisor's work in relation to the CVA, from the security bond of the original supervisor. The court was willing to direct that the supervisors be permitted to charge a reasonable fee in circumstances for their investigation work.

4.037 The court is not empowered to authorise the supervisor of a CVA to breach the trust of the CVA assets for the benefit of the CVA creditors.[51]

4.038 The availability of the right under section 7(3) means that any dissatisfied applicant who is entitled to bring such an application is precluded from any rights of action against the supervisor.[52] There is no authority which informs us whether a dissatisfied applicant is akin to an aggrieved person, the term used in relation to other parts of the Act when dealing with office-holders[53] and their decisions or failure to make decisions, but it is likely that the cases that have explained 'aggrieved' in this context (for example, in relation to s 168(5) of the Act) will be applied. It has been suggested that the existing authorities that have dealt with office-holder decisions might bear directly on applications in respect of acts, omissions and decisions of supervisors while implementing a voluntary arrangement where a composition that involves assets being assigned to the supervisor to realise and distribute the proceeds as the supervisor's task will be regarded as being similar to that of a liquidator's decisions.[54] However, where a scheme of arrangement type CVA is involved, the supervisor may have to undertake a more commercial role and may have to deal with a wide variety of third parties over a range of matters and it would not be inappropriate to stop third parties from being able to complain to the

49 [2001] 1 BCLC 530, [2001] BPIR 203.

50 [2007] BPIR 1322.

51 *Re Beloit Walmsley Ltd* [2008] EWHC 1888 (Ch), [2008] BPIR 1445.

52 *King v Anthony* [1998] 2 BCLC 517.

53 Such as s 168(5) of the Insolvency Act 1986 in relation to a liquidator.

54 E Bailey, *Bailey: Voluntary Arrangements*, LexisNexis, [10.4].

court about the supervisor simply because that person is a third party to the voluntary arrangement, particularly when one considers the fact that they will be unable to challenge the supervisor by private right of action.[55]

4.039 There appears to be a reluctance on the part of judges to question and disagree with actions that are proposed by a supervisor where he or she seems to be proceeding according to the terms of the arrangement and is doing so in good faith. As is the case with other office-holders, courts tend to defer to the commercial decisions of supervisors. There has been no indication given by the courts as to when they might interfere with the commercial aspects of the supervisor's actions in the course of implementing a CVA that involves trading.[56] It is likely that similar principles will be applied as those which apply to the control of other office-holders by the court. In formal insolvency regimes, the courts have been slow to act, being concerned to allow office-holders to exercise their powers and their discretion without placing undue limits on them.[57] The supervisor's judgment, as is the situation with other office-holders, will be, as long as it is bona fide and rational, likely to carry considerable weight,[58] and it is reflected in cases such as *Re Edennote Ltd*[59] and *Re Longmeade Limited (in liquidation)*.[60] The courts are reluctant to second-guess the judgment of office-holders like supervisors and will only do so where the decision of the office-holder is perverse, namely so utterly unreasonable and absurd that no reasonable person would have done it. Thus, save where there is fraud or mala fides, an application against supervisors is unlikely to succeed. Supervisors, again as with other office-holders, must exercise their powers in good faith and for a proper purpose.[61] Thus, if supervisors exercise their commercial judgment and a loss is made, their actions will not be able to be successfully challenged provided that they had behaved rationally.[62] They are prohibited from acting perversely or irrationally or for extraneous reasons, and this includes the requirement for office-holders to take reasonable steps to acquire information on relevant matters and, where appropriate, to follow professional advice.[63] It should be noted that the deferential approach will not

55 Ibid.

56 Ibid., [10.5].

57 *Pitman v Top Business Systems* [1984] BCLC 593, 597.

58 See *Davey v Money* [2018] EWHC 766, [255], in the context of administration.

59 [1996] BCC 718.

60 [2016] EWHC 356 (Ch), [2017] 2 All ER 244.

61 *Davey v Money* [2018] EWHC 766 (Ch), [622]–[623].

62 *Re Capitol Films Ltd (in administration)* [2010] EWHC 3223 (Ch), [83].

63 G Lightman, G Moss, H Anderson, I Fletcher and R Snowden, *Lightman & Moss on the Law of Administrators and Receivers of Companies*, 6th ed (Sweet & Maxwell, 2017), [12-037].

apply to a decision that is based on a question of law rather than one based on commercial reasons.[64]

4.040 If a creditor feels that he or she must seek court involvement because the supervisor has not responded to his or her inquiries, then it is quite likely that a court would award costs of any hearing against the supervisor personally.[65]

H. CONSTRUCTION OF THE CVA

4.041 For a host of reasons, it may well be critical during the CVA's life for its terms to be construed. As discussed in Chapter 2, a CVA is a statutory hypothesis and not a contract per se, but the rules of construction for contracts have been employed. When construing the terms of a CVA, courts must take care not to be overly strict. It came down to a construction of the CVA in *Alman v Approach Housing Ltd*,[66] where the CVA terms provided that the supervisor's express powers empowered him, on the company's behalf, to 'agree' the claims of the creditors, and Rimer J was of the opinion that the most obvious purpose of that was to ensure that his agreement as to the debt of any one creditor would be binding on the other creditors as well.[67] In this case, the claimant was the former employee of the company that had entered into a CVA. The claimant had been dismissed, and he was able to secure a judgment against the company. His judgment debt was admitted at the meeting held to consider whether to approve the CVA. However, his pending claim for unliquidated damages was not admitted and was given only a nominal value, so the claimant was going to pursue the claim in the courts. The supervisor argued that it was an implied term of the CVA that a creditor was not permitted to do so. Rimer J rejected that argument and said that it was not necessary to imply any such term. He went on to say that he could not see any basis at all for doing so, and as the terms contained no machinery for the determination of disputed claims, there appeared to the judge to be everything to be said for not implying any such term.[68]

---

64 *Re Buckingham International plc (in liquidation) (No.2); Mitchell v Buckingham* [1998] BCC 943.

65 Geoffrey Weisgard, Michael Griffiths and Louis Doyle, *Company Voluntary Arrangements and Administrations*, 3rd ed (LexisNexis, 2013), [8.16].

66 [2001] 1 BCLC 530, [2001] BPIR 203.

67 Ibid., [10].

68 Ibid., [16].

In *Welsby v Brelec Installations Ltd*[69] Blackburne J was concerned with the construction of certain express terms employed in a CVA for the purpose of determining if and when there had been a failure for the purposes of that arrangement. His Lordship accepted the arguments of counsel for the supervisors who sought directions as to how certain money held by them should be dealt with following the placing of the company in a creditors' voluntary liquidation.[70] The judge then went on to say that: **4.042**

> An arrangement is usually put together with some haste. Modifications to it are frequently made at the statutory meeting of creditors with little time to reflect on how they relate to the other terms of the debtor's proposal. Quite often, as this case demonstrates, the resulting terms are clumsily worded. The arrangement ought therefore to be construed in a practical fashion. Otherwise, there is a risk that careless drafting coupled with a too-literal approach to its construction will serve to frustrate rather than achieve the purpose of the arrangement.[71]

CVAs must be construed as a whole,[72] and 'it must be borne in mind that the CVA must be read as a whole, and further that specific terms must not be analysed so closely as to overlook the overall commercial context or the practical consequences'.[73] Having said that, in *Re MF Global UK Ltd (in special administration)*; *Heis v Financial Services Compensation Scheme Ltd*[74] Sir Colin Rimer (with whom McFarlane and Asplin LJJ concurred) agreed with the parties that the general principles of interpretation applying to contracts, as summarised by the Supreme Court in *Wood v Capita Insurance Services Ltd*,[75] apply to CVAs.[76] Sir Colin Rimer said: **4.043**

> When interpreting a written contract, the court is concerned to identify the intention of the parties by reference to 'what a reasonable person having all the background knowledge which would have been available to the parties would have understood the language in the contract to mean' [....] and it does so by focusing on the meaning of the relevant words ... in their documentary, factual and commercial context. That meaning has to be assessed in light of (i) the natural and ordinary meaning of the clause, (ii) any other relevant provisions of the [contract], (iii) the overall purpose of the clause and the [contract], (iv) the facts and circumstances known or assumed by the parties at the time the document was

69 [2000] 2 BCLC 576.

70 Ibid., 585.

71 Ibid., 585–586.

72 *Tucker and Spratt (Joint Supervisors of Energy Holdings (No 3) (In Liquidation) v Gold Fields Mining LLC* [2009] EWCA Civ 173, [2009] 1 BCLC 567; [2010] BCC 544; [2009] BPIR 704, [36].

73 L Doyle KC, A Keay and J Curl KC (eds), *Annotated Insolvency Legislation 2025*, 13th ed, LexisNexis, [1.64].

74 [2018] EWCA Civ 1327, [2018] BPIR 1142

75 [2017] UKSC 24.

76 [2018] EWCA Civ 1327, [2018] BPIR 1142, [22].

executed, and (v) commercial common sense, but (vi) disregarding subjective evidence of any party's intentions.[77]

4.044 In *Johnson v Davies*[78] Chadwick LJ said, in the context of a case which considered whether an IVA was capable of releasing a co-debtor from liability, that:

> Under Part VIII of the 1986 Act, the discharge of the debtor depends entirely on the terms of the arrangement. One must look at the arrangement, and nothing else, in order to find the terms (if any) under which the debtor is discharged. This is emphasised by the words in s 260(2) (s 5(2) in the case of a CVA) of the 1986 Act: 'The approved arrangement ... (b) binds every person ... as if he were a party to the arrangement.'[79]

4.045 Thus, the courts are going to be slow to imply terms, although in *El Ajou v Stern*[80] Kitchin J accepted the argument that the IVA in that case was subject to an implied term that creditors who were subject to the IVA would take no action to enforce their claim against the debtor, as this kind of term was necessary to give business efficacy to the arrangement. Terms have been implied in other decisions.[81]

4.046 The courts do not have the power to amend or modify the terms of a CVA.[82]

I. DIVIDENDS

4.047 During the course of the life of a CVA, the supervisor is likely to need to pay out dividends to creditors from the funds generated by the debtor company. Proposals, if well drafted, will usually state plainly when creditors can expect to receive dividends and, as far as is practicable, to state what the likely quantum would be. On the declaration and payment of dividends, the rules applied to liquidations and administrations are usually incorporated by reference. The relevant rules are rules 14.26–14.45.

4.048 The arrangement itself may spell out the procedure for dividends. R3's Standard Conditions for CVAs provide that:

> At the time or times specified in the Proposal or, if none, whenever the Supervisor has sufficient funds in hand for the purpose, the Supervisor shall, subject to the retention of such sums as may be necessary for payment of the expenses of the Arrangement, declare

77 Ibid.
78 [1999] Ch 117.
79 Ibid., 138.
80 [2006] EWHC 3067 (Ch), [2007] BPIR 693.
81 Ibid., [31]–[34]. See *Re Hellard and Goldfarb* [2007] BPIR 1322, [17]; *The Co-operative Bank plc v Phillips* [2017] EWHC 1320 (Ch), [2017] BPIR 1156.
82 *Re Alpa Lighting Ltd* [1997] BPIR 341.

and distribute Dividends among the Creditors in respect of the Debts which they have proved.[83]

J. PROOFS OF DEBT

Creditors will need to submit proofs before they can claim in the CVA. **4.049**

There are no express provisions in the Rules governing proofs of debt in CVAs, **4.050** and commonly the terms of arrangements incorporate the winding-up rules as to proof. Paragraph 26 of R3's Standard Conditions for Company Voluntary Arrangements provides that:

> As soon as practicable after the commencement of the Arrangement, and provided no application under Section 6 of the Act (*challenge of decisions*) or an appeal under Rule 15.35 (*appeals against decisions*) is pending, the Supervisor shall send a notice ('Notice to Submit Proofs') to every Creditor and other person to whom the Company may be indebted of whom the Supervisor has notice requiring them to provide such details of their Debts as the Supervisor thinks fit.

When it comes to proofs, the task of supervisors will be to ascertain claims **4.051** made by creditors for the purpose of dividends in the voluntary arrangement, particularly where nominal or minimum values were placed on the claim for voting purposes at the decision procedure that led to approval of the proposal. The supervisor will decide whether or not a person is a creditor, and that decision may be challenged by the creditor concerned or any other creditor.[84] Where a creditor is appealing against the decision of the supervisor concerning a proof, the disgruntled creditor has the burden of establishing that the supervisor was wrong and the court would consider whether, on the balance of probabilities, the debt was established and was not limited to reviewing the decision.[85]

It will be dependent on the terms of the arrangement, but a creditor might **4.052** seek to revalue or add to his or her claim for the purpose of dividend. In *Meisels v Martin*[86] Warren J said by way of obiter that it may well be correct, and he thought it was probably correct, that 'where a single claim is submitted, that claim can only be increased by variation of the original proof and not by

83 Paragraph 46.1 of the *R3 Standard Conditions for CVAs* (n 34) and available at: https://www.r3.org.uk/technical-library/england-wales/technical-guidance/r3-standard-form-covid-19-cva-proposal/

84 *Re Timothy* [2005] EWHC 1885 (Ch), [2006] BPIR 329, [48].

85 *Re Rossi* [2022] EWHC 1053 (Ch), [2022] BPIR 1241, [28].

86 [2005] EWHC 845 (Ch), [2005] BPIR 1151.

submission of a new proof'.[87] The judge went on to say that: 'It does not follow from that, where there are two completely independent claims, that they cannot form the subject-matter of separate proofs.'[88] He did not have to decide the issue and he said that he expressed no view on the matter. In varying a claim, the creditor needs the consent of the supervisor.

4.053 Some creditors might challenge the proofs of other creditors. The burden of proof in respect of a proof of debt submitted by a creditor which is challenged by another creditor is on the creditor whose proof is challenged.[89] Any abuse of the procedure by a rival creditor can be controlled by the court by summary disposal of an improper application. If there is a bona fide challenge to the admission of a proof and this leads to a court hearing, the challenged creditor should have to make good their claim. The legal burden and the evidential burden will coincide.[90]

4.054 The task of the court was simply to examine the evidence placed before it on the matter and come to a conclusion whether, on balance, the claim against the debtor was established and if so, in what amount. In considering the matter, the court was not confined to the evidence that was before the chairman at the time that decision was made but was entitled to consider whatever admissible evidence on the issue the parties to the appeal chose to place before the court.[91]

K. ESSENTIAL SUPPLIES

4.055 In commercial contracts for the supply of goods and/or services, a standard practice has developed where the contracts provide for an automatic termination provision if the purchaser of the goods and/or services enters some form of insolvency regime. Of course, this can be not only terribly inconvenient but also prevent a company from carrying on business. To thwart the effect of these kinds of provisions in contracts, the legislature introduced certain sections into the Act. Section 233, which applies to CVAs that have taken effect,[92] provides that those who supply 'essential services' may not make it a condition of the supply, or do anything which has the effect of making it a

---

87 Ibid., [35].

88 Ibid.

89 *Farrar Construction Limited, Levi Solicitors LLP v Wilson and JKR Property Development Limited* [2022] EWHC 24 (Ch), [19]–[20].

90 Ibid.

91 *Re A Company (No 004539 of 1993)* [1995] 1 BCLC 459, 466, *Moorgate Industries UK Ltd v Mittal* [2022] EWHC 3009 (Ch), [2023] BPIR 476, [69].

92 Insolvency Act 1986, s 233(1)(c). It applies to other insolvency regimes as well.

condition of the supply, that any outstanding charges in respect of a supply given to the company before the effective date are paid. The notion of essential services covers the supplies of electricity, gas, water and communications services[93] and point of sale terminals, computer hardware and software, information, advice and technical assistance in connection with the use of information technology, data storage and processing and website hosting.[94] The effective date for CVAs is when the CVA comes into effect.[95]

Since section 233 became law, the legislature introduced a new provision, section 233A, to provide further protections as far as essential supplies are concerned. Section 233A only applies to companies in administration or voluntary arrangements. The new provision prevents suppliers of the same essential services that apply to section 233 from relying on their insolvency-related contractual terms to charge higher prices, terminate the contract or do any other thing merely because the company has entered a voluntary arrangement.[96] An insolvency-related term of a contract for the supply of essential goods or services to a company is a provision of the contract under which: **4.056**

(a) the contract or the supply would terminate, or any other thing would take place, because the company enters administration or the voluntary arrangement takes effect,
(b) the supplier would be entitled to terminate the contract or the supply, or to do any other thing, because the company enters administration or the voluntary arrangement takes effect, or
(c) the supplier would be entitled to terminate the contract or the supply because of an event that occurred before the company enters administration or the voluntary arrangement takes effect.[97]

It has been suggested that this would: **4.057**

> cover situations where, for example, the company had breached the terms of its computer software licence before entering a voluntary arrangement, but by simply entering into the voluntary arrangement, the company could prevent the supplier from exercising its right to terminate the licence. Instead, the supplier's usual rights of termination are replaced by a new right to terminate the contract where, in the case of a company voluntary arrangement, the supervisor consents, the court grants permission (which it may only do if satisfied that the continuation of the contract would cause the supplier hardship) or where any

93 Ibid., s 233(3).
94 Ibid., s 233(3A).
95 Ibid., s 233(4)(c).
96 Ibid., s 233A(1).
97 Ibid., s 233A(8).

charges in respect of the supply that are incurred after the voluntary arrangement takes effect are not paid within 28 days of the day on which payment is due.[98]

4.058 According to section 233A(2), an insolvency-related term of a contract does not cease to have effect to the extent that: (1) it provides for the contract or the supply to terminate, or any other thing to take place, because the company becomes subject to an insolvency procedure other than a voluntary arrangement; (2) it entitles a supplier to terminate the contract or the supply, or do any other thing, because the company becomes subject to an insolvency procedure other than a voluntary arrangement; or (3) it entitles a supplier to terminate the contract or the supply because of an event that occurs, or may occur, after the company enters and the voluntary arrangement takes effect.

4.059 Where an insolvency-related term of a contract ceases to have effect because of section 233A, the supplier may terminate the contract if the supervisor consents to the termination of the contract, the court grants permission for the termination of the contract,[99] or any charges in respect of the supply that are incurred after the company entered the voluntary arrangement took effect are not paid within the period of 28 days beginning with the day on which payment is due.[100]

4.060 Again, where an insolvency-related term of a contract ceases to have effect because of section 233A, suppliers are not required to continue to supply the essential goods or services during the period of the voluntary arrangement unless the supervisor personally guarantees the payment of any charges for future supplies. To avoid the right to terminate the supply returning to the supplier, the supervisor must provide a personal guarantee within 14 days of receiving a notice from the supplier advising that if the supervisor fails to do so, the supply will be terminated.[101]

4.061 To provide even greater protection for supervisors (and other office-holders), section 233B was inserted by the Corporate Insolvency and Governance Act 2020. The provision proscribes paragraphs in contracts that allow the supplier of goods or services to terminate or do any other thing in relation to the contract if the company enters into, amongst other regimes, a CVA. These paragraphs are known as ipso facto paragraphs. Thus, the provision stops suppliers

98 M Mullen (ed), *Tolley's Insolvency Law*, LexisNexis [V4031.1].

99 The court may grant permission under para (b) only if satisfied that the continuation of the contract would cause the supplier hardship (s 233(4)).

100 Insolvency Act 1986, ss 233A(3)(a) and (4).

101 Ibid., ss 233A(3)(b) and (5).

from terminating a supply when a company enters a CVA. Furthermore, it prevents suppliers from making it a condition of continued supply that arrears incurred before the debtor company enters the CVA are paid and from making other changes to the contract, such as increasing prices.

Section 233B(5) allows for a contract to be terminated by a supplier under the kind of paragraph referred to in section 233B(4). This latter subsection provides that where, under a provision of a contract for the supply of goods or services to the company, the supplier is entitled to terminate the contract or the supply because of an event occurring before the start of the period during which the company was subject to a CVA, and the entitlement arises before the start of that period, the entitlement may not be exercised during that period. Section 233B(5) provides, as far as a CVA is concerned, that where a provision of a contract ceases to have effect under one entitlement and another entitlement under the provision of a contract is not exercisable under section 233B(4), the supplier may terminate the contract if the company consents to the termination of the contract, or the court is satisfied that the continuation of the contract would cause the supplier hardship and grants permission for the termination of the contract. **4.062**

L. VARIATION OF THE TERMS OF A CVA

During the period in which a CVA operates, and of course it may be implemented over several years, circumstances may change which require some changes to the terms of the arrangement. For instance, 'the projected income of the business or proceeds of sale of certain assets may not be as high as originally forecast'.[102] If that is the case, then some variation to the terms of the CVA may need to be implemented. One of the benefits of a CVA is that it provides flexibility, and its terms may be able to be varied. **4.063**

To have a variation demands the approval of the creditors and members, being the parties to the statutory hypothesis to the arrangement. However, there is no provision in the Act dealing with variation and the court does not have the power to order a variation.[103] In relation to this latter point, Nourse LJ (with whom Saville and Hutchison LJJ concurred) in *Re Alpa Lighting Ltd*[104] said, in relation to an application for a variation under section 7(4)(a), that: **4.064**

102 Andrew Keay and Peter Walton, *Insolvency Law: Corporate and Personal*, 6th ed (LexisNexis, 2024), [8.56].
103 *Re Alpa Lighting Ltd* [1997] BPIR 341, CA.
104 [1997] BPIR 341.

> The only power conferred on the court pursuant to s 7(4)(a) is to give directions in relation to any particular matter arising *under* the voluntary arrangement. That wording presupposes the continuation of the voluntary arrangement in the form in which it is. Moreover and more significantly, I have never heard it suggested, and no authority has now been cited for the suggestion, that a power to give directions under an instrument, whether it be a voluntary arrangement under the 1986 Act, a trust instrument or the like, includes a power to amend it (emphasis in original).[105]

4.065 Consequently, it is advisable that provisions be included in the CVA to permit a variation. The proposal should also give the supervisor the power to convene a decision procedure to enable a variation to be voted on and establish on what basis a variation will be allowed. Many arrangements will contain an express provision for variation, usually requiring a 75 per cent vote of the creditors in accordance with the provisions of the Rules, and as per the process needed for the approval of the original CVA, although the requisite majority will depend upon the facts. Such express provisions for variation are valid. Paragraph 72.1 of R3's Standard Conditions for CVAs[106] provides that an arrangement may be amended by Decision Procedure of the Creditors. Then, paragraph 72.2 states that: 'No variation of the terms of the Arrangement shall be of any effect unless made with the consent of the Company (acting by its Directors) and any third party affected thereby.' Any variation will be of no effect if it unfairly prejudices the rights of any creditor or if there has been any material irregularity in the operation of the provisions,[107] or it causes the arrangement to cease to be a voluntary arrangement within Part I of the Act.[108]

4.066 The voting rights of specific creditors may well be different when a variation is considered compared with the point at which the CVA was approved.

4.067 According to the court in *Horrocks v Broome*,[109] on an application for directions from supervisors in an IVA, it could not be argued that the general scheme of the Act prevented any variation to an arrangement.[110] In this case, the IVA contained a variation paragraph. It provided that subsequent variations to the CVA were permitted if it was approved by a majority in value of over 75 per cent of the participating creditors at their meeting or by a postal vote. The variation proposed, and it was by the debtor, was for the debtor's early release

105 Ibid., 346.

106 *R3 Standard Conditions for CVAs* (n 34) and available at: https://www.r3.org.uk/technical-library/england-wales/technical-guidance/r3-standard-form-covid-19-cva-proposal/

107 Ibid., para 72.4.

108 Ibid., para 72.5.

109 [1999] BPIR 66.

110 Ibid., 69, 71.

from the arrangement on the basis that some cash payments were to be made by third parties. Of those creditors circulated with the variation proposal, 95.5 per cent in value (29 per cent in number) voted on the proposals. Of those voting, 96 per cent in value, representing some £15,000,102, voted in favour and 4 per cent in value, representing some £613,079, voted against. The numbers in favour were 34 and those against 30.[111] The court held the paragraph to be valid and that the arrangement could be varied under the procedure contained in the terms of the arrangement even if a variation might prejudice the interests of a particular creditor, but it noted that it only permitted variations or modifications which could have been validly included in the original proposal by the debtor. Hart J in this case said that:

> It is possible to envisage circumstances where a modification does produce a prejudice to an individual creditor, but where the supervisor, taking account of that prejudice, nevertheless concludes that an exercise of the power will be in the best interests of the creditors generally. In those circumstances, it may be difficult or impossible for the court to interfere, on a s 263 application [the IVA equivalent of s 7(3)], with the exercise by the supervisor of his discretion. In my judgment, this is a real difficulty, which has to be faced. However, it does not lead to the conclusion that the paragraph is bad ab initio.[112]

Hart J said that great caution should be exercised before including any variation that did prejudice creditors as they could seek to challenge the variation on the basis that that were unfairly prejudiced.[113] To be borne in mind when including the power to vary is the fact that the criminal sanction, now contained in section 6A of the Act, that can be imposed on a company officer who makes a false representation or fraudulently does anything in relation to the gaining of an approval of a CVA, may not apply where there is such behaviour in respect of a variation. It has been suggested that nominees should consider including in the terms of the arrangement a provision that provides that the company's officers are to disclose, before a proposal to vary the arrangement is put before the creditors.[114] Another matter to bear in mind is that a creditor who is dissatisfied with, and has voted against, the variation would not have, as he or she would with the vote for the original proposal, the right to challenge the variation under section 6 on the basis of unfair prejudice or material irregularity. A creditor would also not have a right to challenge provided the supervisor is acting correctly and reasonably in implementing the variation, under section 7(3). It has been suggested that one resolution is for **4.068**

111 Ibid., 66, 67.

112 Ibid., 71.

113 Ibid.

114 E Bailey, *Bailey: Voluntary Arrangements* (LexisNexis), [10.7].

the variation paragraph to state that no variation is permitted which, if it had been included in the original proposal that was approved and had been challenged under section 6, would have become the subject of any order of the court under section 6(4).[115] If this were implemented, then it may entitle a dissatisfied creditor to challenge the variation under section 7(3) on the basis that 'the supervisor is implementing or attempting to implement the variation not authorised by the variation paragraph'.[116]

4.069 If it is intended to extend the duration of the arrangement, then that amounts to a variation, so any provision covering variation must be complied with.[117]

4.070 Where minor variations are concerned, for example, the grant of a grace period to the company to comply with its payment or other obligations, the CVA may give discretion to the supervisor, and unless the supervisor acts irrationally, one would think that it would be difficult to challenge the exercise of that discretion. With respect to more substantive variations, but which do not fundamentally affect the essence of the scheme or constitute a substantial reduction or delay in what creditors will receive, it has been suggested that the power to agree to the variations with the company's board of directors can be delegated to the supervisor and the committee of creditors jointly.[118]

4.071 The safest course of action is, naturally, to have an express provision in the terms of the CVA allowing for variation. However, what if there is no express power in the terms of the CVA to make a variation? This was the case in *Raja v Rubin*,[119] a case involving an IVA. Here the supervisor had concluded that it would be in the interests of creditors to vary the terms of the IVA by providing for a release of debts and an extension of the term of the IVA so as to permit the debtor to effect a partial surrender of a retirement annuity for the benefit of his creditors within the extended period. All but one creditor, at a creditors' meeting, approved this variation. The disgruntled creditor, X, applied for a declaration pursuant to the Act, that, in effect, the resolution was void. At first instance, the judge, Sir John Vinelott (sitting as a High Court judge), held that it was not possible to imply a term into the IVA that it could be varied by a specific majority. However, as X had waived his right to a dividend, he had no interest in the IVA, and consequently, all the parties who had a legitimate interest had agreed to vary their rights as between themselves. X appealed.

115 Jeremy Kutner (ed), *Tolley's Company Law* (Lexis, 2023), [V6039].
116 Ibid.
117 *Re Alpa Lighting Ltd* [1997] BPIR 341, CA.
118 Kutner (ed), *Tolley's Company Law* (n 115), [V6039].
119 [1999] BPIR 565.

His appeal was dismissed. The Court of Appeal held that as the IVA was contractual in nature, all the parties bound under the terms were in effect bound by a contract and that where there was no express term in an IVA for its variation, there was no power in the creditors to unanimously vary the IVA as approved pursuant to the statutory procedure.[120] However, on the creditors agreeing to the variation, the IVA continued in its original form as between X and the other creditors and the debtor, but as between the other creditors and the debtor, performance in the varied manner was agreed to constitute performance of the IVA.[121] Peter Gibson LJ (with whom Hirst and Clarke LJJ agreed) recognised that this may cause difficulty in particular cases, although he saw no such difficulty arising in the case before the Court.[122] His Lordship also said that: 'the court when invited to consider what order or other direction to make need not shut its eyes to the fact of a relevant consensual variation.'[123] Thus, where only a class of creditors agrees to a variation, this variation will not affect the rights of creditors not in the class. The arrangement continues as it was first approved as between the debtor and any creditor not in the aforementioned class, but in its varied form as between the class creditors and the debtor. Any creditor who is not content with a variation, where there is not a power to vary in the CVA, and the creditor is affected by the variation, will be entitled to apply to the court to complain concerning what the supervisor has done where the supervisor has permitted the variation to proceed. The court is empowered to disallow the variation.

After a variation decision has been called for and voted on, copies of a report on the outcome of the voting should be sent to the creditors and members, the company itself, the court and the registrar of companies. **4.072**

M. THE SUPERVISOR

A number of issues related to the supervisor are discussed in Chapter 7, but we make a few points in the context of this chapter. We have already made many references to the supervisor, who is the main player in the implementation of a CVA. The primary function of the supervisor is to supervise the performance **4.073**

120 Ibid., 586.
121 Ibid.
122 Ibid., 584.
123 Ibid.

of the company's obligations under the arrangement and to administer the arrangement.[124]

4.074 It was held in *Varden Nuttall Ltd v Nuttall*,[125] by HHJ Pelling QC (sitting as a High Court judge) that SIP 9 governs the way in which the supervisors of voluntary arrangements should conduct themselves.[126] As already indicated, the supervisor implements the arrangement, and the terms of the arrangement will provide what the supervisor must do. In *Appleyard Ltd v Ritecrown Ltd*[127] Lewison J (as he then was) said that:

> The primary duty of the supervisor is to implement the CVA in accordance with the Insolvency Act, the Insolvency Rules, and the terms of the proposals as modified. Any power or discretion given to him under those proposals is in my judgment to be exercised for that purpose, and that purpose only, and not for a collateral purpose. It is common ground that as an officer of the court the supervisor must also act reasonably.[128]

4.075 While he or she is an officer of the court, the supervisor is not an officer of the company. The appointment of a licensed insolvency practitioner as a supervisor is personal to that individual and is not an appointment by the firm of which he or she is a member or by which he or she is employed.[129]

4.076 Where appropriate, a supervisor may institute legal proceedings under section 423 of the Act, which permits a court to make orders where transactions have been found to defraud creditors.[130]

4.077 Like a nominee, a supervisor owes no free-standing duty, statutory or otherwise, to creditors. In the IVA case of *King v Anthony*[131] the Court of Appeal said that the part of the Act that addressed IVAs was a self-contained scheme and precluded the existence of private rights of action against the supervisor.[132] This would apply to CVAs. Thus, liability in respect of post-CVA debts could only occur where the supervisor made a negligent representation when

---

124 See para 12.1 of *R3 Standard Conditions for CVAs* (n 34) and available at: https://www.r3.org.uk/technical-library/england-wales/technical-guidance/r3-standard-form-covid-19-cva-proposal/

125 [2018] EWHC 3868 (Ch), [2019] BPIR 738.

126 Ibid., [63].

127 [2007] EWHC 3515 (Ch), [2009] BPIR 235.

128 Ibid., [38].

129 *Re Sankey Furniture Ltd ex parte Harding* [1995] 2 BCLC 594, 600, *Irvine v Duff and Phelps Ltd* [2019] EWHC 2780 (Ch), [2020] BPIR 158, [27], [28].

130 Insolvency Act 1986, s 424(1)(b).

131 [1999] BPIR 73.

132 Ibid., [78] and followed in *Irvine v Duff and Phelps Ltd* [2019] EWHC 2780 (Ch), [2020] BPIR 158.

he or she was under a duty not to do so and when the supervisor thereby made himself or herself liable for damages.[133]

4.078 Theoretically, a supervisor could be held to be a shadow director if he or she could be said to be 'a person in accordance with whose directions or instructions the directors of the company are accustomed to act'.[134] However, it must be noted that section 251(2) of the Companies Act 2006 states that persons are not deemed to be shadow directors just because the directors act on their advice, in situations where the advice is given in a person's professional capacity. Ordinarily, this will exclude, as shadow directors, people undertaking roles like supervisors of CVAs. To be liable, a supervisor would have to have exercised influence over a narrow range of matters.[135] In determining whether a supervisor was a shadow director, courts will look at the communications between the alleged shadow and the board, and ascertain, from an objective perspective, whether those communications might be able to be regarded as directions or instructions.[136] In this regard, the outcome of the communication is the important element on which to focus.[137]

1. Remuneration

4.079 Rule 2.45 applies where the remuneration of the supervisor has been fixed on the basis of the time spent. A supervisor who has acted, or has acted within the previous two years, must, within 28 days of receipt of a request from any director of the company or, where the proposal has been approved, deliver free of charge a statement[138] that covers the period which, in the case of a person who has ceased to act as a supervisor in relation to a company, begins with the date of appointment as supervisor and ends with the date of ceasing to act; and in any other case, consists of one or more complete periods of six months beginning with the date of appointment and ending most nearly before the date of receiving the request.[139] The statement must also set out the total number of hours spent on the matter during that period by the supervisor and any staff, and for each grade of staff engaged on the matter, the average hourly rate at

133 See *Heritage Joinery v Krasner* [1999] BPIR 683, 690.

134 See Companies Act 2006, s 251.

135 *McKillen v Misland (Cyprus) Investments Ltd* [2012] EWHC 521 (Ch).

136 *Secretary of State for Trade and Industry v Deverell* [2001] Ch 340, [2000] 2 WLR 907, [2000] 2 BCLC 133 (CA), [35].

137 Ibid.

138 Insolvency Rules 2016, r 2.45(2)(3).

139 Ibid., r 2.45(4).

which work carried out by staff in that grade is charged, and the number of hours spent on the matter by each grade of staff during that period.[140]

4.080 The R3 Standard Conditions for CVAs state that the supervisor shall be entitled to charge fees for services in accordance with the time actually and reasonably expended by the supervisor and the supervisor's staff in carrying out the supervisor's functions under the arrangement by reference to the ordinary hourly rates of the supervisor and the supervisor's staff as shall apply from time to time.[141]

2. Powers

4.081 The legislation provides supervisors with limited powers (adumbrated below), and so it is necessary that terms of the arrangement provide for the powers of the supervisor. The nature of the powers is a matter for negotiation. R3's Standard Conditions for CVAs provide that the supervisor is to have the following powers:

(a) take possession, collect, get in and hold any or all of the assets subject to the CVA;
(b) dispose of assets;
(c) put funds on deposit with any established clearing bank or building society;
(d) pay the costs and expenses of the arrangement;
(e) agree creditor claims;
(f) distribute funds in line with the arrangement;
(g) appoint agents;
(h) delegate to the supervisor's firm and others any or all of the supervisor's duties and functions under the arrangement;
(i) ensure any assets subject to the arrangement;
(j) claim a dividend in respect of such debts owed to the company and which fall within the arrangement;
(k) direct the company to do any act or thing if the supervisor is unable or it is impracticable to do it and which the supervisor is empowered to do;
(l) petition for the winding up of the company pursuant to the terms of the arrangement;
(m) make any necessary or incidental payments and do any other act or thing which is necessary or expedient for the purpose of exercising the above powers or for carrying out the supervisor's functions under the arrangement.

---

140 Ibid., r 2.43(5).

141 Paragraph 22.1, *R3 Standard Conditions for CVAs* (n 34) and accessible at: https://www.r3.org.uk/technical-library/england-wales/technical-guidance/r3-standard-form-covid-19-cva-proposal/

It is critical that the arrangement includes adequate powers to enable the supervisor to get the job done and to implement the arrangement. If the supervisor decides that he or she has not been endowed with any necessary powers, then he or she should contact the creditors and express his or her concern and the need for changes to the powers.[142] If all the creditors, or at least all the creditors who are affected by the changes, agree, or the terms of any express provision in the arrangement as to variation are complied with, then the arrangement can be amended to give the supervisor what he or she believes is needed.[143] The supervisor is allowed to apply, pursuant to section 7(4), to the court for directions that may accommodate the supervisor. **4.082**

As mentioned earlier, the courts are going to be slow to imply terms, and they will only do so when it is necessary to ensure the efficacy of the arrangement. Courts will not be ready to imply terms, even if might produce a convenient and tidy result, unless it is necessary in order to give efficacy to the arrangement.[144] **4.083**

The R3 Standard Conditions for CVAs provide that the expiry, full implementation or termination of the arrangement shall not affect the powers which the supervisor has in order to carry out his or her functions and to exercise such powers as are necessary for the supervisor to fully carry out his or her duties, obligations and responsibilities pursuant to the arrangement, Act and Rules and to resolve any issues that may have arisen during the course of the arrangement. This includes, but is not limited to, any duties, obligations and responsibilities in respect of assets held by the supervisor on trust.[145] **4.084**

The supervisor has the power to petition for the debtor's administration or liquidation.[146] **4.085**

142 Bailey, *Bailey: Voluntary Arrangements* (n 54), [10.2].

143 Ibid. and citing *Raja v Rubin* [1999] BPIR 565.

144 *Johnson v Davies* [1999] Ch 117, 128, [1998] BPIR 607, 614.

145 Paragraph 14.1, *R3 Standard Conditions for CVAs* (n 34) and accessible at: https://www.r3.org.uk/technical-library/england-wales/technical-guidance/r3-standard-form-covid-19-cva-proposal/

146 Insolvency Act 1986, s 7(4)(b).

5

ENDING THE CVA

A. INTRODUCTION

5.001 This chapter examines the law where there has been a CVA approved and not challenged, and it comes to an end due either to the successful completion of its terms or a failure of the CVA, that is, where the company fails to comply with its terms. One of the primary issues in this context is the effects resulting from the termination of the CVA, particularly where there has been a failure to perform the terms of the CVA. Thus, a major portion of the chapter deals with this issue. First, the chapter deals with the successful completion of CVAs and then considers the position where there is a premature end of the CVA. Next, the chapter turns to a consideration of the situation where the company fails to comply with the CVA's terms. Lastly, there is a consideration of the effect of winding up on an arrangement.

B. COMPLETION OF AN ARRANGEMENT

5.002 It may be that the CVA states that it is to exist for a set period. For instance, paragraph 8.1 of R3's Standard Conditions[1] for CVAs provides that: 'Unless extended under the provisions of these Conditions, the Arrangement shall continue until the end of the period stated in the Proposal at which time it

1 *R3 Standard Conditions for CVAs*, September 2020 and available at: https://www.r3.org.uk/technical-library/england-wales/technical-guidance/r3-standard-form-covid-19-cva-proposal/

shall expire by effluxion of time.' Although the provisions also provide that the duration of the arrangement may be extended by the supervisor, creditors' committee and creditors in accordance with the terms of the proposal.[2]

Alternatively, if the terms of a CVA are complied with, the arrangement will therefore be completed and thus end. If this is the case, then not more than 28 days after the final completion of the arrangement (often this will be following the payment of the final distribution), the supervisor shall send to all the creditors and members of the company who are bound by it, a notice that the voluntary arrangement has been fully implemented.[3] The notice must state the date the CVA took effect and must be accompanied by a copy of a report by the supervisor which: summarises all receipts and payments in relation to the CVA; explains any departure from the terms of the CVA as it originally had effect; if the CVA has terminated, sets out the reasons why; and includes (if applicable) a statement as to the amount paid to any unsecured creditors by virtue of section 176A of the Insolvency Act 1986 ('the Act') (dealing with the prescribed part).[4] If any creditor or any other person is dissatisfied with the supervisor's report, an application may be made to the court for an appropriate order or directions.[5] The supervisor is required, within the 28 days mentioned above, to send to the registrar of companies and file with the court a copy of the notice to creditors and of the supervisor's report.[6] The supervisor is not permitted to vacate office until after the copies of the notice and report have been delivered to the registrar of companies and filed with the court.[7] **5.003**

The standard practice is for the terms of a CVA to provide that the debtor company is released from the creditors' debts when it has completed its payments due under the arrangement. R3's standard Conditions for CVAs provide for this in paragraph 9.2.[8] **5.004**

According to paragraph 19 of Statement of Practice ('SIP') 3.2, the CVA should be closed promptly on completion. **5.005**

2 Paragraph 8.2.
3 Insolvency Rules 2016, r 2.44(1).
4 Ibid., r 2.44(2).
5 Insolvency Act 1986, s 7(3).
6 Insolvency Rules 2016, r 2.44(3).
7 Ibid., r 2.44(4).
8 *R3 Standard Conditions for CVAs* (n 1) and available at: https://www.r3.org.uk/technical-library/england-wales/technical-guidance/r3-standard-form-covid-19-cva-proposal/

C. PREMATURE END OF AN ARRANGEMENT

5.006 Several provisions in the Act consider the situation where a CVA terminates prematurely. Section 7B of the Act specifically addresses this matter. The provision states that for the purposes of Part I of the Act, a voluntary arrangement, the approval of which has taken effect under section 4A, comes to an end prematurely if, when it ceases to have effect, it has not been fully implemented in respect of all persons bound by the arrangement by virtue of section 5(2)(b)(i). This includes every person who in accordance with the rules was entitled to vote in the qualifying decision procedure by which the creditors' decision to approve the voluntary arrangement was made.

D. FAILURE OF AN ARRANGEMENT

5.007 Naturally, everyone hopes that a CVA will be successfully completed. However, that is not always the case. This part of the chapter examines the situation where an arrangement fails to complete and terminates. It is in this area where the most difficulty has been experienced.

5.008 It could be that the company's business does not provide sufficient income to satisfy the payments that are scheduled for the CVA creditors and the terms of the CVA are, therefore, breached. Another scenario that causes problems is that although the CVA creditors have received what they are owed under the arrangement, not enough money has been made by the company in order to satisfy those who have become unsecured creditors after the commencement of the CVA.

5.009 Where there has been a failure in complying with the CVA, the supervisor must follow the provisions in it concerning any such failure.

5.010 Whether a CVA has failed or not depends on a construction of the terms of the CVA. Neither culpability on the part of the debtor nor the views of the creditors are issues that are relevant in undertaking a proper construction of the terms.[9] If the CVA fails because of a breach of the CVA, for whatever reason, the supervisor can petition for a winding-up order or apply for an administration order.[10] In *Re Arthur Rathbone Kitchens Ltd*[11] Roger Kaye QC (sitting as a Deputy High Court judge) (as he then was) rejected submissions to the

9 *Re Keenan* [1998] BPIR 205, 209.

10 Insolvency Rules 2016, s 7(4)(b).

11 [1997] 2 BCLC 280.

effect that a supervisor could not petition for winding up under section 7(4)(b) of the Act if the CVA had ended and therefore deprived the supervisor of locus standi as 'supervisor' within the meaning of section 7(2).[12] The deputy judge said that the supervisor still had functions to fulfil following the ending of the CVA, namely adhering to the wishes of certain CVA creditors who wished him to petition for compulsory liquidation and to apply for directions.[13] This approach was also taken in the IVA case of *Harris v Gross*.[14]

In *Re Maple Environmental Services Ltd* the court said that any failure by the company to comply with its ongoing obligations would represent a failure of the voluntary arrangement, whether or not the supervisor was aware of the failure. Blackburne J, in *Welsby v Brelec Installations Ltd*[15] said that an event that caused failure would only provoke a termination of the CVA if it came to the notice of the supervisor and the supervisor, in response, took a step to indicate that the CVA would terminate and the effects of the arrangement failing would be enlivened.[16] Blackburne J went on to say that it was not to be supposed that the creditors in approving the arrangement had contemplated that any default, however trivial, might bring the arrangement to an end, and indeed do so without the supervisor or the creditors being aware of the fact.[17] The judge said that: 'I certainly do not consider that the fact that an arrangement has continued to function at the expense of the debtor's post-arrangement creditors, of itself, constitutes some special circumstance which results in the termination of the arrangement and revocation of the trusts.'[18] **5.011**

His Lordship opined that if a liquidator is subsequently appointed, he or she, if considering that the company was wrong to continue making payments to fund the CVA, has at his or her disposal the antecedent transaction provisions of the Act and may then seek recovery of any money which should not have been paid to CVA creditors. In addition, the liquidator can seek to claim that the directors are personally accountable under section 214 of the Act for any wrongful trading that may have occurred.[19] **5.012**

12 Ibid., 290–291.
13 Ibid., 292.
14 [2001] BPIR 586.
15 [2000] 2 BCLC 576.
16 Ibid., 585, 586.
17 Ibid., 586.
18 Ibid., 589.
19 Ibid.

5.013 However, the judge thought that it was likely that the terms of the CVA would be critical.

5.014 Bailey has submitted that:

> It may well be that if a supervisor allows a voluntary arrangement to continue and accepts further contributions from the debtor after the debtor is in breach of obligation despite a requirement to petition for insolvency, creditors whose debts post date the voluntary arrangement are likely to be prejudiced in an eventual insolvency where the trusts on which the voluntary arrangement contributions are held survive the insolvency. It should be open to such creditors to apply to the court as persons dissatisfied with the acts of the supervisor in the expectation that the court would order that all 'post failure' contributions should be held for the benefit of all the debtors' creditors and not just those creditors who are bound to the voluntary arrangement.[20] (footnote omitted)

5.015 It would be possible to draft the terms of an arrangement in such a way as to make it mandatory for a supervisor to present a petition for winding up in the case of a breach of certain terms, but to make it a matter of discretion when other terms are contravened.

5.016 The CVA may require a supervisor to ascertain the view of the creditors before presenting a winding-up order. However, it was held in *Everitt v Floyd*,[21] an IVA case, that the inclusion of such a provision was not a condition precedent to obtaining a bankruptcy order, and so if a supervisor neglects to do so and petitions, the court was entitled to make a bankruptcy order notwithstanding the failure of the supervisor to ascertain creditor views. Thus, a court could make a winding-up order in relation to a company that was subject to a CVA.

5.017 Unlike section 264(1) of the Act, which, when read with section 276, expressly provides the circumstances in which a supervisor or a creditor bound by an IVA may petition for the debtor's bankruptcy, there is nothing in the legislation explaining the grounds that enable a winding-up petition to be presented where a CVA is involved. Although a supervisor of a CVA can, as noted above, petition under section 7(4), the grounds are not set out. Consequently, if the parties to a CVA envisage that a winding up is to be an option on a breach occurring and the CVA failing, the CVA should express that in its terms.

5.018 Paragraph 11.1 of R3's Standard Conditions for CVAs provides that an arrangement ends if in any of the following situations:

---

20 E Bailey, *Bailey: Voluntary Arrangements* (LexisNexis), [11.1].

21 [2000] 10 WLUK 722.

- the supervisor issues a Notice of Termination after it appeared to the supervisor that the company was in breach of the arrangement, and such breach was not remedied forthwith or the supervisor had not already presented a petition for the company's winding up. After giving the company a notice of breach identifying the breach and requiring the company to rectify it within one month, the company failed to rectify the breach;
- the making of a winding-up order against the company;
- the passing of a resolution for the voluntary winding up of the company;
- the dissolution of the company; or
- the company enters administration.

If there is a failure, creditors bound by the CVA would also be entitled to enforce their debt or present a petition for winding up on the basis of the company being unable to pay their debts.[22] Further, post-CVA creditors whose debts have not been paid may also petition for a winding up on the basis that the company is not able to pay its debts. **5.019**

If, following a failure of the CVA, a winding-up order is made, the supervisor may be appointed liquidator.[23] The supervisor would, of course, be disqualified from taking on the role in certain circumstances, such as where he or she would have a conflict of interests. However, it is likely that this would not be common. **5.020**

It might be possible for a supervisor to persuade the directors of the company to move a members' resolution that the company winds up voluntarily, as this would reduce costs and give creditors, potentially, a greater dividend. **5.021**

Where the terms of a CVA provide for the supervisor to petition for compulsory liquidation on a breach, then there should be a court winding up even if the company has entered voluntary liquidation, and this even though the latter would present a more inexpensive way of addressing the affairs of the company.[24] Nevertheless, where the company has entered voluntary liquidation and the CVA allowed for court winding up, provided that no action is taken to obtain a winding-up order, the voluntary liquidation is not invalidated.[25] **5.022**

Jacob J held, in a case dealing with an IVA, *Re Keenan*,[26] that in the exercise of the discretion of the court it was appropriate for bankruptcy orders to be **5.023**

22 Insolvency Act 1986, s 122.
23 Ibid., s 140(2).
24 *Souster v Carman Construction Ltd* [2000] BPIR 371.
25 *Re Arthur Rathbone Kitchens Ltd* [1997] 2 BCLC 280.
26 [1998] BPIR 205, 210.

made even though the debtors were not at fault, having particular regard to the fact that all the creditors wanted bankruptcy. This applies to CVAs in like measure.

5.024 If failure occurs, standard conditions 'usually require the supervisor to report the fact to the creditors and distribute any funds in his possession under the terms of the arrangement, and further provide that individual creditors cease to be bound by the arrangement'.[27] Where the CVA cannot continue to operate, questions have been asked as to what exactly happens to the CVA. If the company is wound up and the supervisor is still holding assets under the terms of the CVA to distribute to the CVA creditors, what is the supervisor to do with the funds: pass them to the liquidator or pay CVA creditors? Does a liquidation terminate the CVA or does the CVA survive?[28] These and other issues are discussed below under the heading of 'Effect of a Failure of an Arrangement.'

5.025 Where a CVA's terms provide that it should last for a fixed period, subject to extension with the consent of the creditors in a creditors' meeting, the creditors are not entitled to extend the arrangement after the fixed period expires because the arrangement will have ceased to exist.[29] The arrangement would be regarded as failing.

5.026 The arrangement would also be regarded as failing if there was a breach of it as provided for in the terms of the arrangement. Paragraph 66 of R3's Standard Conditions for CVAs[30] provides that the company shall be regarded as in breach of the arrangement if:

> (a) the Company fails to comply with any obligation under the Arrangement;
> (b) information which was false or misleading in any material particular or contained any material omissions:
>   (i) was contained in any statement of affairs or other document supplied by the company or its directors under Part I of the Act to any person, or
>   (ii) was otherwise made available by the company or its directors to the creditors or shareholders at or in connection with any meeting of creditors or shareholders held, or any decision taken, in connection with the arrangement; or

27 Bailey, *Bailey: Voluntary Arrangements* (n 20), para 11.1.
28 Andrew Keay and Peter Walton, *Insolvency Law: Corporate and Personal*, 6th ed (LexisNexis, 2024), [8.58].
29 *Strongmaster Ltd v Stephen Kaye* [2002] EWHC 444 (Ch), [2002] BPIR 1259.
30 *R3 Standard Conditions for CVAs* (n 1) and available at: https://www.r3.org.uk/technical-library/england-wales/technical-guidance/r3-standard-form-covid-19-cva-proposal/

(c) the company or its directors fail to do all such things as may, for the purposes of the arrangement have been reasonably required by the supervisor.

E. EFFECT OF A FAILURE OF AN ARRANGEMENT

1. Introduction

As intimated in the previous part of the chapter, the main issue that emanates from the failure of a CVA is ascertaining what the effects of the failure are. This is mainly concerned with what happens to the company's assets. As some commentators have said: 'The courts have considered this problem a number of times. Initially, and for several years, the courts' approach to the law on termination of voluntary arrangements was somewhat complex and illogical.'[31] The following seeks to provide both an exposition of the case law, as this is necessary to appreciate the issues involved, and some conclusions. 5.027

This issue is commonly considered in the context of a company that was subject to a CVA entering liquidation. Most of the case law considers this scenario. If a winding-up order is made on a petition, the issue that preoccupied courts for some time was what the effect of the order was on the existing voluntary arrangement. The Act does not provide an answer to this issue. 5.028

As explained below, the general rule is that the assets which are included in the CVA are regarded as trust assets in the hands of the supervisor when a CVA fails. 5.029

2. The High Court decisions

The terms of the CVA may well provide that property owned by or vested in the company at the date of commencement of the arrangement will be subject to the arrangement and be an asset of it. The terms might proceed to provide, as paragraph 27.1 of R3's Standard Conditions on CVAs[32] does, that: 'Property constituting an asset of the Arrangement in the possession, custody or control of the Company shall be held by the Company upon trust for the purposes of the Arrangement during the Trust Realisation Period in accordance with this Arrangement.' 5.030

31 Keay and Walton, *Insolvency Law: Corporate and Personal* (n 28), [8.58].

32 *R3 Standard Conditions for CVAs* (n 1) and available at: https://www.r3.org.uk/technical-library/england-wales/technical-guidance/r3-standard-form-covid-19-cva-proposal/

5.031 We can say that even though the terms of a CVA do not state that a supervisor is to hold assets and funds on trust so that they might be applied in accordance with the terms of the arrangement, the courts will do so if it can be determined from the scheme provided for in the CVA.

5.032 In *Re Arthur Rathbone Kitchens Ltd*[33] the company was unable to keep up with the monthly payments required by the CVA's terms, and the company entered creditors' voluntary liquidation, which in turn was followed by a compulsory liquidation. Roger Kaye QC (sitting as a Deputy High Court judge) (as he then was) found that although there was no express provision creating a trust of the assets in the supervisor's hands, 'it is clear that the scheme as a whole imposes a trust on the supervisor to receive and apply the funds he receives in accordance with the terms of the CVA'.[34] The deputy judge thus was of the view that the CVA implicitly created a trust as to any assets held by the supervisor. The CVA did not state this, but the deputy judge was of the opinion that it was clear that the scheme, provided for under the arrangement as a whole, imposed a trust on the supervisor to receive and apply the funds he received in accordance with the terms of the CVA.[35] Mr Kaye adverted to the fact that Harman J in *Re Leisure Study Group Ltd*[36] came to a similar conclusion.[37] Harman J had held that notwithstanding the fact that no express words of trust were used, the effect of the arrangement in that case was to create a trust of the funds in the hands of the supervisor so as not to be available to a receiver subsequently appointed under a floating charge.

5.033 In *Re McKeen (a debtor)*[38] a post-IVA creditor obtained a bankruptcy order. The debtor applied to the court for the annulment of the order under section 282(1)(b) of the Act. Morritt J held that the IVA was not terminated by the making of the bankruptcy order and that the debts of the IVA creditors were not 'bankruptcy debts' to which the debtor was subject. Accordingly, the annulment was allowed.

5.034 In another case dealing with an IVA, *Re Bradley-Hole*,[39] Rimer J said that the assets held by the supervisor on the terms of the arrangement, together with any unrealised assets of the debtor (now a bankrupt) as of the date of the

33 [1998] BPIR 1.
34 Ibid., 18.
35 Ibid.
36 [1994] 2 BCLC 65.
37 [1998] BPIR 1, 18.
38 [1995] BCC 412.
39 [1995] 2 BCLC 163.

arrangement, were impressed with a trust for the benefit of the creditors who were party to the arrangement. Such trust continued notwithstanding the fact that a bankruptcy order was made on the petition of a creditor in respect of a post-IVA debt as the bankruptcy did not bring the arrangement to an end. The bankrupt consequently retained no beneficial interest in the trust assets save an interest in any surplus after the payment of the creditors in full, and none of those assets vested in the trustee in bankruptcy. Also, the assets were not available to post-IVA creditors unless the creditors had obtained a security interest over the assets as a condition of granting credit. This reasoning could equally apply to the corporate situation with a CVA, in line with what the Court of Appeal said in *Re NT Gallagher & Sons Ltd*,[40] discussed later.

It is notable, though, that in *Davis v Martin-Sklan*,[41] an IVA case, Blackburne J held that where a bankruptcy order was made on the petition of the supervisor pursuant to section 264(1)(c) of the Act, in circumstances where the debtor had entered into an IVA but had failed to make payments and provide information as required under the arrangement, the bankruptcy order terminated the voluntary arrangement and the trust. Section 7(4)(b) gives the same power to a supervisor of a CVA as section 264 does for a supervisor of an IVA. Blackburne J distinguished *Re Bradley-Hole* on the basis that Rimer J said that there was no provision in the Act that warranted an inference that a bankruptcy order, at any rate one made on a petition presented by someone other than a section 264(1)(c) petitioner, was intended to have the effect of automatically terminating a prior voluntary arrangement.[42] **5.035**

Nevertheless, a different view to that of Blackburne J was expressed in *Re Halson Packaging Ltd*[43] where a CVA had been approved by creditors on terms that the company would continue to trade, making monthly contributions to the supervisors which would be held in trust to be applied in accordance with the CVA. The CVA provided that after the payment of costs and of preferential debts, there would be a dividend for unsecured creditors. The CVA failed and the company went into a creditors' voluntary liquidation. At the time of the commencement of the winding up, the supervisors held approximately £80,000 under the CVA. The cessation of business and liquidation of the company necessarily brought the arrangement to an end in the sense that there could be no further payments made to the supervisors. HHJ Maddocks **5.036**

40 [2002] EWCA Civ 404, [2002] 1 WLR 2380, [2002] BPIR 565.

41 [1995] BCC 1122.

42 Ibid., 1127.

43 [1997] BCC 993.

(sitting as a High Court judge) held that a valid trust had been created by the CVA of the funds in favour of the creditors and that trust had not failed nor was it revoked by the terms of the CVA nor by the winding up of the company even though the CVA had failed. There was no provision in the terms of the CVA terminating this trust in the event of liquidation. The consequence was that the fund held by the supervisor was not determined by the winding up of the debtor company and thus the fund was to be distributed in accordance with the CVA. According to the judge, the effect of the arrangement was 'of a contract as between the creditors, and as between the creditors as a class, and the company'.[44] Except where there were clear reasons not to do so, according to the judge, the terms of the CVA contract would be given effect. The funds held by the supervisors remained subject to the trust created by the CVA in favour of the CVA creditors and could not be claimed by the liquidator. In the course of coming to this view, the judge distinguished *Davis v Martin-Sklan* on its facts.

5.037 In *Re Arthur Rathbone Kitchens Ltd*[45] the deputy judge said that if there was no specific provision in the arrangement, a voluntary winding up did not determine the trusts of a CVA, but a compulsory winding-up order would determine the same, at least where the creditors bound by the arrangement wanted the supervisor to petition because wanting the presentation of a petition was inconsistent with the continuation of the CVA.[46] Shortly afterwards, in *Re Excalibur Airways Ltd*,[47] Jonathan Parker J (as he then was) held, however, that a winding-up order made on the petition of the directors of the company did not have the effect of terminating a subsisting CVA unless there was an express provision in the terms of the arrangement to that effect. The judge said that there would be a different result if it was the creditors who had backed the presentation of a petition. This accords with the approach taken by Blackburne J as the petition in this matter was not presented by the supervisor, as was the case in *Davis v Martin-Sklan*.[48] A different position was taken in *Kings v Cleghorn*[49] by HHJ Behrens (sitting as a High Court judge), who held that an IVA terminated on the making of a bankruptcy order made on the petition of a post-IVA creditor, and that moneys held by the supervisor on trust for the CVA creditors should be handed to the trustee in bankruptcy.

44 Ibid., 995.
45 [1998] BPIR 1.
46 Ibid., 21.
47 [1998] 1 BCLC 436.
48 [1995] BCC 1122, [1996] BPIR 160.
49 [1998] BPIR 463.

In *Re Maple Environmental Services Ltd*[50] the CVA contained an express term that moneys paid to the supervisor should, in the event of failure of the CVA and an ensuing winding up, be paid to the liquidator. The CVA failed in that the company was placed into liquidation by the company's members. The supervisor had a substantial sum left in his hands and the issue was whether he should pay it out to arrangement creditors or over to the liquidator. HHJ Boggis QC (sitting as a High Court judge) held that the CVA failed, that the supervisor should have petitioned for the winding up of the company but did not do so, and that the fact that the company went into a creditors' voluntary liquidation did not affect the conclusion that the trust of the moneys paid to the supervisor ended and that the money should be paid to the liquidator. His Lordship said that the following principles should be applied in the kind of case before him: 5.038

- if a CVA is followed by a liquidation, the devolution of the funds held by the supervisor depends on whether the trust has come to an end;
- if the petition is brought by the supervisor, it necessarily follows that the scheme has come to an end;[51]
- if the petition is brought by someone else and there is no breach of the scheme, the scheme continues, and the trust is not broken;
- but, if the petition is brought by someone else and the scheme has been broken so that the supervisor might have brought the petition, it depends on the circumstances, the terms of the scheme, the conduct of the bound creditors and the legislation in order to decide what implications are to be drawn as to the state of the trust.[52]

Subsequently, in *Re Welsby v Brelec Installations Ltd*[53] Blackburne J, after saying that it was necessary to decide whether the CVA had failed by primarily considering the terms of the CVA, held that in deciding what happened to undistributed moneys or other assets held by or under the control of the supervisors and whether they were to be paid to creditors in accordance with the terms of the arrangement or held for the benefit of the company as a whole, the provisions of the particular arrangement were to be considered and were the prime determinant of what happened to the assets.[54] In this case, the CVA provided for the payment by the company of contributions to the supervisors and for distribution to creditors. The company went into a creditors' voluntary 5.039

50 [2001] BPIR 321.

51 This appears to be consistent with the view expressed by Blackburne J in *Davis v Martin-Sklan* [1995] BCC 1122, and discussed earlier. Also, see, *Re Kudos Glass Ltd* [2001] 1 BCLC 390.

52 [2001] BPIR 321, 324, 325.

53 [2000] 2 BCLC 576.

54 Ibid., 579.

liquidation, and Blackburne J held that the sums held by the supervisors in trust for the CVA creditors remained subject to that trust notwithstanding the liquidation. The judge went on to say that it was necessary in construing the terms of the CVA to give the arrangement a sensible and workable meaning and to interpret it in a practical fashion in order to achieve rather than frustrate the CVA's purpose.[55] Following this, in the case of *Re Kudos Glass Ltd (in liq)*[56] there was a CVA which provided that funds that came into the hands of the supervisors were to be held by the supervisors as trustees. Further, the terms of the CVA provided that if the CVA should fail, the supervisors should distribute the moneys to the CVA creditors. Mr Richard McCombe QC (sitting as a Deputy High Court judge) held that the trust continued, notwithstanding the fact that a winding-up order was obtained by a post-CVA creditor. The deputy judge said that the case law provided that the identity of the petitioner for the compulsory winding-up order was normally crucial to the question of whether the trusts arising under the scheme were held to have determined.

3. The Court of Appeal cases

5.040 It is fair to say that the case law just discussed, as well as other decisions, did not provide the certainty that all craved. However, the Court of Appeal brought a semblance of certainty to the area in *Re NT Gallagher & Sons Ltd.*[57] In this case, the Court of Appeal agreed with counsel that the cases displayed a misplaced concentration on the form of liquidation (in CVA cases) and the identity of the petitioner in bankruptcy petitions following an IVA.[58] The Court said that:

> We would question whether the mere fact that a supervisor presents a petition entails that the CVA or IVA creditors have elected to terminate the CVA or IVA trust in their favour. Even if there is evidence that all the CVA or IVA creditors supported the presentation of a petition, it does not follow that they were thereby evincing an intention that the trust should come to an end and that the trust assets should revert to the company or debtor.[59]

5.041 The Court also said that it made little sense for the form of the liquidation to affect the question of the effect of liquidation on trusts created by a CVA.[60]

55 Ibid., 585.
56 [2001] 1 BCLC 390.
57 [2002] EWCA Civ 404, [2002] 1 WLR 2380, [2002] BPIR 565.
58 Ibid., [42]–[43].
59 Ibid., [43].
60 Ibid.

5.042 Besides stating that similar provisions in relation to IVAs should apply to CVAs and vice versa, the Court of Appeal in *Re NT Gallagher & Sons Ltd*, with Peter Gibson LJ giving the judgment of the Court (which also comprised Ward and Dyson LJJ), considered the issue of whether arrangement assets held in trust for CVA creditors survived liquidation and whether the arrangement creditors were entitled to prove in the liquidation that was entered into subsequent to the CVA. In this case, an engineering company experienced financial difficulty due principally to a significant dispute with one of its customers concerning a contract that had been entered into with them. A CVA was approved with the expectation that this would enable the company to continue trading until the proceedings relating to the dispute were resolved. The terms of the CVA provided that new debts were to be paid out of trading income and monthly payments were to be made to the supervisor for distribution to the creditors bound by the CVA, although it was indicated that the amount that the creditors would receive would depend on the outcome of the proceedings relating to the contractual dispute. The CVA was to end on the resolution of the contractual dispute proceedings. The terms of the CVA provided that the supervisor was to petition for the company's winding up if the company did not meet its obligations under the CVA.

5.043 Notwithstanding several company defaults, the supervisor did not present a petition. The company was struggling and asked the CVA creditors to return some of the contributions made to them by the company, but the creditors refused. The supervisors, in conjunction with the directors, considered that the only options available were either that the supervisors should petition for the winding up of the company by the court or that the directors should put the company into voluntary liquidation. The directors chose the latter because this would both result in the speedier appointment of a liquidator and be less expensive. The contractual dispute had not been resolved at this point. The supervisor held over £500,000 under the CVA, money which had not been distributed to the CVA creditors. The company's post-CVA debts were owed a little in excess of £2.5 million and the company's total liabilities were a little over £5 million. Besides the company's contractual claims, its assets were valued at £98,000. The liquidators issued an originating application, to which the supervisors were made respondents and by which the liquidators sought a direction. The appeal to the Court of Appeal considered two of the orders sought by the supervisors, namely whether (1) the sum of £571,141.87 retained by the supervisors or (2) the benefit of the proceedings related to the contractual dispute and any sums recovered pursuant thereto was (a) held on trust for the sole benefit of the creditors bound by the CVA, or (b) available for the purposes of the liquidation. Thus, the primary matter for the Court was to determine who should be paid the funds held by the supervisor. It was the first time that this issue had come before the Court of Appeal, and Peter Gibson LJ adverted to the fact that the High Court decisions to this point had not provided much needed consistency.[61] His Lordship said that although the CVA did not expressly use the language of trusts, the supervisors were trustees of the assets in their hands.[62] In *Re Leisure Study Group Ltd*[63] Harman J had similarly held that a supervisor receiving contributions for distribution to the creditors of the company pursuant to a CVA was a trustee of those moneys for the CVA creditors.

5.044 The Court of Appeal said that it could not see why a fully constituted trust created by a CVA should terminate on the CVA failing or terminating in the absence of any provisions requiring the trust to terminate and specifying what is to happen to the trust assets.[64] Peter Gibson LJ went on to say that the fact that the debtor company was in breach of its obligations under the statutory contract constituted by the CVA and went into liquidation, which meant it could not fulfil any further the purpose of the CVA, did not produce the consequence that the trust also failed when plainly it could still be carried into effect.[65]

5.045 The Court said that as a matter of policy, where there is no provision in the CVA as to what should happen to trust assets on liquidation of the company, the courts should prefer a default rule which furthers rather than hinders what might be taken to be the statutory purpose of Part I of the Act. The policy evident was that companies and creditors were encouraged to enter into CVAs so as to provide creditors with a way of recovering what they are owed without having to have recourse to more expensive means provided by winding up or administration, thereby giving many companies the opportunity to continue to trade.[66]

5.046 In relation to the case before it, the Court held that the trusts of the CVA had not been terminated by the liquidation and, therefore, the money in the hands of the supervisors and any benefit from the proceedings were to be distributed under the terms of the CVA.

---

61 Ibid., [1].
62 Ibid., [29].
63 [1994] 2 BCLC 65.
64 Ibid., [48].
65 Ibid.
66 Ibid., [50].

Peter Gibson LJ, speaking for the Court, helpfully summarised the Court's conclusions on the points raised on the appeal before it as follows: **5.047**

> (1) Where a CVA or IVA provides for money or other assets to be paid to or transferred or held for the benefit of CVA or IVA creditors, this will create a trust of those moneys or assets for those creditors. (2) The effect of the liquidation of the company or the bankruptcy of the debtor on a trust created by the CVA or IVA will depend on the provision of the CVA or IVA relating thereto. (3) If the CVA or IVA provides what is to happen on liquidation or bankruptcy (or a failure of the CVA or IVA), effect must be given thereto. (4) If the CVA or IVA does not so provide, the trust will continue notwithstanding the liquidation, bankruptcy or failure and must take effect according to its terms. (5) The CVA or IVA creditors can prove in the liquidation or bankruptcy for so much of their debt as remains after payment of what has been or will be recovered under the trust.[67]

What is notable from points (3) and (4) is that: **5.048**

> arrangement assets will remain ring-fenced for arrangement creditors on a liquidation or bankruptcy or failure of the arrangement unless the arrangement itself specifically provides that the arrangement assets are to be treated differently, most obviously by way of falling into the liquidation or bankruptcy for the benefit of liquidation or bankruptcy creditors.[68]

Shortly afterwards, a differently constituted Court of Appeal in *Welburn v Dibb Lupton Broomhead*[69] said that whether the trust created in an IVA survived a subsequent bankruptcy depended on the intention of the parties, something that was to be ascertained from the terms of the arrangement as a whole.[70] The Court applied the reasoning in *Re NT Gallagher & Sons Ltd.* **5.049**

The decision in *Re NT Gallagher & Sons Ltd*[71] has been applied on many occasions, including in recent years by a differently constituted Court of Appeal in *Green v Wright*,[72] although in this later case, one involving an IVA, the courts were considering the situation where an arrangement was completed and not where the debtor had entered bankruptcy. In this case, an IVA had been completed and following the supervisor giving a certificate of completion, he received two payments from banks in respect of compensation for the banks previously mis-selling payment protection insurance policies to the debtor. While it was agreed by the supervisor and the debtor that the **5.050**

67 Ibid., [54].

68 L Doyle KC, A Keay and J Curl KC (eds), *Doyle, Keay and Curl: Annotated Insolvency Legislation*, 13th ed (LexisNexis, 2025), [1.59].

69 [2002] EWCA Civ 1601, [2003] BPIR 768.

70 Ibid., [14].

71 [2002] EWCA Civ 404, [2002] 1 WLR 2380, [2002] BPIR 565.

72 [2017] EWCA Civ 111, [2017] BPIR 430.

claims constituted arrangement assets, the debtor claimed the compensation funds for himself while the supervisor claimed it for the IVA creditors. The supervisor applied to the courts for directions as to whether the sums paid by the banks were subject to the trust. At first instance and on appeal to the High Court, the debtor succeeded, but the supervisor appealed to the Court of Appeal which allowed the supervisor's appeal.

5.051 The issue before the Court of Appeal was whether a trust in favour of creditors constituted by an IVA survived the issue of a certificate of completion of the IVA, so that the property of the debtor, which was subject to the trust but was discovered only after the issue of the certificate, remained subject to the trust once the property was discovered.[73] David Richards LJ (as he then was) (with whom Irwin LJ agreed) held that the trusts over the debtor's assets constituted by the IVA did not come to an end on the completion of the IVA, and, consequently, the proceeds of claims that had been assets of the arrangement, but which were only paid out after the notice of completion had been given, were distributable to creditors pursuant to the terms of the IVA. His Lordship said that while the debtor was released from his debts on completion of the IVA, this was not the same as the extinction or discharge of the debt, particularly in a bankruptcy context.[74] The judge saw an IVA as analogous to bankruptcy and noted that where a bankrupt is discharged, the discharge released him or her from all bankruptcy debts but had no effect on the trustee's functions or the operation of the Act as regards those functions, including, in particular, the right of any creditor to prove in the bankruptcy.[75] His Lordship went on to say that:

> The debts continue to exist for the purposes of proof in the bankruptcy and payment out of the realisation proceeds of the assets subject to the bankruptcy. The effect is to separate the debtor from his bankruptcy estate which continues to be administered for the benefit of his creditors as at the date of bankruptcy. The debts continue to exist as the means of defining the rights and interests of creditors in the bankruptcy but they cease to be the debtor's personal obligations.[76]

5.052 David Richards LJ said that this was the same effect produced by the IVA provisions.[77] The effect of the completion of the IVA was that the debtor had fully performed all his or her obligations under the IVA, and the minimum

73 Ibid., [1].
74 Ibid., [30].
75 Ibid., [32].
76 Ibid.
77 Ibid., [33].

distribution had been made to creditors. However, it did not mean that the trusts came to an end.[78] The judge appeared to suggest that if there had been a provision in the IVA that the trusts were to come to an end when the IVA had been completed, then the trust would have come to an end.[79] Thus, the upshot is that an arrangement may come to an end, but the trusts continue.

4. Some reflections

Clearly, the starting point in determining whether a CVA has failed is to give effect to the provisions of the arrangement. Commonly, creditors would require a provision included in the terms of the arrangement that provides that the assets held by the supervisor are to be held for the creditors' benefit if and when the company is wound up (or the CVA comes to an end in some other way). As a general rule, the assets included in the CVA are trust assets in the hands of the supervisor. **5.053**

It has been suggested that the decision in *Re NT Gallagher & Sons Ltd* 'may lead to difficulties in companies obtaining continued financing during the CVA where prospective lenders are almost certain to be aware of the CVA'.[80] This is exacerbated by the fact that creditors participating in the trust created by the CVA will be entitled to prove in a subsequent liquidation for such part of their debt which remains unpaid after the trust assets have been distributed. **5.054**

As one learned commentary notes, while the clarity given by the judgment in *Re NT Gallagher & Sons Ltd:* **5.055**

> is welcomed, it does lead to some complex practical difficulties, with two insolvency regimes running in parallel and some creditors being entitled to two 'bites of the cherry'. Similarly, the decision provides no guidance on who should act as trustee when the termination of the arrangement has removed the supervisor. In many cases, the supervisors will become liquidators, and may simply be prepared to take a pragmatic approach and, in effect, act as trustees de son tort by administrating the trust assets in accordance with the terms of the voluntary arrangement. As ever, careful and explicit drafting can assist.[81]

F. WINDING UP SUBSEQUENT TO AN ARRANGEMENT

We have already considered what happens when a CVA fails, and in examining what happens to the company's assets we noted that a liquidation might be **5.056**

78 Ibid.

79 Ibid.

80 Keay and Walton, *Insolvency Law: Corporate and Personal* (n 28), [8.59].

81 M Mullen (ed), *Tolleys Insolvency Law*, LexisNexis [V4038].

entered into. This part focuses on the instigation of a subsequent liquidation. It is quite possible that during the life of the CVA, even where the company is fulfilling its obligations under the arrangement, creditors who are not bound by the CVA will be able to apply successfully for a winding-up order, usually because the debts owed to the post-CVA creditors are payable and have not been paid.

5.057 If someone other than the supervisor, such as a post-CVA creditor, presents a petition, then the petition must be served on the supervisor.[82] If a winding-up order is secured by a post-CVA creditor, then, according to *Re Bradley-Hole*[83] and *Re McKeen*,[84] and applying what was said in the cases to a corporate context, there is nothing in the Act to warrant the inference that a winding-up order (or at any rate one made on a petition presented by someone other than the supervisor of the arrangement or any creditor bound by the arrangement) was intended to have the effect of automatically terminating a prior voluntary arrangement. Thus, the CVA could continue, and the supervisor would commonly apply arrangement assets in favour of the CVA creditors under existing trusts. The CVA could include a provision that provides for its termination in the event of winding up. If it does not, then the CVA continues to run. The estate of a company in liquidation is subject to the rights that any other person may have in the property comprising the estate. Thus, a liquidator would take the company's estate subject to the rights of the creditors under the CVA.

5.058 Very often, to approve a CVA, creditors will require a substantial proportion of the company's assets to form part of the voluntary arrangement. If the company were to enter liquidation shortly after the approval of the CVA, it is quite possible that there will be few assets of the company available to a liquidator (and hence to the non-CVA creditors and the post-CVA creditors) if the trust over assets to the supervisor cannot be challenged by the liquidator. This presents a matter of concern for creditors whose debts arise after the arrangement and who may be unaware of the arrangement or its terms.[85] The liquidator may have little hope of having the transfer of assets under the arrangement set aside as transactions at an undervalue under section 238 of the Act, or as

82 Insolvency Rules 2016, r 7.9(3)(c).
83 [1995] 4 All ER 865, [1995] 1 WLR 1097, [1995] 2 BCLC 163.
84 [1995] BCC 412.
85 Bailey, *Bailey: Voluntary Arrangements* (n 20), [11.3].

transactions defrauding creditors under section 423 of the Act.[86] It is unlikely that the arrangement could be regarded as a preference under section 239 of the Act.[87]

As considered earlier in the chapter, a supervisor of the company subject to a CVA may present a petition against the company if the company fails to fulfil its obligations under the arrangement. The supervisor must present the petition to the court or hearing centre to which the nominee's report under section 2 was submitted.[88] Section 140(2) of the Act provides that the supervisor may be appointed liquidator in a compulsory liquidation, but he or she must comply with rule 7.30(2) of the Rules. **5.059**

86 Ibid., [11.3].

87 Ibid.

88 Insolvency Rules 2016, r 7.8(1).

6

REGULATION OF THE INSOLVENCY PRACTITIONER

A. INTRODUCTION

6.001 As was mentioned in Chapter 1, one of the foundational recommendations of the Cork Committee[1] was that the insolvency profession required effective regulation so that stakeholders could have trust in the competence and impartiality of those tasked with giving effect to the procedures under what became the Insolvency Act 1986 ('the Act'). It had historically been a real weakness of all previous UK insolvency regimes that those appointed by creditors were not always trusted. Cork recognised that the lack of minimum professional qualifications had been the subject of much criticism[2] and concluded that such qualifications, as well as effective licensing and regulation, were essential in order to command public confidence.[3]

1 *Insolvency Law and Practice: Report of the Review Committee*, Cmnd 8558, 1982 ('Cork Report').
2 Cork Report, para 735.
3 Cork Report, para 756.

Legislation provides for a regulatory regime whereby insolvency practitioners ('IPs') are required to be suitably qualified[4] and to be members of a Recognised Professional Body ('RPB'), which is responsible for their licensing and regulation. The Act gives power to the Secretary of State for Business and Trade to authorise (or revoke authorisation) of RPBs.[5] The functions of the Secretary of State under the Act are discharged by the Insolvency Service, which is an Executive Agency within the Department of Business and Trade.[6] The Insolvency Practitioner Regulations 2005[7] require an IP to have passed the Joint Insolvency Examination Board examination,[8] provide security[9] and maintain records for inspection.[10] A person acts as an IP in relation to a company when, among other offices held, they act as a monitor of a Moratorium under Part A1 of the Act or as the nominee or supervisor of an approved CVA.[11] A person who acts as an IP without being qualified commits an offence.[12] **6.002**

In practical terms, it is crucial that the RPBs adopt consistent approaches to their function. The necessary coordination between the RPBs is maintained by the Joint Insolvency Committee ('JIC'), which is comprised of a mixture of RPB representatives, lay members (most of whom represent creditors), and representatives from the Insolvency Service and the Insolvency Service Northern Ireland.[13] The JIC is a significant body as it issues (and updates) the Insolvency Code of Ethics ('the Code'). The JIC also issues Statements of Insolvency Practice ('SIPs') and specifically for our purposes, has issued SIP 3.2, which deals with CVAs. Both the Code and SIP 3.2 are considered below.[14] **6.003**

4 The Insolvency Practitioner Regulations 2005 require IPs, among other things, to have passed the Joint Insolvency Examination Board examination, to provide security for office-holder posts they are appointed to and to maintain certain records for inspection.

5 Sections 391–398. Of the original seven RPBs, only four have retained that status today – the Insolvency Practitioners' Association, the Institute of Chartered Accountants in England and Wales, the Institute of Chartered Accountants in Ireland and the Institute of Chartered Accountants of Scotland.

6 See *Insolvency Service as oversight regulator of the insolvency profession: in detail* (17 February 2017).

7 SI 2005/524.

8 Ibid., Part 2.

9 Ibid., Part 3 and Sch 2.

10 Ibid., Part 4.

11 Section 388(1). The other corporate office-holder appointments, which can only be held by an IP, are as liquidator, provisional liquidator, administrator and administrative receiver.

12 Section 389.

13 Observers may, and do, attend JIC meetings by invitation.

14 The JIC also issues non-mandatory guidance in the form of Insolvency Guidance Papers, which cover such matters as Succession Planning for IPs, Dealing with Complaints and Control of Cases. The Insolvency Service issues Dear IP letters periodically, which contain technical updates and revisions to legislation, together with updates from policy and other departments within the Insolvency Service. Dear IP also contains guidance for insolvency practitioners, although none is directly relevant to CVAs.

6.004 After a recap on the role an IP plays in a CVA, this chapter will concentrate on the regulatory position of IPs as it applies in the context of CVAs. The interaction between the courts[15] and the regulatory regime in the context of CVAs will be considered at the end of this chapter.

B. THE ROLE OF AN IP IN A CVA

6.005 As we have seen,[16] there are various statutory duties owed by the nominee, the chair of the members' meeting, the convener of the creditors' decision and subsequently the supervisor. These duties include the initial appraisal of the proposal, the calling and holding of meetings, the convening of qualifying decision procedures and supervising the voluntary arrangement in accordance with the Act, the Insolvency (England and Wales) Rules 2016[17] and the terms of the arrangement.

6.006 The role of an IP in a CVA changes as the CVA progresses. The court discussed this in the individual voluntary arrangement case of *Paymex Ltd v HMRC*[18] where it considered the IP's different functions, which may include initial advice, planning, obtaining approval, and supervision. The court opined that the IP's principal activities in the context of a voluntary arrangement are negotiation and payment handling.

6.007 The negotiation aspect involves acting as an intermediary between the debtor and the creditors. This role continues throughout the whole process but is particularly evident at the nominee stage, where the proposal is formulated with the knowledge of creditors' likely positions regarding voting intentions and required standard modifications. Negotiation is a core element of the IP's role.

6.008 Once in office as supervisor, payment handling (under the terms of the arrangement) forms a major part of the IP's role. The role of the supervisor is not limited to the mechanical process of money handling. The supervisor needs to agree on creditors' claims and pay creditors in accordance with the terms of the arrangement. The supervisor does not act to enforce payment from the company, and although not an adviser to the company, they will advise the

---

15 The courts have on occasion intervened in the activities, including decision-making, of nominees and supervisors. These matters are discussed in earlier chapters: see, in particular Chapter 2, D The Nominee and Chapter 4, Court Involvement.

16 See generally Chapters 2 and 4.

17 SI 2016/1024, Pt 2 ('the Rules' or 'the Insolvency Rules').

18 [2012] BPIR 178.

company of the consequences of failing to keep to the terms of the arrangement. If, during the supervisory stage, variations to the voluntary arrangement are subsequently needed, the negotiation element of what the practitioner does may return to the fore.

There are other elements that occur along the way, such as initial advice to the debtor and fact-finding to ensure a voluntary arrangement is appropriate in the circumstances, the organisation of decision-making processes and reporting to members and creditors. **6.009**

Any breach of the statutory duties owed by a person acting in any of these official capacities gives creditors the right to apply to court. As discussed earlier in Chapters 2 and 4, the court has wide powers, for example, to remove and replace a nominee or supervisor, to overturn a decision of the supervisor and to regulate the supervision of the arrangement generally.[19] **6.010**

Although an IP must exercise professional independent judgement throughout their involvement as a nominee or supervisor of a CVA, somewhat surprisingly, any breach of that duty will not lead to private law liability to creditors for breach of trust or negligence. The duties owed by a nominee/chair/convener/supervisor were created by statute, and only if the statute did not contain a remedy for creditors could they maintain a private law action. Under the Act, there are provisions that permit a creditor (and others) to complain of the acts of the nominee/chair/convener/supervisor, who is an officer of the court. As an officer of the court, the court itself has wide powers to control the proper performance of the statutory powers. There can be no private law action for breach of these statutory duties.[20] **6.011**

Despite what appears to be a blanket ban on private law actions against IPs in relation to their actions as office-holders in relation to CVAs, the courts have confirmed that an action may still lie where the acts complained of are carried out by the nominee or supervisor, but in some other capacity, such as a professional adviser. The problem often facing a nominee/chair/convener/supervisor is that they may have a long-standing professional relationship with the debtor company. In such cases, they need to be careful to make it clear in what capacity they are acting. If the court thinks the IP has returned to acting as an adviser to the company, even though they have been appointed as nominee or **6.012**

---

19 Rule 2.41.

20 See *King v Anthony* [1998] 2 BCLC 517 and *Irvine v Duff & Phelps Ltd* [2019] EWHC 2780 (Ch).

supervisor, they will be open to a private law action based upon their actions as adviser.[21]

6.013 This discussion of the legal position of the IP leads us now to consider how the professional regulatory regime[22] governs the role of the IP in the context of CVAs.

C. INSOLVENCY CODE OF ETHICS

6.014 The Insolvency Code of Ethics ('the Code')[23] is the primary source of mandatory professional regulatory guidance for IPs. It applies to all professional work relating to an insolvency appointment, including work which may lead to such an appointment, and so covers the activities of IPs both before and during any appointment (as nominee or supervisor in relation to a CVA or as monitor in a Moratorium). The Code is based on the International Ethics Standards Board for Accountants Code. The Code has five 'Fundamental Principles',[24] which are supplemented by a 'Conceptual Framework' that identifies a number of threats to those principles.[25]

1. The fundamental principles

(a) Integrity

6.015 This principle requires an IP to be straightforward and honest in all professional and business relationships.[26] The Code states that an IP must not knowingly be associated with reports, returns, communications or other information that are false or misleading, contain statements or information provided recklessly or omit or obscure required information where such omission or obscurity would be misleading. If an IP becomes aware of having been associated with such matters, they should take steps to become dissociated from them, and if they have provided a report with such information in it, they should

21 See, e.g., *Prosser v Castle Sanderson* [2002] EWCA Civ 1140 and *Smurthwaite v Simpson-Smith and Mond* [2006] BPIR 1504.

22 Since June 2013, the Insolvency Service has operated an online function known as the 'Complaints Gateway'. This is a single point of entry for those wishing to complain about IPs, regardless of which RPB regulates them. The Insolvency Service then refers to the relevant RPB those cases that require consideration by that RPB but otherwise rejects them.

23 The latest version dates from 1 May 2020.

24 The Code, 2100.1 A1 and 2100.2. The numbering used here is taken from the version of the Code available on the Institute of Chartered Accountants in England and Wales website.

25 Ibid., 2110.1.

26 Ibid., 2101.1.

provide a modified report to correct the misinformation.[27] Consistently with this principle, the courts have commented that, when acting as a nominee for a CVA, if the fullness and candour of the information provided by the company is called into question, the nominee must take reasonable steps to be satisfied as to the true position.[28]

(b) Objectivity

Objectivity is described by the Code as 'the state of mind which has regard to all considerations relevant to the task in hand but no other'.[29] This principle requires an IP not to compromise professional or business judgement because of bias, conflict of interest or undue influence of others.[30] The threats to compliance with the Fundamental Principles that are identified in the Conceptual Framework[31] focus specifically on issues relating to objectivity, and a further section of the Code is specifically devoted to conflicts of interest.[32] It is a particular risk for an IP who has previously acted as an adviser to a company to then take on the role of nominee (and supervisor). Consistently with this principle, the courts have identified the need for IPs in these cases to preserve their objectivity and independence from any party, either the debtor company or a creditor.[33] **6.016**

(c) Professional competence and due care

This principle requires an IP to attain and maintain professional knowledge and skill, based on current technical and professional standards and relevant legislation, and to act diligently and in accordance with applicable technical and professional standards.[34] The IP must exercise sound judgement in applying their professional knowledge and skill. An IP is also required to take reasonable steps to ensure that those working under their authority have appropriate training and supervision.[35] Where appropriate, an IP must make users of their services aware of any limitations inherent in the services provided.[36] This may be relevant in the context of a CVA where a company's directors **6.017**

27 Ibid., 2101.2.
28 *Greystoke v Hamilton-Smith* [1997] BPIR 24.
29 The Code, 2102.1 A1.
30 Ibid., 2102.1.
31 Ibid., 2110.1 to 2116.2.
32 Ibid., 2310.1 to 2316.1.
33 *Smurthwaite v Simpson-Smith and Mond* (n 21), [33].
34 The Code, 2103.1.
35 Ibid., 2103.2. Further regulatory guidance on the delegation or sharing of workloads, either within firms or between them, with staff or other IPs, is provided by the Insolvency Guidance Paper – Control of Cases (April 2014).
36 The Code, 2103.3.

look to the supervisor for advice on how to rescue their company. This type of advice would be outside the remit of the supervisor and so the company should have this limitation confirmed.

(d) Confidentiality

6.018 The principle of confidentiality is owed by all professionals but applies to IPs in a slightly different way as they are required by this principle to provide transparency in reporting on their acts and dealings as fully as possible given the circumstances of the case.[37] In doing so, the IP must respect the confidentiality of information acquired as a result of professional and business relationships.[38] In order to allow the IP to carry out their role, there are various exceptions to the general confidentiality requirement, such as producing statutory reports for the creditors, submitting reports on the conduct of the directors or producing documents in the course of legal proceedings.[39]

(e) Professional behaviour

6.019 An IP must comply with relevant laws and regulations and avoid any conduct that the IP knows or should know might discredit the profession. They may not knowingly engage in any business, occupation or activity that impairs or might impair the integrity, objectivity or good reputation of the insolvency profession.[40] This would seem to include providing a positive report as a nominee on a CVA proposal which the IP knows would be inherently unfairly prejudicial to certain creditors.[41]

2. The conceptual framework

6.020 The Conceptual Framework begins by observing that the 'circumstances in which insolvency practitioners operate might create threats to compliance with the fundamental principles'.[42] It provides an approach designed to identify such threats, evaluate the threats identified and address them by eliminating them or reducing them to an acceptable level.[43] It is significant that the Code does not look to eliminate all of these threats but instead, where appropriate, it provides means to manage those threats. If these threats are present, it

---

37 Ibid., 2104.2.

38 Ibid., 2104.3.

39 Ibid., 2104.3 A1.

40 Ibid., 2105.1.

41 See, e.g., *Mourant v Sixty UK Ltd* [2010] BCC 882, where the court reported the IPs to their professional bodies. The judgment was admissible in subsequent disciplinary proceedings (*R (on the application of Hollis) v ACCA* [2014] BPIR 1317).

42 The Code, 2110.1.

43 Ibid., 2110.2.

does not necessarily preclude the IP from taking an appointment, but it does highlight the threat and indicates that something needs to be done about it. It may be that the threat can be managed, but where it cannot, the IP will need to decline the appointment.

Five specific categories of threats to the Fundamental Principles are identified in the Conceptual Framework. Some of the examples given in the Code for each of the threats are summarised below. The Code recognises that a circumstance may create more than one threat, and a threat might affect compliance with more than one of the Fundamental Principles.[44] **6.021**

(a) Self-interest threat

Examples of the self-interest threat include an individual within the IP's firm having an interest in a creditor or potential creditor with a claim that requires subjective adjudication, for example, in considering how to distribute funds to creditors under the terms of a CVA. It may also include situations where an IP discovers a significant error when evaluating the provision of previous services performed by an individual within the IP's firm.[45] This may be the case where the IP's firm has, prior to the CVA being entered into, provided inadequate or negligent advice. **6.022**

(b) Self-review threat

An example provided in the Code is where an IP has previously carried out professional work of any description, including sequential insolvency appointments, for an entity.[46] This may be the case where an IP's firm has previously been administrator or monitor in relation to the company where the IP has now become supervisor under a CVA. **6.023**

(c) Advocacy threat

This may arise where an IP has advised a creditor of an insolvent entity or the entity itself prior to its insolvency.[47] It is common for an IP's firm to advise a company prior to its entering into a CVA. **6.024**

(d) Familiarity threat

A familiarity threat may arise where an IP or an individual within their firm or an immediate family member has a close professional or personal relationship **6.025**

44 Ibid., 2114.1 A6.
45 Ibid., 2114.1 A5(a).
46 Ibid., 2114.1 A5(b).
47 Ibid., 2114.1 A5(c).

with the insolvent entity or a purchaser of the insolvent entity's assets.[48] This may arise where a CVA is drafted as a gradual wind-down and sale of a business and the purchaser falls within the class of entity identified in the Code.

(e) Intimidation threat

6.026 An IP may be affected by an intimidation threat where an individual within their firm is threatened with dismissal or replacement, litigation, complaint or adverse publicity, violence or other reprisal.[49] In practice, there is often a risk that large secured creditors will only support the appointment of IPs on their own panel of practitioners, and any threat of de facto removal from that panel, with a consequent loss of potential appointments, may fall within this class of threat.

3. Evaluating the threat and taking action

6.027 Where the IP identifies a threat to compliance with the Fundamental Principles, they must evaluate whether such a threat is at an acceptable level.[50] An IP is required to use the 'reasonable and informed third party test' in considering compliance – that is, would a reasonable and informed third party likely conclude the IP has complied with the Code? Such consideration is one that weighs all the relevant facts and circumstances that the IP knows or could reasonably be expected to know at the time the conclusions are reached. The hypothetical third party need not be an IP but would possess the relevant knowledge and experience to understand and evaluate the appropriateness of the IP's conclusions in an impartial manner.[51] Where the threat cannot be eliminated or reduced to an acceptable level, the IP should decline or end the appointment in question.[52]

6.028 The Code contains a specific section on conflicts of interest which states that they create threats to the principle of objectivity and might also create threats to compliance with other Fundamental Principles.[53] There is a general requirement that an IP 'shall not allow a conflict of interest to compromise professional or business judgment'.[54] The Code uses the concepts of a 'significant professional relationship' or a 'significant personal relationship'. Where such

---

48 Ibid., 2114.1 A5(d).
49 Ibid., 2114.1 A5(e).
50 Ibid., 2115.1.
51 Ibid., 2113.1 A1.
52 Ibid., 2116.1.
53 Ibid., 2310.2.
54 Ibid., 2311.1.

relationships are present, no action can be taken to eliminate a threat or reduce it to an acceptable level. Where such a relationship exists, the IP is therefore prevented from accepting the appointment.[55] Risks of conflict will be increased where IPs or their firm have carried out one or more pre-appointment engagements for the entity, and the IP is appointed as an insolvency office-holder, and they, or another IP in their firm, are subsequently appointed office-holder in a further insolvency process.[56] This type of risk will therefore arise if an IP advises a company which enters a Moratorium followed by a CVA where the IP (or a member of their firm) has acted as Monitor and nominee/supervisor. Although the risk will be increased in such cases, it will usually be reasonable and possible to manage that risk.

The Code requires the IP to assess whether there is any prior relationship that would make it inappropriate to accept an appointment. The IP is required to have policies and procedures to identify such relationships[57] and must take reasonable steps to identify circumstances and relationships that may create conflicts of interest.[58] This obligation is ongoing and must be kept under review throughout the appointment,[59] including changes in circumstance.[60] **6.029**

Where a threat to the Fundamental Principles is identified, one of the ways that it may be possible to manage the threat is to disclose the threat. The Code states that, prior to accepting an appointment, an IP should consider making disclosure to the court or the creditors of the existence of any threat, together with any safeguard identified and applied.[61] It is a matter of professional judgement for the IP to determine whether the nature and significance of any conflict of interest are such that specific disclosure and explicit consent are necessary when addressing the threat created by the conflict of interest.[62] In reaching their view, the IP must always consider the perception of others in deciding whether to accept an appointment.[63] The IP must document their courses of action, judgements made and decisions taken[64] sufficiently to enable **6.030**

55 Ibid., 2312.7.
56 Ibid., 2311.2 A2.
57 Ibid., 2312.3.
58 Ibid., 2312.4.
59 Ibid., 2312.4 A1.
60 Ibid., 2313.1.
61 Ibid., 2210.5 A3.
62 Ibid., 2315.4.
63 Ibid., 2312.8.
64 Ibid., 2312.9.

a reasonable and informed third party to reach a view on the appropriateness of their action.[65]

6.031 The Code deals specifically with the self-interest threat to the Fundamental Principles posed by the payment or receipt of referral fees or commissions for CVA work. IPs are effectively banned from receiving or paying such fees. The Code is very clear that an IP (including their firm or an associate) 'shall not make or offer to make any payment or commission for the introduction of an insolvency appointment'.[66] Slightly less clearly, where an engagement might lead to an insolvency appointment, such as acting as a nominee or supervisor in relation to a CVA, IPs 'shall not accept referral fees or commissions unless they take action to reduce the threats created by such fees or commissions to an acceptable level'. Suggested safeguards to address such a threat include prior disclosure to creditors.[67] In the context of a CVA this may not be realistic and is likely to encourage creditors to vote against any proposal. The Code goes on to state that if, after the receipt of any such payment, the IP accepts an insolvency appointment, the amount and its source must be disclosed to creditors.[68] During an insolvency appointment, any referral fees received by an IP must be paid into the insolvent estate.[69] The sum total of these provisions is that an IP acting in relation to a CVA is not able to pay a referral fee in any cases and if they receive a referral fee, they must account for it to the creditors.

6.032 Although the Code is written in a way that encourages flexibility, there are some specific instances involving sequential appointments that are identified.[70] Relevant to the present discussion, the Code states that an IP 'may normally' accept appointment as an administrator or liquidator where an individual within their firm has previously acted as a supervisor of a CVA.[71] CVAs often terminate prematurely, and in such cases, it may be reasonable for the

---

65 Ibid., 2319.10.

66 Ibid., R2340.4.

67 Ibid., 2340.5 A1.

68 Ibid., R2340.6.

69 Ibid., R2340.7.

70 Ibid., 2510. At 2510.1, the Code considers that a significant personal relationship precluding appointment 'will normally arise' where the IP's firm or an individual within the firm has carried out audit-related work involving the entity within the previous three years. Where the audit work was more than three years before the proposed date of the appointment, the IP must nonetheless evaluate the threat. At 2510.2, the Code highlights cases where an IP proposes to take an appointment, such as nominee or supervisor, where their firm or an individual within the firm was previously instructed by or at the instigation of a creditor or a party with a financial interest in the company to investigate, monitor or advise in relation to its affairs. Whether or not a significant personal relationship arises depends on close scrutiny of the nature of the previous involvement.

71 Ibid., 2520.2.

IP who has acted as supervisor to take on the sequential appointment. The IP must consider whether there are any circumstances that give rise to an unacceptable threat to compliance with the Fundamental Principles. In these categories of cases, the risk of conflict is plainly reduced given the collective nature of the respective processes where the creditors will usually have their say in who is appointed.

4. The Code and the law

The Code is drafted as a professional governance document and thus does not trespass into the area of substantive law beyond pointing out the rather obvious point that IPs are required to comply with statute and secondary legislation,[72] any relevant judicial authority relating to their conduct, any directions given by the court,[73] act in a manner appropriate to their position as an officer of the court (when acting as either nominee or supervisor under a CVA) where applicable, and in accordance with any quasi-judicial, fiduciary or other duties that they may be under.[74] **6.033**

While departure from the Code of Ethics by an IP may give rise to regulatory action by that IP's RPB,[75] such a departure by an office-holder will not, of itself, necessarily give rise to a breach of duty that is susceptible to review by the court. **6.034**

D. STATEMENT OF INSOLVENCY PRACTICE 3.2

Statements of Insolvency Practice are issued to IPs under procedures agreed between the RPBs acting through the JIC.[76] They are individually numbered and act to supplement the Code in providing practical, mandatory guidance to IPs. SIPs are not legally enforceable in the courts, but their breach will form the basis of professional misconduct action by the IP's RPB. **6.035**

SIP 1 (entitled *An introduction to statements of insolvency practice*) states that SIPs set principles and key compliance standards with which IPs are required to comply and, accordingly, compliance with the SIPs is mandatory.[77] SIP **6.036**

72 Ibid., 2200.4.
73 Ibid., 2200.6.
74 Ibid., 2200.7.
75 See, e.g., *Mourant v Sixty UK Ltd* (n 41) and the subsequent related disciplinary proceedings *R (on the application of Hollis) v ACCA* [2014] BPIR 1317.
76 SIP 1, para 9 (1 October 2015).
77 Ibid., para 6.

1 states that the SIPs exist to promote and maintain high standards and to harmonise the approach of IPs. It adds that the SIPs 'apply in parallel to the prevailing statutory framework'.[78] Various significant aspects of insolvency practice have their own individual SIP. The SIP which provides guidance specifically for CVAs is SIP 3.2, which we will concentrate on here.[79]

6.037 SIP 3.2 sets out compliance standards for IPs when dealing at different stages in the CVA process. It deals both with cases where the IP is assisting a company's directors in putting together a CVA and where the IP is putting forward the CVA themselves as an administrator or liquidator.

6.038 An important principle that it highlights is, in identifying that an IP is likely to act in a number of different capacities (the provision of initial advice to the directors, assisting in the preparation of the proposal, acting as nominee and acting as supervisor), the IP must clearly differentiate between these stages and roles.[80] To a similar effect, the IP must explain to the company's directors (where the CVA is being proposed by the directors) what the directors' responsibilities and role are both before and during the CVA, as well as the consequences of the CVA.

6.039 An IP must act with objectivity.[81] A failure to bring objectivity to each role carried out by the IP may prejudice the interests of the company and its creditors and is likely to bring the practitioner and the profession into disrepute. As mentioned above, it may lead to action in the courts where the IP fails to recognise or manage a conflict of interest.

6.040 A common misunderstanding in practice has historically been around the extent to which the IP may become involved in the operation of the company once in post as supervisor.[82] SIP 3.2 provides that when the IP is assisting with the drafting of the proposal, it must be clear what, if any, additional specialist assistance, which will not be provided by the supervisor, will be required.[83] An IP acting as a nominee or supervisor is not an officer of the company or a 'company doctor'. They should not be involved in the day-to-day operation of the company. If the services of a turnaround specialist are needed to give effect

78 Ibid., para 1.
79 SIP 3.2 (1 April 2021).
80 Ibid., para 3.
81 Ibid., para 3.
82 P Walton, C Umfreville and L Jacobs, *Company Voluntary Arrangements: Evaluating Success and Failure* (2018).
83 SIP 3.2, paras 10 and 15.

to the CVA's terms, the directors must be clear that that turnaround specialist needs to be someone separate from the nominee/supervisor.

As part of the IP's duty to act objectively, they must be satisfied that the proposal 'is achievable and that a fair balance is struck between the interests of the company and its creditors'.[84] When acting as nominee, SIP 3.2 replicates the legal duty to ensure they report objectively on the viability of the proposal.[85] A company may or may not be insolvent when it enters a CVA. The SIP's wording here suggests that IPs must follow the law when considering the interests of different stakeholders. When insolvent administration or liquidation is inevitable, the interests of a company's creditors become paramount and the interests of the company and its shareholders fall away. At a time when a company is insolvent or bordering on insolvency but insolvent administration or liquidation is not inevitable, the interests of the shareholders and the creditors must both be considered.[86] It is submitted that most companies considering a CVA are insolvent (or that insolvency is imminent) but that insolvent administration or liquidation is not inevitable; otherwise, the company would not be proposing a CVA. Hence, when considering the terms of a CVA proposal, the IP must consider and balance the interests of both the shareholders and the creditors. **6.041**

When an IP is acting as nominee or supervisor, they need to be satisfied that procedures are in place to ensure an assessment is made of certain key issues.[87] They must assess the actual solutions available and whether they are viable. They must assess whether the directors are being sufficiently cooperative and that they understand the process and are committed to it. In assessing the fairness towards creditors of the proposal, they must assess the likely attitude of key creditors and the general body of creditors. Creditors should be given sufficient time to consider what is being planned and be provided with sufficient information to understand the company's financial and trading history. This speaks to their actions as a 'go-between' considered above. The IP must also assess whether or not a Moratorium is required or available. Research suggests the use of a Moratorium does increase the chances of a successful CVA even though the use of a Moratorium is infrequent in practice.[88] **6.042**

84 Ibid., para 7.
85 Ibid., para 16, the wording of which effectively replicates the test laid down in *Greystoke v Hamilton-Smith* [1997] BPIR 24.
86 *BTI 2014 LLC v Sequana SA* [2022] UKSC 25.
87 SIP 3.2, paras 12, 14 and 15.
88 P Walton, C Umfreville and L Jacobs, *Company Voluntary Arrangements: Evaluating Success and Failure* (May 2018), and See P Walton and L Jacobs, *Insolvency Service Corporate Insolvency and Governance Act*

6.043 As the proposal is put to the creditors and subsequently, where the proposal is approved, the IP has a number of obligations. These are listed in SIP 3.2 and include such matters as the role and powers of the supervisor, which will include monitoring the CVA as it progresses and explaining any powers to terminate the CVA and on what grounds.

6.044 One significant difference between CVAs and other procedures under the Act is how the IP is paid their fee. The fees system under the Insolvency Rules, whereby IPs must estimate their likely costs and have them, and any increase on that estimate, approved by the creditors, does not operate in CVAs.[89] The fee that the IP is paid for acting as nominee and supervisor is a matter which is dealt with under the terms of the CVA itself.[90] It will therefore require the approval of the creditors as part of the approval process of the CVA, but it is not subject to a separate procedure as it is in administration and liquidation. SIP 3.2 goes further than the Rules in that the Rules require the proposal to state the amount of the nominee's fee and expenses and also how the supervisor's fees and expenses will be determined and paid. SIP 3.2 requires, in a nod to the system which applies in administration and liquidation, the IP to ensure the proposal contains a disclosure of the estimated costs of the CVA including the proposed remuneration of the nominee and the supervisor and the bases for those estimates.[91] The SIP therefore requires an estimate of the supervisor's fees, not merely an explanation of the mechanism by which it will be calculated.

6.045 The Insolvency Rules do not specify on what basis the fees of the nominee or supervisor are to be calculated. This will be included in the terms of the proposal and requires the agreement of the company and its creditors. The fees will usually be stated as a fixed sum, as a percentage of funds coming into the arrangement or by reference to the time costs of the nominee or supervisor and their staff (or a combination of these options).

E. THE COURTS AND THE PROFESSIONAL REGULATORY REGIME

6.046 The purpose of the professional regulatory regime is to ensure best practice, professional competence and ethical behaviour. The purpose of litigation is usually to ensure that a claimant with a financial or other economic interest

2020 – Final Evaluation Report (November 2022).

89 Insolvency Rules, r 18.15 et seq.

90 Insolvency Rules, r 2.3 lists the requisite contents of a proposal.

91 SIP 3.2, para 15.

in a breach of the law is able to obtain a remedy against a defendant. There is a clear distinction between the two regimes, and the courts will not usually be drawn into considering professional misconduct evidence when considering legal rights and obligations. Professional misconduct may be serious but, in itself, may not cause loss to a complainant.

In the context of alleged IP conflicts of interest in a CVA, the court has opined that regulatory guidance did not really add anything to the case.[92] The court preferred to concentrate on the statutory provision (the allegation of unfair prejudice under s 6 of the Act). The court disagreed with an argument that evidence of a breach of professional conduct rules was, in itself, sufficient to show unfair prejudice.[93] The question for the court was whether there was unfair prejudice. A breach of the regulatory regime guidance, in itself, did not amount to that. In other, non-CVA cases, the courts have generally followed this approach in distinguishing the two regimes and so have emphasised that they are primarily concerned with the insolvency proceedings, not professional misconduct issues.[94] That is not to say that the courts will entirely ignore breaches of professional conduct as part of the evidence base in making their deliberations.[95] In such cases, the courts appear to have concluded that the objective standard for a competent office-holder would include satisfaction of professional conduct rules. Breach of those rules would suggest a breach of the duty of skill and care (or other duty). As explained earlier, nominees and supervisors cannot usually be sued in negligence by disgruntled creditors, but breach of professional conduct rules may support a case of unfair prejudice, even if, on its own, breach of the regulatory framework would not be sufficient. **6.047**

92 *SISU Capital Fund Ltd v Tucker* [2005] EWHC 2170 (Ch).

93 Ibid., at [91].

94 *Re Zinc Hotels (Holdings) Ltd* [2018] EWHC 1936 (Ch) and *Clydesdale Financial Services Ltd v Smailes* [2009] EWHC 1745 (Ch).

95 In the context of pre-packaged administrations, the courts have found non-compliance with SIP 16 to be a relevant factor: *Re Kayley Vending Ltd* [2009] EWHC 904 (Ch) and *Re Moss Groundworks Ltd* [2019] EWHC 2825 (Ch). In *Brewer v Iqbal* [2019] EWHC 182 (Ch) and *Re One Blackfriars Limited* [2021] EWHC 684 (Ch), the court considered breaches of professional conduct could be evidence of a breach of the duty of skill and care.

6.048 As well as the courts' reluctance to rely on breaches of the regulatory regime in reaching their decisions, the courts are also reluctant to become involved in assessing whether IP conduct amounts to a breach of professional conduct. The court will not be used as a form of insurance for IPs concerned about misconduct proceedings.[96] Indeed, if the court is aware of evidence of professional misconduct, the court may report that to the IP's RPB.[97]

96 *Re Comet Group Ltd* [2018] EWHC 1378 (Ch).

97 *Mourant v Sixty UK Ltd* (n 41).

7

IMPACT ON CREDITORS

A. INTRODUCTION

The purpose of a company voluntary arrangement ('CVA') is usually to rescue the company as a going concern. In a small minority of cases, the object of the CVA is an ordered wind down of the company's business with a consequent realisation and distribution of the company assets.[1] Whatever the motivation behind the CVA, its terms will require that, in general terms, the company's creditors are treated in accordance with their pre-CVA priority. As we have seen in Chapter 2, the rights of secured and preferential creditors are protected in that a CVA cannot prevent a secured creditor enforcing its security unless the secured creditor agrees,[2] and any CVA must respect the relative priority of preferential creditors, again unless the preferential creditor agrees to a modification of their rights.[3] If the company had previously entered into a Moratorium under Part A1 of the Insolvency Act 1986 ('the Act') and the nominee's report is submitted to the court during the 12 weeks after the Moratorium has ended, the CVA must not provide for Moratorium debts or priority pre-Moratorium debts[4] to be paid otherwise than in full (unless the creditors affected agree).[5] **7.001**

1 P Walton, C Umfreville and L Jacobs, *Company Voluntary Arrangements: Evaluating Success and Failure* (May 2018) at [4.1.1].

2 Insolvency Act 1986, s 4(3).

3 Ibid., s 4(4).

4 The meaning of Moratorium and priority pre-Moratorium debts is provided by s 174A. See Chapter 3.

5 Insolvency Act 1986, s 4(4A) and (4B).

7.002 Apart from the above specific exceptions, the terms of the CVA must generally treat unsecured creditors equally (although, as we will see, the courts will allow a divergence from equal treatment in certain circumstances where unequal treatment can be justified). The principle of equality of division among creditors of an insolvent debtor is one of the fundamental principles of insolvency law. The 'pari passu principle' is an example of the equitable maxim 'equity is equality'. It is at the heart of all the collective insolvency procedures including voluntary arrangements. A collective process is generally necessary before any equal division of assets may be accomplished. The collective nature of CVAs requires that all (unsecured) creditors come inside the system to ensure that individual creditors do not act on their own to reward themselves at the cost of the collective good. Creditors who are quick off the mark in enforcing their rights against a debtor can steal an advantage over other creditors as long as they act before a CVA (or other collective process) becomes enforceable against all creditors.

7.003 Creditors who have security are treated well by formal insolvency procedures. As long as the security is adequate, secured creditors will nearly always be guaranteed payment even if there is little if anything left for the unsecured creditors. Preferential creditors are given statutory priority over other unsecured creditors.[6] The most relevant classes of preferential creditors in the CVA context are employees and HMRC. We will consider their position specifically below. Non-preferential unsecured creditors are at the bottom of the priority waterfall. Those that have guaranteed a company's debt have in the past attempted to have the terms of a CVA strip away their liability. This is unlikely to be successful as it will be seen by the courts as unfairly prejudicial to the creditor with the benefit of the guarantee. Landlords have rights peculiar to themselves which may allow them to come out of their tenants' CVA in better shape than other creditors although it is possible under the terms of a CVA for different landlords to be treated differently. This is an exception to the pari passu principle but one which may be justified on the facts of the case. The rights of these different categories of creditor in the context of a CVA will be considered below.

---

6 See the discussion in the administration case *Hobson v OAS Realisations (2022) Limited* [2024] EWHC 1491 (Ch), where preferential creditors were classed as unsecured.

B. SECURED CREDITORS

1. Introduction

Under the Act, security is defined by section 248 as 'any mortgage, charge, lien or other security'. This definition is taken to mean that the rights the creditor has are proprietary in character. The proprietary interest in the debtor's assets allows the creditor to realise the secured assets to discharge the debtor's obligation to the creditor. It is very common for a creditor to take security in the form of a debenture containing both fixed and floating charges over the whole of a company's undertaking (which includes all present and future property)[7]. Lightman J in *Razzaq v Pala*[8] stated that a security interest involves the debtor conferring an interest in their property on the creditor which allows the creditor, following default, to enforce the debt against the property. This right is defeasible upon payment of money. This is consistent with the concepts of mortgages, charges and various types of lien. **7.004**

Secured creditors generally have two rights: a right of action against the property over which they have security and a right of action against the debtor. As long as the security is adequate to pay the amount owed, the creditor will normally look to the secured assets for payment. This may be accomplished by entering into possession of the secured assets if the creditor is a mortgagee but the security will more usually be realised on behalf of the secured creditor by an appointed office-holder of the company such as a receiver, administrator or liquidator. **7.005**

If no office-holder is already in place, the secured creditor will normally look to appoint a receiver (if they have the power to do so) or, more commonly, an administrator.[9] The costs of the realisation of the secured assets which are subject to a form of fixed security, and the distribution of the proceeds, will be paid for separately out of the realised assets and will not be part of the fee chargeable to the company by the office-holder in their office-holder capacity. The realisation occurs outside the insolvency office even though it is conducted by the same person.[10] Assets subject to a floating charge will be subject to the costs and expenses of the office-holder. Assets subject to fixed charges are **7.006**

7 For a discussion of the history as to how this type of security developed, see, e.g., R Gregory and P Walton, 'Fixed and Floating Charges – a Revelation' [2001] LMCLQ 123.

8 [1998] BCC 66. See also *Re Lomax Leisure Ltd* [1999] 2 BCLC 126.

9 Insolvency Act 1986, Sch B1, para 14.

10 See the explanation in *Pagden v Ridgley* [2024] EWHC 3047 (Ch).

seen as falling outside the insolvency procedure and so are not used to pay the office-holder's costs and expenses.

7.007 In the context of a CVA, it is usual for the secured assets (whether subject to fixed or floating security) not to be realised as this is likely to have an adverse effect on the company continuing to trade. Where secured assets are realised during a CVA, the secured creditor will have agreed how and who conducts the realisation.

7.008 In practice, most secured creditors are supportive of attempts by companies to enter into CVAs. They do not usually take enforcement action once they have notice of a CVA proposal. In order to protect their position, they will often not consent to their rights of enforcement being affected by the CVA, and so hold such enforcement powers in reserve in case the CVA is not a success.

2. Execution creditors

7.009 The category of 'secured creditors' includes execution creditors whose execution has progressed to the point where they have been converted from an unsecured into a secured creditor.[11] An unsecured creditor who has obtained judgment against a debtor will usually want to execute that judgment. Depending upon which type of execution is chosen and whether the debtor subsequently enters a formal insolvency procedure, the execution creditor may remain in the ranks of the unsecured creditors or may be able to show that the judgment debt has become a secured debt.

7.010 Once the voluntary arrangement is approved, it is given effect to under its own terms and will expressly prevent creditors bound under it from enforcing their rights against the debtor while the voluntary arrangement remains in force.[12] In the context of an individual voluntary arrangement, *Peck v Craighead*[13] considered the status of an execution creditor under a writ of fieri facias (the predecessor of today's writ of control[14]) after seizure of the debtor's assets but prior to sale. In this case, the debtor proposed an individual voluntary arrangement but prior to the creditors' meeting held to consider his proposal, a judgment creditor proceeded to issue a writ of fieri facias under which goods were

11 See generally the discussion in P Walton, 'Execution Creditors – (almost) the Last Rights in Insolvency' (2003) 32 *Common Law World Review* 179.

12 *R3 Standard Conditions for Company Voluntary Arrangements*, clauses 4, 5 and 6.

13 [1995] 1 BCLC 337.

14 See generally A Keay and P Walton, *Insolvency Law Corporate and Personal* 6th ed (LexisNexis, 2024), Chapter 33.

seized. The issue was whether or not the creditor became a secured creditor for the purposes of voting on the voluntary arrangement. The court held that the judgment creditor became a secured creditor upon seizure of the goods. In the context of a CVA, therefore, an execution creditor who has become secured before the voluntary arrangement is approved, is not bound by its terms unless it has agreed to be bound. The creditor can continue with the execution. It should be borne in mind that the execution creditor's secured creditor status could be sidestepped by the company entering liquidation[15] which would avoid the secured creditor status of the creditor and return them to the ranks of unsecured creditors.[16]

If the CVA goes ahead but terminates prematurely with the company then entering into liquidation the result is again that the execution creditor is no longer in the position of a secured creditor. In liquidation the creditor would be unable to continue with the execution (without leave of the court) and would be reduced to the ranks of unsecured creditors. **7.011**

An execution creditor who has achieved secured creditor status for the purposes of a CVA would be in a safer position if they did not agree to the proposal at all. As a secured creditor the CVA cannot prevent their continued enforcement action without their consent and so, they are able to forge ahead with the execution to ensure payment. **7.012**

R3's Standard Conditions for Company Voluntary Arrangements[17] relegate execution creditors, who have not completed their execution by the time the CVA is effective, to the status of unsecured creditors and prevent further enforcement action by execution creditors. This might be challenged by an execution creditor who has achieved secured creditor status by the time of the creditor decision on the CVA proposal. **7.013**

3. Assignment of debts

In addition to taking traditional security over a company's assets, in the form of a debenture containing fixed and floating charges,[18] it is common for some finance providers to require an assignment of a company's book debts. The financial arrangement is in effect a sale of the company's future book debts. The assignment of the book debts may be by way of either (i) an equitable **7.014**

15 Insolvency Act 1986, s 130.

16 See generally Walton, 'Execution Creditors – (almost) the Last Rights in Insolvency' (n 11).

17 Clauses 4, 5 and 6.

18 See, e.g., Keay and Walton, *Insolvency Law Corporate and Personal* (LexisNexis) (n 14), Chapter 6.

assignment which does not require that notice be given to the company's debtors (this practice is usually referred to as invoice discounting); or (ii) a statutory or legal assignment effective under section 136 of the Law of Property Act 1925 which does require notice to be given to the debtor (this practice is usually referred to as debt factoring). Where a company has a strong debt ledger, a finance provider will often prefer to take an assignment of the debts rather than a mere charge over the debts, as the assignment is not subject to registration under the Companies Act 2006 and if the company enters a formal insolvency procedure such as a CVA, the assignee will be able to retain the value of all the debts as it owns them either at law or in equity.

4. Vulnerable security

7.015 Only if the security is inadequate or vulnerable to attack will the creditor consider surrendering the security. This may work to the advantage of the secured creditor if its security is worthless as by choosing to become an unsecured creditor it will then be able to participate in voting upon the CVA proposal and in any distribution under the terms of the CVA. Creditors' votes on a resolution considering a proposal for a voluntary arrangement are calculated according to the amount of a creditor's unsecured debt. If a creditor's debt is partly secured, they can vote in respect of the unsecured part.[19]

7.016 A security may be vulnerable in a subsequent administration or liquidation of the company as a preference under section 239 of the Act, a transaction at an undervalue under section 238 or in the case of a floating charge under section 245 of the Act. *Re Leisure Study Group Ltd*[20] is an example of a potential pitfall for floating charge holders who agree to the CVA. If the CVA fails prematurely, it will usually be the case that some, if not all, of the floating charge assets will have been transferred to the supervisor on trust for the unsecured creditors. The floating charge holder may not have any claim to such assets. Careful consideration needs to be taken by a floating charge holder of the terms of the CVA prior to giving consent to it in order to avoid this result.

C. GUARANTORS

7.017 As well as demanding security over a company's assets, a lender will usually also demand that either the company's directors or, if there is one, the

19 See Insolvency (England and Wales) Rules 2016 (SI 2016/1024) r 15.31(5) and *Calor Gas v Piercy* [1994] BCC 69.

20 [1994] 2 BCLC 65.

company's parent company, guarantee the company's debt. In practice guarantees are frequently entered into at the same time as, and in order to support the principal debt under, a secured loan. A guarantee creates a contractual liability in the guarantor but is not a form of security as defined by section 248 of the Act. It is not a 'mortgage, charge, lien or other security'.

A guarantee is a tripartite agreement entered by the principal debtor (the company), the creditor (often a bank or other institutional lender) and the guarantor. The purpose of taking the guarantee is that if the company fails to repay the loan (or if the security taken by the bank proves to be inadequate), the bank can enforce the debt against the guarantor. Guarantee documents vary in terms of how they are drafted but they will be drafted with the intention of protecting the bank's interest as far as possible. The law applicable to guarantees is complex. The explanation provided here is only an outline designed to explain some of the basic issues.[21] **7.018**

According to Patten LJ in *McGuinness v Norwich and Peterborough Building Society*,[22] a guarantee may impose one or more of the following types of liability on the guarantor: **7.019**

(1) a 'see to it' obligation: i.e., an undertaking by the guarantor that the principal debtor will perform his own contract with the creditor;
(2) a conditional payment obligation: i.e., a promise by the guarantor to pay the instalments of principal and interest which fall due if the principal debtor fails to make those payments;
(3) an indemnity; and
(4) a concurrent liability with the debtor for what is due under the contract of loan.

Guarantees falling within classes (2) and (4) create a liability in debt whereas those falling within (1) and (3) create a liability enforceable by way of action for unliquidated damages. A guarantee is often referred to as a secondary obligation. It is related to the primary liability owed by the principal debtor to the creditor and is secondary in that it is contingent on the principal debtor failing to perform its obligations. A guarantor's liability will fall away if the liability of the principal debtor is extinguished, for example, if the debt is paid off or void for some reason. If the obligations of the principal debtor are varied, for example, the debtor is given longer to pay than originally agreed, the guarantee will also lapse. Where a guarantor pays out on a guarantee, they will **7.020**

---

21 For a full consideration see, e.g., G Andrews and R Millett, *Law of Guarantees* 7th ed (Sweet & Maxwell, 2015).

22 [2011] EWCA 1286, [2010] EWHC 2989 (Ch).

usually be entitled to an indemnity from the principal debtor and so can sue the principal debtor for the amount paid out under the guarantee. Such a right may not prove to be particularly beneficial if the principal debtor is insolvent but the guarantor will often be subrogated to the rights of the creditor whom the guarantor has paid off. This permits the guarantor to enforce the rights the creditor had against the principal debtor (and so, may include the benefit of any security).

7.021 A guarantee must be in writing.[23] Where companies within a group structure guarantee one another's debts, there may be a concern that the contract of guarantee is not supported by consideration if there is no discernible benefit to one company guaranteeing another company's debt. For this reason, guarantees are usually executed by way of deed as the Common Law has historically enforced any contract under seal without the need for further consideration.

7.022 A guarantee is sometimes referred to as a contract of suretyship. The other main type of surety contract is an indemnity and it is often the difficulty of distinguishing between guarantees and indemnities which causes problems in practice. An indemnity is a primary obligation, expressed to be independent from the obligations of the principal debtor and its enforcement is not dependent upon the failure of the principal debtor to pay the debt. If a creditor has the benefit of an indemnity rather than a guarantee and, if the principal debtor's liability is set aside or altered, a person who has provided an indemnity to the creditor will usually still be liable to pay.

7.023 It is often a challenge to know whether a particular document has created a guarantee or an indemnity (or a combination of the two). Many precedent documents are themselves headed 'Guarantee and Indemnity' which does little to make their interpretation straightforward. From a bank's point of view, it is common to insist on a guarantor having a primary obligation to pay the debt. If this is the case, an indemnity has probably been created. From the bank's point of view, this is beneficial as it permits the bank to enforce the debt against the guarantor without the need to attempt first to enforce the obligation against the principal debtor. An indemnity does not fall away if the obligation owed by the principal debtor to the creditor is varied or extinguished. Much will depend upon the wording of the document and as mentioned above a guarantee agreement may be interpreted as creating any one (or more) of four classes of obligation.

23 Statute of Frauds Act 1677, s 4.

A guarantor will usually remain liable on a guarantee in the event of the formal insolvency of the principal debtor. This is really the whole point of a creditor taking the guarantee. The terms of a voluntary arrangement may attempt to restrict a creditor's right to enforce a guarantee against a third party. This may be intended to protect the guarantor or to restrict the amount the guarantor may claim under its indemnity as a creditor bound by the voluntary arrangement. Such attempts are usually seen as unfairly prejudicial to the interests of the creditor in question and so not enforceable. An insolvency practitioner who approves a CVA proposal with such guarantee-stripping provisions is likely to be in breach of the Insolvency Code of Ethics.[24] 7.024

D. PREFERENTIAL CREDITORS

There has long been, in one form or another, a class of unsecured creditors which is given priority or preferential rights in any insolvency. There are two types of preferential debt: ordinary and secondary. Ordinary preferential debts rank equally among themselves and are paid in full, unless the assets are insufficient to meet them, in which case they abate in equal proportions. Secondary preferential debts rank equally among themselves after the ordinary preferential debts and are paid in full, unless the assets are insufficient to meet them, in which case they too abate in equal proportions. 7.025

Historically, the most significant preferential creditor was the Crown in the form of His Majesty's Revenue and Customs ('HMRC'). HMRC's preferential status was abolished by the Enterprise Act 2002, but was reintroduced by the Finance Act 2020 (as a secondary preferential debt). Employees have long been given limited rights as preferential creditors (and are ordinary preferential debts). 7.026

The current preferential creditor regime is found in section 386 and Schedule 6 to the Act. It applies to all formal procedures under the Act, including CVAs. The concept of the regime is that certain unsecured creditors, while having no priority under the general law, are given express priority by legislation to payment from an insolvent estate. Bestowing favoured status on particular kinds 7.027

24 See *Mourant v Sixty UK Ltd* [2010] BCC 882 and the subsequent disciplinary proceedings reported in *R (on the application of Hollis) v Association of Chartered Certified Accountants* [2014] BPIR 1317. See also the failed attempt to strip away the guarantee of a parent company in exchange for the payment of a sum representing a relatively small percentage of the guaranteed debt in *Re Mizen Design/Build Ltd* [2023] EWHC 127 (Ch).

of debts is a statutory exception to the pari passu principle and has been a matter of controversy for some time.[25]

7.028 Section 4(7) of the Act applies the general scheme of preferential debts which applies in liquidation and administration to CVAs. Those debts are set out in section 386 and Schedule 6 to the Act. Ordinary preferential debts (these are set out, according to s 386(1A), in paras 8–15B of Sch 6 to the Act) relate mainly to debts owed to employees and rank equally among themselves and are to be paid in full unless the assets are insufficient to meet them when the debts abate in equal proportions. Secondary preferential debts, which mainly comprise debts owed to HMRC, are set out in paragraphs 15BA, 15BB or 15D of Schedule 6 to the Act (s 386(1B)) and again rank equally among themselves and are to be paid in full (after the ordinary preferential debts are paid in full) unless the assets are insufficient to meet them when the debts abate in equal proportions.

7.029 If there are insufficient funds to pay preferential creditors from the funds available to the unsecured creditors then the preferential creditors are paid from funds that would ordinarily go to secured creditors who hold floating charges.[26] Preferential creditors therefore have priority over floating charge holders.

7.030 The date on which preferential debts are determined is known as the 'relevant date' and is defined in section 387. Where the company which enters a CVA is not being wound up,[27] the relevant date under section 387(2) and (2A) is:

1. where the company is in administration the date on which the company entered administration;
2. if the company is not in administration the relevant date is the date on which the voluntary arrangement takes effect.

7.031 As mentioned above, Schedule 6 to the Act divides preferential debts into different categories. The most significant of these categories fall into two broad

25 For a discussion of the history behind preferential debts and the development of the law, see A Keay and P Walton, 'The Preferential Debts' Regime in Liquidation Law: In the Public Interest?' (1999) 3 Cfi LR 84 at 86–91.

26 See Insolvency Act 1986, s 175(2) for details. Also, where goods or effects of the company have been distrained within three months of the date of any winding-up order, the goods and effects or the proceeds from their sale are the subject of a charge to the preferential debts if there are not sufficient funds held by the company to pay these debts (s 176(2), (2A)).

27 It is extremely rare for a company in liquidation to enter into a CVA, but where it does, the date for identifying preferential debts will generally be the commencement of the winding up (see the detailed provisions in s 387(3)).

groups – the first deals with employee benefits and the second relates to debts owed to HMRC.[28]

1. Employees

Category 4 includes any sum which is owed by the company in relation to unpaid contributions to the occupational pension schemes and state scheme premiums. Category 5 addresses employee remuneration[29] and related matters. It includes: unpaid remuneration of employees for up to four months prior to the relevant date but subject to a maximum payment of £800.[30] It also includes any amount of employee holiday pay accrued prior to the relevant date.[31] In order not to discourage those who are willing to fund an ailing company, any sum loaned and used for the specific purpose of paying employees' remuneration is also preferential debt.[32] **7.032**

Although the preferential status of some of the debt owed to employees is helpful to employees, due to the financial limit of £800 in total for unpaid wages or salary, their rights to distribution as preferential creditors under a CVA are restricted. Any additional unpaid remuneration will rank as unsecured debt.[33] Having stated that, it should be borne in mind that CVAs often ensure employees are paid in full, in order to encourage them to continue to work for the company as it attempts its rescue plan. The courts are unlikely to find that paying employees in full is unfairly prejudicial to other creditors. **7.033**

There is often an issue as to whether a person is actually an employee employed under a contract of service with the company or is an independent contractor **7.034**

---

28 The other significant group of preferential debts relates to certain debts owed to, and deposits covered by, the Financial Services Compensation Scheme under the Financial Services and Markets Act 2000, which were added to the classes of preferential debts in 2015.

29 Remuneration is widely defined by Insolvency Act 1986, Sch 6, para 13.

30 Insolvency Act, Sch 6, para 9. The £800 figure has not been increased since 1976. It is found in Insolvency Proceedings (Monetary Limits) Order 1986 (SI 1986/1996), art 4. In addition, under Sch 6, para 12, any amount which is ordered to be paid by the company under the Reserve Forces (Safeguard of Employment) Act 1985 and is ordered in respect of a default by the company in respect of the employee's obligations under that Act, not exceeding £800, is also preferential.

31 Insolvency Act 1986, Sch 6, para 10. See generally *Chief Constable of the Police Service of Northern Ireland v Agnew* [2023] UKSC 33.

32 Insolvency Act 1986, Sch 6, para 11.

33 Outside the Act, employees also have the benefit of an additional and separate statutory scheme that provides for their protection when their employers are unable or unwilling to meet certain of their liabilities. Payments are made to employees by the Secretary of State out of the National Insurance Fund under the Employment Rights Act 1996. The Secretary of State is then able to step into the shoes of the employees and take over their preferential rights to the extent that the payments made are in respect of the insolvent employers' liabilities, which have preferential status under the Act.

contracting with the company or is a director of the company. Much will depend upon the contractual terms under which the worker operates. The nature of the company's business will also be relevant. In assessing whether a worker is or is not an employee all relevant factors will be taken into account in reaching a balanced view. In carrying out this balancing exercise, the court in *Ivey v Secretary of State for Employment*[34] identified the following questions which need consideration:

- Is the person under the control of another?
- Is the person an integral part of another's organisation?
- Is the person in business on their own account?
- What is the economic reality between the person and the alleged employer?
- Is there mutuality of obligation between the person and the alleged employer?
- What are the respective bargaining powers of the person and the alleged employer?

7.035 In cases where a shareholder (and/or director) of the company claims to be an employee the court has provided the following guidelines for factual enquiry:[35]

- whether there was a genuine contract between the company and the shareholder;
- how and for what reasons the contract came into existence (for example, whether it was made at a time when insolvency was looming);
- what each party actually did pursuant to the contract;
- if the contract was not a sham, whether it actually gave rise to an employer/employee relationship;
- the relevant factors to consider were the degree of control exercised by the company over the shareholder employee, whether there were other directors and whether the constitution of the company gave the shareholder rights such that they were answerable only to themselves and incapable of being dismissed;
- if they were a director, whether they were able, under the articles of association, to vote on matters in which they were personally interested, for example, the termination of their contract of employment;
- all the relevant factors needed to be taken into account and given such weight as was considered appropriate.

2. HMRC

7.036 Prior to the Enterprise Act 2002, the revenue authorities (now HMRC) had certain preferential rights (known as the 'Crown preference') which were abolished by the 2002 Act. In relation to formal insolvencies commenced on or after 1 December 2020 Parliament reintroduced a level of revenue priority (as

34 [1997] BCC 145.

35 *Secretary of State for Trade and Industry v Bottrill* [1999] BCC 177.

a secondary preferential creditor). The Crown debts which are preferential are limited to certain taxation debts where the debtor effectively collects tax (or other payments) on behalf of HMRC. The taxes included under Schedule 6, Category 9 are: PAYE income tax deductions; national insurance deductions; VAT payments; Construction Industry Scheme deductions; and student loan repayments. The debts rank as secondary preferential debts after ordinary preferential debts such as those relating to liabilities to (mainly) employees.

As explained above, a CVA cannot alter the priority position of preferential creditors without their consent. In most corporate insolvencies, the main preferential creditor is HMRC. One obvious consequence of this is that in practical terms, a CVA will usually need to provide for full payment of any such preferential debt before any payments are to be made to the other unsecured creditors. HMRC is often the most significant creditor where a CVA proposal is voted upon. If it is not promised full payment (or some agreement can be agreed upon) HMRC will often prevent a CVA being approved. Although HMRC has suggested it will support attempts to rescue companies such as by using a CVA, and be proactive in using its vote,[36] there will be limits to that support. HMRC will commonly require the inclusion of specific provisions in a CVA proposal which favour its position. HMRC takes a commercial view of any CVA proposal. If a company has a history of poor tax compliance, even if HMRC is promised full payment under the terms of a CVA, it is likely that HMRC will not support the proposal. As HMRC is often the most significant unsecured (albeit preferential) creditor, its vote will usually be crucial in securing the 75 per cent majority needed to approve the CVA. **7.037**

E. LANDLORDS

Landlords are unusual creditors as, at the time of a CVA proposal being voted upon, they may be unsecured creditors for past rent which has not been paid, but, where it is intended that a lease will continue during the CVA, they will also be unsecured contingent creditors for the future rent and therefore will be able to vote on the basis of that debt too and be bound by the CVA.[37] A further significant issue which arises in practice, is whether attempts under the terms of a CVA to amend the terms of a lease, for example, by reducing rent during the CVA period, will be unfairly prejudicial. **7.038**

---

36 See Dear IP Issue 148, July 2022.

37 *Discovery (Northampton) Ltd v Debenhams Retail Ltd* [2019] EWHC 2441 (Ch). See also *Lazari Properties Ltd v New Look Retailers Ltd* [2021] EWHC 1209 (Ch).

7.039 Although landlords have two distinct remedies available to them, neither constitutes them as secured creditors.[38] The remedies are Commercial Rent Arrears Recovery ('CRAR') in relation to commercial but not residential leases and the right to forfeit a lease either by obtaining a court order or by self-help through the process of peaceable re-entry. If the tenant subsequently enters a formal insolvency procedure, this may impact on the landlord's rights to carry on with, or retain, the benefits of such remedies.

7.040 CRAR is the modern replacement for the ancient power to distrain for unpaid rent (referred to as the remedy of 'distress') which had enabled landlords for centuries to recover arrears of rent, without going to court, by taking goods from the leased property without notice and selling them to cover unpaid rent. The remedy of distress was abolished by section 71 of the Tribunals, Courts and Enforcement Act 2007. Section 72 of the 2007 Act introduced the remedy of CRAR which is only available to commercial landlords. CRAR adopts the procedure under Schedule 12 to the 2007 Act which itself introduced a new form of execution for judgment creditors looking to enforce their judgment which involves taking control of the debtor's goods and selling them. Landlords may only carry out CRAR through appropriately licensed enforcement agents and must serve a minimum period of notice on the tenant. The 2007 Act and regulations created under it provide in detail the procedure which a landlord must follow in order to carry out CRAR.[39] With the abolition of the former common law remedy of distress, landlords no longer have the element of surprise on their side when they decide to recover rent arrears as notice must be served on the tenant prior to any exercise of CRAR. This does restrict the power of landlords to undermine a CVA when they receive a proposal. They cannot immediately and without notice exercise their CRAR remedy. They must first give the company notice of their intention so to do.

7.041 Where a lease has a substantial capital value, the landlord may prefer to take action to forfeit the lease which brings the lease to an end and enables the landlord to grant a new lease to a new tenant. Leases will commonly contain a clause permitting forfeiture in the event of a company entering or proposing formal insolvency procedures such as a CVA. Although this may be attractive to a landlord, it pre-supposes that it will be straightforward to find a new tenant. In the post-pandemic world, this is not always possible and landlords may prefer to accept a reduced rent rather than lose the tenant.

---

38 *Razzaq v Pala* [1998] BCC 66 and *Re Lomax Leisure Ltd* [1999] 2 BCLC 126.

39 Taking Control of Goods Regulations 2013 (SI 2013/1894) which also apply to judgment creditors executing their judgment by writ of control.

7.042 It will usually be expressly stated in any lease that the insolvency of the tenant will give rise to a power in the landlord to forfeit the lease.[40] Failure to pay rent or the tenant entering a formal insolvency procedure will almost always be listed as events triggering the right to forfeit. Things are not though, so weighted in favour of the landlord as this might suggest. If the effect of forfeiture would deprive the tenant's other creditors of a valuable asset, such as a long lease with a capital value on a sale, the court may not permit forfeiture. The landlord's ability to forfeit may, in such circumstances, be viewed as an act which unjustly enriches the landlord and so relief against forfeiture will be ordered.

7.043 If a CVA covers rent owing to the landlord at the date of the arrangement, it will be drafted so as to prevent the landlord from exercising CRAR on the basis of it, even if the landlord voted against the arrangement proposal. Unless a moratorium has been imposed, there is nothing to prevent the landlord from exercising CRAR prior to the decision of the creditors to approve the arrangement, if rent is unpaid, but it will need to give at least seven days' notice of its intention to carry out CRAR. By doing so, the landlord will avoid being bound by the arrangement. The exercise of CRAR at this time may well have the knock-on effect of destroying any possibility of the arrangement being workable.

7.044 If a CVA has been entered into which covers rent owing at the date of the arrangement's approval, the terms of the CVA should prevent the landlord from forfeiting on the basis of that rent. The landlord may be able to forfeit subsequently for non-payment of future rent not covered by the arrangement.[41] Even where a voluntary arrangement is not unfairly prejudicial to the landlord by reducing the future rent payable, the provisions of the voluntary arrangement cannot remove the landlord's right of forfeiture.[42]

7.045 CVAs are most commonly used in attempts to rescue small- or medium-sized companies, but CVAs have been used by large undertakings especially in the retail sector. The proposal for such complex CVAs often puts the company's

---

40 The standard provision for forfeiture in a lease allows the landlord to be able to re-enter the premises upon the occurrence of various events of default. Once the right to forfeit has arisen, the landlord may exercise it by either making a peaceable re-entry or by bringing an action by way of a writ of possession. Peaceable re-entry has the advantage of being an out-of-court action by the landlord. If the writ is issued, the forfeiture only becomes final once a judgment for possession is obtained, which has the effect of establishing that the forfeiture is justified and that no relief against it will be granted. If the tenant is able to pay, they will be able to obtain relief from forfeiture, virtually as a right.

41 See, e.g., *Thomas v Ken Thomas Ltd* [2007] BPIR 959.

42 *Discovery (Northampton) Ltd v Debenhams Retail Ltd* [2019] EWHC 2441 (Ch).

leasehold retail units into different categories based upon their individual profitability.[43] The terms of the CVA in such cases treats the landlords of the most profitable units more favourably than those of the less profitable. Some are promised the full rent due under the lease during the CVA whilst others are paid only a percentage of the contract rent during the CVA. This differential treatment looks at first blush to be unfairly prejudicial to the landlords who receive a lesser percentage. The court's approach to such CVAs is seen in the leading case of *Discovery (Northampton) Ltd v Debenhams Retail Ltd.*[44] The CVA's terms created five classes of landlord depending upon the financial performance of each unit. Those units which were financially sustainable at the contracted rent remained largely unaffected by the CVA with full rent continuing to be paid during the CVA. Those units which were shown to be not sustainable at the contract rate had their respective rents reduced to a level which made them financially sustainable. The reduction in rent payable for the duration of the CVA was not lower than the market rent available at the time of the CVA. All landlords were given the right to terminate their leases if they did not wish to accept the lower rent. The court looked at the 'basic fairness' of the CVA and judged it fair. The court was satisfied that the differential treatment of the landlords was justified on the facts to secure continuation of the business.

43 See generally *Discovery (Northampton) Ltd v Debenhams Retail Ltd*, ibid.; *Re SHB Realisations Ltd* [2018] EWHC 1294 (Ch); *Lazari Properties Ltd v New Look Retailers Ltd* (n 36); *Re Regis UK Ltd* [2021] EWHC 1294 (Ch); and *Young v Nero Holdings Ltd* [2021] EWHC 2600 (Ch).

44 [2019] EWHC 2441 (Ch).

APPENDIX

Covid-19

Standard Conditions for Company Voluntary Arrangements

Produced by

Association of Business Recovery Professionals

Version 1

September 2020

CONTENTS

PART 1: INTERPRETATION

1. Miscellaneous Definitions

1.1 In the Arrangement, except where the context otherwise demands:

'Act' means the Insolvency Act 1986 as amended;

'Arrangement' means the Proposal and the Conditions read together;

'Conditions' are these Conditions;

'Connected' shall have the meaning given to it in section 249 of the Act;

'Court' means any court having jurisdiction in respect of the Arrangement;

'Creditor' is a person bound by the Arrangement to whom a Debt is owed;

'Debt' has the meaning given to it in Part 14 of the Rules with the modifications necessary to refer to a voluntary arrangement, and an HMRC Debt;

'Decision Date' has the meaning given by Rule 15.2(1) of the Rules with the modifications necessary to refer to a voluntary arrangement;

'Decision Procedure' has the meaning given to a Qualifying Decision Procedure by Section 246ZE of the Act and that given to a Decision Procedure by Rule 15.3 of the Rules with the modifications necessary to refer to a voluntary arrangement;

'Directors' means all the directors of the Company at the time that the Proposal was made or at the time of the event described, where relevant in the context;

'Dividend' means a distribution to Creditors;

'Excluded Assets' are those assets identified in the Proposal as being excluded from the Arrangement;

'Hire Purchase Agreement' has the same meaning as found in paragraph 111(1) of Schedule B1 to the Insolvency Act 1986;

'HMRC Debt' means the HMRC claim in the arrangement including corporation tax, PAYE/NIC, VAT and any other assessed tax, levy or duty due (with the exception of corporation tax) to the day before the approval of the Arrangement and in respect of corporation tax in respect of any accounting period ended on or before the day before the approval of the Arrangement;

'Ordinary Preferential Creditor' is a Creditor with a Debt falling within section 175 of the Act, and whose Debt falls within the definition of an 'ordinary preferential debt' as given to that term in section 386 of the Act, and 'Ordinary Preferential Debt' shall be construed accordingly;

'Paragraphs' are Paragraphs of these Conditions, and 'Sub-paragraph' shall be construed accordingly;

'Preferential Creditor' is an Ordinary Preferential Creditor or a Secondary Preferential Creditor and 'Preferential Debt' shall be construed accordingly;

'Proof' means a proof of claim in accordance with Rules 14.3 to 14.4 of the Rules with the modifications necessary to refer to a voluntary arrangement.

'Property' has the meaning given to it in section 436 of the Act;

'Rules' means the Insolvency (England and Wales) Rules 2016 as amended;

'Secondary Preferential Creditor' is a Creditor with a Debt falling within section 175 of the Act, and whose Debt falls within the definition of a 'secondary preferential debt' as given to that term in section 386 of the Act, and 'Secondary Preferential Debt' shall be construed accordingly;

'Secured Creditor' and 'Security' have the meaning given to them in section 248 of the Act;

'Secretary of State' means the Secretary of State for Business, Energy and Industrial Strategy or any successor office;

'Shareholders' are the holders of ordinary or preference shares in the Company;

'Supervisor' is the person or persons for the time being appointed to supervise the implementation of the Arrangement;

'Trust Realisation Period' is the period of time from commencement of the Arrangement and continues, notwithstanding expiry, termination or full implementation of the Arrangement until the realisation and distribution of sums due to Creditors under the Arrangement terms.

1.2 References in the Arrangement to any statutory provision shall include a reference to any modification or re-enactment thereof for the time being in force

2. The Conditions

The Conditions are an integral part of the Arrangement. In the event of any ambiguity or conflict between the Conditions and the Proposal and any modifications to it, the Proposal as modified shall prevail.

PART 2: COMMENCEMENT, EFFECT, AND DURATION OF ARRANGEMENT

3. Commencement of Arrangement

The Arrangement shall come into effect upon the approval thereof by the Creditors pursuant to the provisions of the Act and Rules.

4. Nature and Effect of the Arrangement

4.1 [Nature of Arrangement]

The Arrangement is a proposal under Part I of the Act for a scheme of arrangement of the Company's affairs or a composition in full and final satisfaction of the Company's Debts.

4.2 [Claims against third parties]

Unless the Proposal indicates to the contrary, nothing in the Arrangement shall be construed as effecting a composition or satisfaction of any Debt owed by a person other than the Company, whether that Debt is owed jointly by the Company or otherwise. Therefore, the release of the Company from its debts by the terms of Arrangement shall not operate as a release of any co-debtor for the same debts.

4.3 [Restriction on Creditors' rights]

After the commencement of the Arrangement, no Creditor shall (save with the consent of the Supervisor), in respect of any Debt which is subject to the Arrangement:

(a) have any remedy against the property of the Company;
(b) commence or continue any action or other legal proceeding against the Company.

4.4 [Suspension of limitation period]

The Company agrees that any limitation period accruing in respect of a Debt which is subject to the Arrangement shall be suspended until expiry, termination or full implementation of the Arrangement, whichever is sooner.

4.5 [Saving for certain rights]

Nothing in this Paragraph or elsewhere in the Conditions shall be construed as affecting the following rights:

(a) the right of any Secured Creditor to enforce its Security, except with the Secured Creditor's consent;

(b) the right of the Supervisor to present a winding-up petition under section 7(4)(b) of the Act for default in connection with the Arrangement;

(c) the right of any Creditor to bring or continue legal proceedings against the Company and to obtain a judgment against the Company in the full amount of its Debt for the sole purpose of making a claim against an insurer of the Company by virtue of the Third Party (Rights Against Insurers) Act 2010.

5. Existing Proceedings against Company

5.1 [Discontinuance of existing proceedings]

Legal proceedings against the Company in existence at the commencement of the Arrangement in respect of Debts which are subject to the Arrangement shall, unless they are of a type contemplated by Paragraph 4.5 or the Supervisor otherwise directs, be discontinued by the Creditor with no order as to costs as soon after the commencement of the Arrangement as is practicable.

5.2 [Waiver of Company's costs entitlement on discontinuance]

The Company confirms that no costs entitlement arising as a result of the discontinuance of any legal action in accordance with Sub-paragraph 5.1 will be enforced and the Company waives any such rights.

5.3 [Costs of existing proceedings]

Legal costs of a Creditor in proceedings other than winding-up referred to in Sub-paragraph 5.1 shall be a Debt falling within the Arrangement.

5.4 [Costs of winding-up proceedings]

Petition costs of a Creditor who presented a winding-up petition against the Company prior to the commencement of the Arrangement shall be treated as an expense of the Arrangement to rank after the costs of the Nominee but before those of the Supervisor.

6. Existing Execution Against Company's Assets

6.1 [Partly-completed execution]

A Creditor who, before the commencement of the Arrangement, has issued execution against the property of the Company in respect of a Debt which is subject to the Arrangement, or has attached a Debt due to the Company from another person in respect of such a Debt shall, unless the execution or attachment was completed before the commencement of the Arrangement, discontinue the execution or attachment as soon after the commencement of the Arrangement as is practicable.

6.2 [Completion of execution or attachment]

For the purposes of Sub-paragraph 6.1:

(a) an execution against chattels is completed by seizure and sale or by the making of a charging order absolute under section 1 of the Charging Orders Act 1979;
(b) an execution against land is completed by seizure, by the appointment of a receiver or by the making of a charging order absolute under section 1 of the Charging Orders Act 1979;
(c) an attachment of a Debt is completed by the receipt of the Debt.

7. Mutual Credit and Set-off

7.1 [Application]

This Paragraph applies where before the commencement of the Arrangement there have been mutual credits, mutual debts or other mutual dealings between the Company and any Creditor.

7.2 [Account to be taken]

An account shall be taken of what is due from each party to the other in respect of the mutual dealings and the sums due from one party shall be set-off against the sums due from the other.

7.3 [No account where Creditor has notice]

Sums due from the Company to another party shall not be included in the account taken under Sub-paragraph 7.2 if that other party had notice at the time they became due that a winding-up petition relating to the Company was pending, an application for an administration order was pending, a notice of intention to appoint an administrator was pending or that a moratorium under Part A1 of the Act was in force.

7.4 [Restriction on post-commencement set-off]

Other than as provided for in this Paragraph, set-off shall not be available in respect of any Debt or item of Property.

7.5 [Balance provable or to be paid]

Only the balance (if any) of the account taken under Sub-paragraph 7.2) is provable in the Arrangement or, as the case may be, to be paid to the Company or, if the Proposal so provides, to the Supervisor.

8. Duration and Expiry of Arrangement

8.1 [General rule]

Unless extended under the provisions of these Conditions, the Arrangement shall continue until the end of the period stated in the Proposal at which time it shall expire by effluxion of time.

8.2 [Extension of duration by Supervisor or Creditors' Committee]

The Supervisor, Creditors' Committee and Creditors may extend the duration of the Arrangement in accordance with the terms of the Proposal and the Supervisor shall send a notice of any extension ('Extension Notice') to the Company and all Creditors and Shareholders.

8.3 [Extension Notice]

An Extension Notice shall be sent not less than 7 days prior to the date upon which the Arrangement is otherwise due to be fully implemented and must state the reason or reasons for the extension.

8.4 [Effect of extension]

In the event of an Extension Notice being sent, the Arrangement shall continue for the period specified therein, or for the maximum allowable period for that extension commencing on the date immediately after that on which the Arrangement would otherwise have been fully implemented, whichever is sooner.

8.5 [Supervening notice of a decision procedure]

If a Decision Procedure has been initiated by the Supervisor with a Decision Date after the Arrangement would otherwise have expired, the duration of the Arrangement shall be extended to the Decision Date.

8.6 [Further extension]

Any extension for a period longer than that provided for in the Proposal shall require approval as a variation of the Arrangement.

9. Full Implementation of Arrangement

9.1 [Certificate of full implementation]

Upon the full implementation of the Arrangement, the Supervisor shall, if the Company has complied with its obligations under the Arrangement, issue a notice ('Certificate of Full Implementation') stating that the Arrangement has been fully implemented.

9.2 [Effect of full implementation]

Save to the extent provided in these Condition or the Proposal, upon the issue by the Supervisor of a Certificate of Full Implementation, the Company shall be released from all Debts which are subject to the Arrangement.

9.3 [Notification of full implementation]

Copies of the Certificate of Full Implementation issued under this Paragraph shall be sent by the Supervisor to the Company, the Creditors and the Shareholders together with the Supervisor's report under Rule 2.44 (termination or full implementation of the CVA).

10. Substantial Compliance

10.1 [Issue of notice where substantial compliance]

The Supervisor may issue a Certificate of Full Implementation notwithstanding that the Company has not complied with all of its obligations under the Arrangement provided the Company has:

(a) made all the payments required under the terms of the Arrangement;
(b) provided a full explanation of any breach of the terms of the Arrangement required by the Supervisor;
(c) paid to the Supervisor such sum (if any) as the Supervisor shall reasonably have required to compensate the Creditors for any reduction in Dividend caused by the Company's breach of the terms of the Arrangement.

10.2 [Notification to creditors]

Where the Supervisor proposes to issue a Certificate of Full Implementation under Sub-paragraph 10.1, the Supervisor shall notify the Creditors and invite them to submit any comments within 21 days from the date of notification.

10.3 [Treatment as full implementation]

If the Supervisor issues a Certificate of Full Implementation under Sub-paragraph 10.1, the Arrangement shall be treated as fully implemented for the purposes of Rule 2.44 (termination or full implementation of the CVA).

11. Termination of Arrangement

11.1 [Termination in certain circumstances]

The Arrangement shall terminate upon the earlier of:

(a) the Supervisor issuing a Notice of Termination under Paragraph 67;
(b) the making of a winding-up order against the Company;
(c) the passing of a resolution for the voluntary winding-up of the Company;
(d) the dissolution of the Company; or
(e) the Company entering administration.

11.2 [Notice of termination]

The Supervisor shall, on discovering the occurrence of a terminating event, but in any event not more than 28 days after such discovery, give notice of such termination and its reason to the Company, the Directors of the Company, Shareholders, Creditors and the Secretary of State, together with the Supervisor's report under Rule 2.44 (termination or full implementation of the CVA).

PART 3: SUPERVISOR'S FUNCTIONS, POWERS ETC

12. Supervisor's Functions

12.1 [Primary function]

The Supervisor's primary function is to supervise performance of the Company's obligations under the Arrangement and to administer the Arrangement.

12.2 [Other functions]

The Supervisor shall also undertake such functions as are provided for in the Proposal, Act and Rules. In addition, the Supervisor shall place money coming into the Supervisor's hands during the course of the Arrangement on deposit with any established United Kingdom clearing bank or building society.

13. Supervisor's Powers

Subject to those powers more particularly given in the Arrangement, Act and Rules, the Supervisor shall have the following powers:

(a) [Getting in assets]

(b) power to take possession of, collect, get in and hold any or all of the assets which, under the terms of the Arrangement, the Supervisor is to hold as trustee, including any instalment payments;
(c) [Realisation of assets]
(d) power to sell or otherwise dispose of any asset referred to in Sub-paragraph 13.1(a) in such manner as may seem to the Supervisor expedient;
(e) [Putting funds on deposit]
(f) power to place money coming into the Supervisor's hands during the course of the Arrangement on deposit with any established United Kingdom clearing bank or building society;
(g) [Payment]
(h) power to pay the costs and expenses of the Arrangement;
(i) [Agreement of Creditor claims]
(j) power to determine Creditors' claims and enter into any compromise or arrangement with any creditor alleging that they have a claim;
(k) [Distribution]
(l) power to make payments to Creditors pursuant to the terms of the Arrangement;
(m) [Appointing agents]
(n) power to engage legal representatives, managers, agents and other persons to assist in the performance of the Supervisor's functions under the Arrangement;
(o) [Delegation]
(p) power to delegate to the Supervisor's firm and any appropriate partner, director, employee or agent thereof any or all of the Supervisor's duties and functions under the Arrangement save those which by law the Supervisor is required to perform personally;
(q) [Insurance]
(r) power to effect and maintain insurances in respect of any asset subject to the Arrangement;
(s) [Power to claim]
(t) power to prove, rank, claim and draw a dividend in respect of such debts owed to the Company as fall within the Arrangement;
(u) [Power to direct Company]
(v) power, in the event that the Supervisor is unable or it is impracticable to do any act or thing which the Supervisor is empowered to do, to direct the Company to do that act or thing;
(w) [Winding up]
(x) power to commence winding-up proceedings in respect of the Company pursuant to the terms of the Arrangement;
(y) [Ancillary power]
(z) power to make any necessary or incidental payments and to do any other act or thing which is necessary or expedient for the purposes of exercising the above powers or for carrying out the Supervisor's functions under the Arrangement.

Where more than one person is appointed as Supervisor, any act required or authorised to be done under any enactment or otherwise may be done by all or any one or more of the persons for the time being holding office.

14. Supervisor's Powers After Expiry, Full Implementation or Termination

14.1 [Exercise of powers]

The expiry, full implementation or termination of the Arrangement shall not affect the Supervisor's power to carry out such functions and to exercise such powers as are necessary for the Supervisor to fully carry out the duties, obligations and responsibilities of the Supervisor under the Arrangement, Act and Rules and to resolve such matters as may have arisen during the course of the Arrangement. This includes, but is not limited to, any duties, obligations and responsibilities in respect of assets held by the Supervisor on trust.

14.2 [Retention of funds by Supervisor]

Upon the expiry, full implementation or termination of the Arrangement, the Supervisor shall be entitled to retain, for such period as is reasonably necessary and from any funds under the Supervisor's control, such monies as the Supervisor reasonably thinks fit on account of fees, costs, charges, liabilities and expenses, and the Supervisor shall advise Creditors and the Company in writing of the quantum of the funds so retained and the reasons why.

15. Exercise of Supervisor's Functions and Powers

15.1 [Application of winding-up provisions]

In the event that the Arrangement does not provide guidance to the Supervisor as to what action should be taken in any given situation, the Supervisor shall apply the provisions of the Act and Rules in so far as they relate to winding-up with necessary modifications to refer to a voluntary arrangement.

15.2 [Consultation of Creditors]

If the Supervisor is uncertain as to what action should be taken in any situation, or wishes to ascertain the wishes of Creditors on a matter concerning the Arrangement, the Supervisor may seek the advice and/or direction of the Creditors' Committee and/or the majority or most material of the Creditors and may act upon such advice and/or direction.

15.3 [Directions from the Court]

This Paragraph is without prejudice to the Supervisor's right to refer matters concerning the Arrangement to the Court for guidance and/or directions.

16. Restriction upon Supervisor's Duty and Liability

16.1 [Supervisor's duty]

The Supervisor shall be under no obligation to perform any act or carry out any function nor take part in the management of the Company in any way and will have no duties or responsibilities except as expressly set out in the Arrangement or imposed under the Act or Rules.

16.2 [Supervisor's liability]

Neither the Supervisor, the Supervisor's firm or any of that firm's or the Supervisor's agents or employees shall incur any personal liability in negligence or otherwise for any act or omission in connection with the Arrangement, unless such act or omission constitutes one of dishonesty or a breach of the Supervisor's obligations under the Act, Rules or the Arrangement.

17. Supervisor's Resignation

17.1 [Methods of resignation]

A Supervisor may resign from office with the approval of Creditors sought via a Decision Procedure, with the permission of the Court or in the circumstances set out in Paragraph 17.3 below.

17.2 [Grounds of Supervisor's resignation]

The sole Supervisor may only resign from office on one or more of the following grounds:

(a) ill health;
(b) cessation of practice as an insolvency practitioner;
(c) change of circumstances rendering it impracticable to continue in office;

17.3 [More than one supervisor]

Where there is more than one supervisor in office, a Supervisor may resign without seeking the approval of the Creditors or permission of the court where it is considered to be impracticable or no longer necessary to have the present number of persons acting as Supervisor to the Arrangement and at least one supervisor shall remain in office notwithstanding the resignation. In these circumstances notice of the resignation of a Supervisor shall be given in the next report to Creditors when otherwise due.

17.4 [Report of Supervisor's administration]

The notice to Creditors in a Decision Procedure for the purpose of receiving the resignation of a Supervisor shall specify the grounds upon which the Supervisor wishes to resign and shall be accompanied by a report of the

Supervisor's administration of the Arrangement which includes an up to date summary of receipts and payments.

18. Removal of Supervisor From Office

18.1 [Methods of removal]

The Supervisor may be removed from office only by an order of the Court, or by a decision of the Creditors requested specifically for that purpose.

18.2 [Notice of requisitioned decision procedure]

Any notice served by a Creditor upon the Supervisor under Paragraph 57.5 (content of notice requisitioning a decision) for the purpose of initiating a decision of Creditors to remove the Supervisor from office must set out the grounds upon which removal is sought.

18.3 [Report of Supervisor's administration]

The notice sent out by the Supervisor to Creditors convening such a Decision Procedure shall specify the grounds upon which removal is sought and shall be accompanied by a report of the Supervisor's administration of the Arrangement including an up to date summary of receipts and payments.

19. Vacation of Office by Supervisor

19.1 [Resignation/removal of Supervisor where more than one acting]

If the Creditors resolve to remove a Supervisor from office, or a joint Supervisor resigns, and there will be another person in the office of Supervisor for the time being, the Supervisor who is resigning or being removed shall vacate office immediately.

19.2 [Resignation/removal of Supervisor where no other acting]

If the Creditors resolve to accept a Supervisor's resignation or to remove a Supervisor from office, and there is no other person in the office of Supervisor for the time being, that resignation and/or removal shall not take effect and the Supervisor shall not vacate office unless and until the Creditors by a Decision Procedure, or the Court, appoints a replacement Supervisor.

19.3 [Loss of qualification]

The Supervisor shall vacate office immediately if the Supervisor ceases to be a person who is for the time being qualified to act.

19.4 [Notice of vacation of office]

A Supervisor who, for any reason other than as set out in Paragraph 17.3, vacates office shall forthwith give notice of that fact to the Company, the Shareholders and the Creditors.

19.5 [Duties of Supervisor upon vacation of office]

A Supervisor who, for any reason, vacates office shall, as soon as practicable, deliver up to any successor all books, records and papers relating to the Arrangement and the Supervisor's administration thereof together with all assets of which the Supervisor is a trustee under the terms of the Arrangement.

19.6 [Continuing duty of former Supervisor]

Former Supervisors shall be obliged to give such assistance to the Supervisor of the Arrangement from time to time as may be reasonably required for ascertaining what transpired during the tenure of office by the former Supervisor.

20. Vacancy in the Office of Supervisor

20.1 [Decision of Creditors to fill vacancy]

If, for any reason, there is a vacancy in the office of Supervisor, that vacancy may be filled by the Creditors by way of a Decision Procedure, or by the Court.

20.2 [Seeking appointment where no Supervisor acting]

If no Supervisor is in office, the Company, any Director, any Creditor, any person who was in partnership with the Supervisor immediately before the vacancy occurred, the former Supervisor's authorising body, or any other interested party may convene a Decision Procedure to fill the vacancy.

20.3 [Chair where no Supervisor acting]

In the event that a meeting of Creditors is called when no Supervisor is in office, the convenor shall act as chair of the meeting.

21. Release of Supervisor

Upon the termination or full implementation of the Arrangement and the Supervisor having dealt with the assets in the Supervisor's possession in accordance with the terms of the Arrangement, the Supervisor shall be released by each Creditor from any further obligations or liability in respect of the Arrangement or any trusts created thereby and in respect of acts and omissions of theirs or otherwise in relation to his conduct as Supervisor. Each Creditor shall and hereby does waive all claims or rights which the Creditor may have against the Supervisor in respect of such matters.

22. Supervisor's Fees, Costs and Expenses

22.1 [Amount of fees]

The Supervisor shall be entitled to charge fees for services in accordance with the time actually and reasonably expended by the Supervisor and the Supervisor's staff in carrying out the Supervisor's functions under the Arrangement by reference to the ordinary hourly rates of the Supervisor and the Supervisor's staff as shall apply from time to time.

22.2 [Payment of fees, costs and expenses]

The fees, costs, charges and expenses of the Supervisor shall be paid out of the assets of the Arrangement from time to time as the Supervisor thinks fit. The Supervisor shall provide such information to any Creditors' Committee appointed in relation to the Arrangement as is reasonably necessary to explain how the fees, costs, charges and expenses were determined or incurred, as the case may be.

22.3 [Supervisor's right of recourse to Court]

If the Supervisor is dissatisfied with a determination of the Creditors' Committee or a decision of Creditors on a matter involving fees, costs, charges and/or expenses, the Supervisor shall have the right to refer the matter to the Court, whose decision on the matter shall bind all parties.

PART 4: COMPANY'S WARRANTY, DUTIES AND OBLIGATIONS

23. Company's Warranty

23.1 [Disclosure in Proposal]

The Directors of the Company warrant that the Proposal discloses full and complete particulars of all matters required under the Act and Rules including (without prejudice to the generality of the foregoing) particulars of all of the Company's assets, debts and liabilities, whether actual, contingent or prospective.

23.2 [Accuracy of Proposal]

The Directors of the Company warrant that the contents of the Proposal are true and accurate in all material respects as at the date of the commencement of the Arrangement, subject only to those qualifications that may be disclosed by the Directors of the Company to the Creditors considering the approval of the Arrangement and recorded by the Supervisor in reporting under Rule 2.38 (report of the consideration of a proposal).

23.3 [Disclosure of third-party information]

The Company authorises any Creditor to disclose to the Supervisor such information relating to the Company and the Company's dealings or property as may reasonably be required to assist in the implementation of the Arrangement.

24. Company's Duties in relation to the Supervisor

24.1 [Duty to co-operate with Supervisor]

The Directors of the Company undertake and agree to:

(a) give to the Supervisor such information as to the Company's assets, liabilities and other affairs;
(b) attend on the Supervisor and the Supervisor's agents, representatives or nominees at such times; and
(c) do all such other things;

as the Supervisor shall reasonably require for the purpose of carrying out the Supervisor's functions and duties under the Arrangement, including as trustee and/or following the expiry, full implementation or termination of the Arrangement.

24.2 [Duty to submit accounts]

The Directors of the Company undertake and agree to furnish the Supervisor with accounts relating to the Company's affairs of such nature, as at such date and for such period as the Supervisor may reasonably require.

25. Further Documents

Without prejudice to the generality of the Company's other duties under the Arrangement, the Company or its Directors shall, at the request of the Supervisor, execute such Mortgages, Charges, Deeds, Transfers, Trusts, Powers of Attorney or other documents as may reasonably be required by the Supervisor for the protection and/or realisation of assets, to secure the Company's compliance with the Company's obligations under the Arrangement, or otherwise to facilitate the implementation of the Arrangement.

26. Company's Acknowledgement

26.1 [Agreement to be bound]

The Directors of the Company undertake to procure that the Company shall carry out the obligations imposed upon the Company under the Arrangement in full and at the times provided for.

26.2 [Consequences of breach]

The Directors of the Company acknowledge that a likely consequence of the Company's failure to comply with the Company's obligations hereunder in full and at the times provided for is that the Arrangement will fail and the Company will be wound up on a petition presented by the Supervisor.

26.3 [Section 6A]

Each of the Directors of the Company acknowledge that they commit an offence if any false representation is made or any other fraud is committed for the purpose of obtaining the approval of Shareholders or Creditors to the Arrangement.

PART 5: ARRANGEMENT ASSETS

27. Trust of Arrangement Assets

27.1 [Company Assets and Excluded Assets]

Property other than Excluded Assets belonging to or vested in the Company at the date of commencement of the Arrangement shall be subject to the Arrangement and be an asset thereof. Property constituting an asset of the Arrangement in the possession, custody or control of the Company shall be held by the Company upon trust for the purposes of the Arrangement during the Trust Realisation Period in accordance with this Arrangement.

27.2 [Assets in the possession of the Supervisor]

Property constituting an asset of the Arrangement in the possession, custody or control of the Supervisor shall be held by the Supervisor upon trust for the purposes of the Arrangement.

27.3 [Actions during the Trust Realisation Period]

The Supervisor will get in and realise assets which are subject to the trust and which are capable of being realised during the Trust Realisation Period.

27.4 [Effect of expiry or termination]

The trusts referred to in Sub-paragraph 27.1 and 27.2 shall not come to an end upon expiry or termination of the Arrangement but such assets as are contained within the trust shall be distributed to Creditors in accordance with the terms of the Proposal. At the expiry of the Trust Realisation Period, the trust shall come to an end.

27.5 [Effect of full implementation]

Upon the issuing of a Certificate of Full Implementation under Paragraph 9, the trusts referred to in Sub-paragraphs 27.2 shall not come to an end but such assets as are contained within the trust shall be paid to the Company. At expiry of the Trust Realisation Period, the trust shall come to an end.

27.6 [Effect of winding-up]

In the event that a Winding-up Order is made against the Company, any assets held by the Supervisor prior to the making of that Order shall be applied and distributed in accordance with the terms of the Arrangement and the trust shall terminate solely in respect of assets of the Company not yet held by the Supervisor.

PART 6: PROOFS OF DEBT

28. Notice to Submit Proofs

As soon as practicable after the commencement of the Arrangement, and provided no application under Section 6 of the Act (challenge of decisions) or an appeal under Rule 15.35 (appeals against decisions) is pending, the Supervisor shall send a notice ('Notice to Submit Proofs') to every Creditor and other person to whom the Company may be indebted of whom the Supervisor has notice requiring them to provide such details of their Debts as the Supervisor thinks fit.

29. Submission of Proofs

Creditors shall submit their Proofs in writing to the Supervisor in the form, if any, required by the Supervisor, or one which is substantially similar.

30. Withdrawal and Variation of Proofs

30.1 [Withdrawal by written notice]

A Creditor may withdraw a Proof at any time by delivering a written notice to the Supervisor.

30.2 [Variation of amount by agreement]

The amount claimed by a Creditor's Proof may be varied at any time by agreement between the Creditor and the Supervisor.

31. Production of Documents

The Supervisor may call for any document or other evidence to be produced for the purpose of substantiating the whole or any part of the Proof.

32. Witness Statement Substantiating Proof

The Supervisor may require a Proof to be verified by witness statement with a statement of truth.

33. Supervisor to Allow Inspection of Proofs

The Supervisor shall, so long as Proofs are in the Supervisor's possession, allow them to be inspected, at all reasonable times on any business day, by:

(a) any Creditor who has delivered a Proof (unless the Proof has been wholly rejected for the purposes of Dividend, or otherwise); and
(b) a person acting on behalf of any such Creditor.

34. Admission and Rejection of Proofs for Dividend

34.1 [Admission]

The Supervisor may admit or reject a Proof for Dividend in whole or in part.

34.2 [Rejection]

If the Supervisor rejects a Proof in whole or in part, the Supervisor must deliver to the Creditor a written statement of reasons for so doing, as soon as reasonably practicable.

35. Appeal Against Decision on Proof

35.1 [Application by Creditor]

If a Creditor is dissatisfied with the Supervisor's decision with respect to the Creditor's own Proof (including a decision whether the Debt is preferential), the Creditor may apply to the Court, within 21 days (or such longer period as the Court shall allow) of receiving the statement sent under Paragraphs 34.2 or 36.2, for the decision to be reversed or varied.

35.2 [Application by other parties]

The Company or any other Creditor may, if dissatisfied with the Supervisor's decision admitting or rejecting the whole or any part of a Proof or agreeing to revalue a Creditor's security, make such an application within 21 days (or such longer period as the Court shall allow) of becoming aware of the Supervisor's decision.

35.3 [Costs of appeal]

The Supervisor is not personally liable for the costs incurred by any person in respect of an appeal under this Paragraph unless the Court so orders.

36. Debts of Uncertain and Small Value

36.1 [Estimation of Debt or liability]

The Supervisor shall estimate the value of any Debt which, by reason of its being subject to a contingency or for any other reason, does not bear a certain value.

36.2 [Notification to Creditor]

The Supervisor shall notify the Creditor in writing of any such estimate. If the Creditor is dissatisfied with the Supervisor's decision the Creditor may exercise the right of appeal under Paragraph 35.

36.3 [Claim of Debts of uncertain value]

Where the value of any Debt is estimated by the Supervisor under Sub-paragraph 36.1, the amount provable in the Arrangement shall be the amount of the estimate.

36.4 [Small Debts]

Any Creditor whose Debt does not exceed £1,000 need not (unless so required by the Supervisor) submit a Proof to the Supervisor and the Supervisor may admit such Debt and pay a Dividend accordingly. Where the Supervisor intends to admit a Debt in that manner, the Supervisor shall send a notice to the Creditor (which may form part of any other notice) stating the amount the Supervisor believes is owed, that the Supervisor intends to treat it as proved for the purposes of the Arrangement, and require the Creditor to notify the Supervisor by the last date for proving if the amount of the Debt is incorrect or if no debt is owed.

37. Secured Creditors

37.1 [Proving for balance of Debt]

A Secured Creditor may submit a Proof for the balance of Debt (if any) after deducting the value of that Creditor's Security.

37.2 [Voluntary surrender of Security]

If a Secured Creditor voluntarily surrenders its Security for the general benefit of the Creditors, that Creditor may submit a Proof for the whole Debt as if it were unsecured.

37.3 [Altering value of Security]

A Secured Creditor may, with the agreement of the Supervisor or the permission of the Court, at any time alter the value put upon that Creditor's Security in a Proof.

37.4 [Test of Security's value]

If the Supervisor is dissatisfied with the value which a Secured Creditor puts on a Security in the Creditor's Proof, the Supervisor may require the Secured Creditor to obtain a professional valuation of any property comprised in the Security by a person agreed as between the Creditor and the Supervisor, or in default of such agreement by the Court. The costs of the valuer shall form part of the Secured Creditor's cost of proving.

37.5 [Professional valuation treated as amended valuation]

Where a professional valuation has been carried out under the previous Sub-paragraph, that valuation shall be treated as an amended valuation of the Creditor.

37.6 [Realisation of Security]

If a Creditor who has valued Security subsequently realises it:

(a) the Creditor shall forthwith notify the Supervisor and shall give the Supervisor such information relating thereto as the Supervisor may reasonably require;
(b) the net amount realised shall be substituted for the value previously put by the Creditor on the Security, and
(c) that amount shall be treated in all respects as the Creditor's amended valuation.

38. Foreign Currency Debts

38.1 [Conversion into sterling]

For the purpose of proving for a Debt incurred or payable in a currency other than sterling, the amount of the Debt shall be converted into sterling at a single rate for each currency determined by the Supervisor by reference to the exchange rate prevailing at the date of commencement of the Arrangement.

39. Interest on Debts

Where a Debt bears interest, that interest is provable as part of the Debt except in so far as it is payable in respect of any period after the commencement of the Arrangement.

40. Cost of Submitting Proofs

40.1 [Creditor bears cost of submitting Proof]

Every Creditor bears the cost of submitting that Creditor's own Proof, including costs incurred in providing any document or evidence to the Supervisor.

40.2 [Supervisor's costs]

Costs incurred by the Supervisor in estimating the value of a Debt of uncertain value shall be an expense of the Arrangement.

PART 7: CREDITORS WHO DO NOT HAVE NOTICE

41. Proof Arising Where Funds Available

If, at the time the Proof is notified to the Supervisor, the Arrangement is continuing and the Supervisor is holding sufficient funds to pay a Dividend to such Creditor or Creditors, then the Supervisor will (subject to agreement of the Proof) forthwith pay to the Creditor a Dividend of an amount which is on the same basis as the Dividends already paid. Such payments will be made before any further payments to any other Creditors and will be paid so as to bring about an equalisation in Dividends between Creditors who fall within section 5(2)(b)(i) of the Act on the one hand and section 5(2)(b)(ii) of the Act on the other hand.

42. Proof Arising Where no funds Available

If a Proof is notified to the Supervisor at a time when the Supervisor is holding no funds available for payment of a Dividend, then as and when any funds are received, the Supervisor will (subject to agreement of the Proof) out of such funds first make such payment to such Creditors so as to bring about an equalisation as aforesaid.

43. Effect of Proof on Company

43.1 [Proof not to constitute default]

The notification to the Supervisor of any such Proof shall not constitute an act of default unless the failure to give notice to such Creditor was a deliberate act on the part of the Directors.

43.2 [Obligation to provide further funds]

Unless the Proposal otherwise provides, there shall be no obligation upon the Company to pay to the Supervisor any further sums of money or make any further assets available (other than already provided for in the Proposal) so as to meet the Proof falling to be dealt with under section 5(2)(b)(ii) of the Act unless the Proposal as agreed provides for a minimum Dividend to be paid to Creditors.

44. Notification of Proof to Creditors

On receipt of any such Proof, the Supervisor will notify all Creditors bound of such receipt, the name of the Creditor, the amount of the Proof and will provide such other information as may be relevant, including particulars as to the Directors' explanation why the Creditor was not given notice and the impact which such Proof is likely to have on the outcome of the Arrangement. Such notification may, if the Supervisor considers it appropriate, be included in the progress report to Creditors, provided that such report is due to be circulated within a period of three months from the date on which the Proof is notified. Where, in the opinion of the Supervisor, the Proof, whether taken alone or in conjunction with other such Proofs, will not materially reduce the amount of the estimated Dividend, the Supervisor may defer notification and include it in the next progress report.

45. Proof Arising After Arrangement Ceases to have Effect

If the Proof is notified to the Supervisor after the date on which the Arrangement ceases to have effect, then the Creditor shall be entitled to rely upon section 5(2A) of the Act and shall be entitled to recover from the Company such sum as the Creditor would have received had the Proof been notified to the Supervisor prior to the date on which the Arrangement ceased to have effect and the Supervisor had been able to include the Proof in the Arrangement for the purpose of payment of Dividends or distributions. The Supervisor shall be under no obligation to agree any such Proof, or take any action in respect thereof, other than to furnish the Creditor who relies on section 5(2A) with a certificate as to the Dividend or distribution the Creditor would have received had the Proof been included in the Arrangement for Dividend or distribution purposes and on the assumption that the Proof would have been agreed in the sum claimed.

PART 8: PAYMENT OF DIVIDENDS

46. Distribution by Dividend

46.1 [Duty to declare and distribute Dividends]

At the time or times specified in the Proposal or, if none, whenever the Supervisor has sufficient funds in hand for the purpose, the Supervisor shall, subject to the retention of such sums as may be necessary for payment of the expenses of the Arrangement, declare and distribute Dividends among the Creditors in respect of the Debts which they have proved.

46.2 [Calculation and distribution of Dividend]

In the calculation and distribution of a Dividend the Supervisor shall make provision:

(a) for any Debts which are the subject of Proofs which have not yet been determined; and
(b) for any disputed Debts.

47. Notice of Intended Dividend

47.1 [Notice to Creditors who have not proved]

No more than three months before declaring a Dividend to non-preferential Creditors, the Supervisor shall give notice of the intention to do so to all such Creditors whose addresses are known to the Supervisor and who have not proved.

47.2 [Last date for submitting proofs]

Any notice sent out to Creditors under Sub-paragraph 47.1 shall specify a date ('Last Date for Submitting Proofs') up to which a Proof may be delivered. The Last Date for Submitting Proofs shall be the same for all Creditors and not less than 21 days from the date of the notice.

48. Notice of declaration

48.1 [Notice to Creditors who have proved]

The Supervisor shall give notice of the Dividend to all Creditors who have proved for their Debts.

48.2 [Particulars in notice]

The notice shall include the following particulars:

(a) amounts realised from the sale of assets subject to the Arrangement, indicating (so far as practicable) amounts realised by the sale of particular assets, and/or amounts paid by the Company to the Supervisor under the Arrangement;

(b) payments made by the Supervisor during the course of the Arrangement;
(c) provision (if any) made for unsettled claims and funds (if any) retained for particular purposes;
(d) the total amount to be distributed and the rate of Dividend;
(e) whether, and if so when, any further Dividend is expected to be declared.

48.3 [Simultaneous distribution]

The Dividend may be distributed simultaneously with the notice declaring it.

48.4 [Method of payment]

Payment of Dividend may be made by post, or arrangements may be made with any Creditor for it to be paid in another way or held for collection. Neither the Supervisor nor the Company shall be responsible for any loss in transmission. The encashment of any cheque shall be a good discharge to the Company for the monies represented thereby.

48.5 [Endorsement in negotiable instrument]

Where a Dividend is paid on a bill of exchange or other negotiable instrument, the amount of the Dividend shall be endorsed on the instrument, or on a certified copy of it, if required to be produced by the holder for that purpose.

49. Proof altered after payment of Dividend

49.1 [Amount claimed increased]

If, after payment of the Dividend, the amount proved for by a Creditor is increased, the Creditor is not entitled to disturb the distribution of the Dividend; but is entitled to be paid, out of any money for the time being available for the payment of any further Dividend, any Dividend or Dividends which the Creditor has failed to receive before that money is applied to the payment of any such further Dividend.

49.2 [Proof withdrawn, disallowed, reduced]

If, after a Creditor's Proof has been admitted, the Proof is withdrawn or disallowed, or the amount of it is reduced, the Creditor shall repay to the Supervisor any amount overpaid by way of Dividend.

50. Secured Creditors

50.1 [Application of Paragraph]

The following applies where a Creditor re-values Security at a time when a Dividend has been declared.

50.2 [Reduction in unsecured claim]

If the re-valuation results in a reduction of the Creditor's unsecured claim ranking for Dividend, the Creditor shall, as soon as practicable, repay to the Supervisor any amount received as Dividend in excess of that to which the Creditor would be entitled having regard to the re-valuation of the Security.

50.3 [Increase of unsecured claim]

If the re-valuation results in an increase of the Creditor's unsecured claim, the Creditor is entitled to receive from the Supervisor, out of any money for the time being available for the payment of a further Dividend, before any such Dividend is paid, any Dividend or Dividends which the Creditor has failed to receive, having regard to the re-valuation of the Security. However, the Creditor is not entitled to disturb any Dividend declared (whether or not distributed) before the date of the revaluation.

51. Assignment of Debts or rights to Dividend

51.1 [Notice of assignment]

If a Creditor entitled to a Dividend gives notice to the Supervisor that the Creditor wishes the Dividend to be paid to another person, or that the Creditor has assigned its entitlement or Debt to another person, the Supervisor shall pay the Dividend to that other person accordingly.

51.2 [Contents of notice]

A notice given under this Paragraph must specify the name and address of the person to whom payment is to be made.

52. Debts payable at future time

52.1 [Debts payable at a future time]

A Creditor may prove for a Debt of which payment was not yet due at the date of commencement of the Arrangement.

52.2 [Entitlement to Dividend]

Where a Creditor has claimed for a Debt of which payment is not due at the date of the declaration of Dividend, the Creditor is entitled to the Dividend equally with other Creditors, but subject as follows.

52.3 [Calculation of amount of reduction]

For the purpose of Dividend (and no other purpose), the amount of the Creditor's admitted Proof (or, if a distribution has previously been made to the Creditor, the amount remaining outstanding in respect of the Creditor's admitted claim) must be discounted by applying the following formula:

$$\frac{X}{1.05^{n}}$$

where X is the value of the admitted Proof; and 'n' is the period beginning with the date of the commencement of the Arrangement and ending with the date on which the payment of the Creditor's Debt would otherwise be due, expressed in years.

53. Debts of unpaid Creditors

53.1 [Creditors not entitled to Dividend]

Creditors who do not prove in the Arrangement (with the exception of any Debts admitted by the Supervisor under Paragraph 36.4) shall not be entitled to receive any Dividend.

53.2 [Unclaimed Dividends paid to the Company]

Dividends due to Creditors who have proved in the Arrangement but to whom the Supervisor has been unable to pay shall, at the end of the Arrangement, be paid to the Company or, if there is one, the Company's liquidator or administrator.

53.3 [Company liable for unclaimed Dividends]

Once a Dividend has been paid to the Company or the Company's liquidator or administrator under the previous Sub-paragraph, the Creditor must claim it from the Company or, as the case may be, the Company's liquidator or administrator and no other person.

PART 9: PRIORITY OF PAYMENTS AND DISTRIBUTIONS

54. Costs and Expenses of the Arrangement

54.1 [Expenses to be paid first]

Subject to Paragraphs 5.4 and 68 the fees, costs, charges, expenses and liabilities properly charged or incurred by or on behalf of the Nominee or the Supervisor are expenses of the Arrangement and shall be paid in priority to all other charges, expenses, liabilities and Debts.

54.2 [Charge in relation to expenses]

The Supervisor shall have a charge on the assets subject to the Arrangement in respect of the expenses of the Arrangement.

PART 10: THE CREDITORS' COMMITTEE, WEBSITES & CREDITOR DECISIONS

55. The Creditors' Committee

In the event that the Nominee has invited creditors to form a committee or the Creditors have so decided, the following provisions will apply:

55.1 [Establishment]

Creditors may establish a committee ('Creditors' Committee'), consisting of not less than 3 and not more than 5 members to represent the interests of the Creditors and to provide such assistance and guidance to the Supervisor as may reasonably be required. The Nominee may invite Creditors to form a committee at the same time the Creditors' approval for the Proposal is sought.

55.2 [Eligibility]

All the members of the Creditors' Committee must be Creditors of the Company; and any Creditor (other than one who is fully secured) may be a member, so long as:

(a) the Creditor has delivered a Proof, and
(b) the Creditor's Proof has neither been wholly disallowed for voting purposes, nor wholly rejected for the purposes of distribution or Dividend.

55.3 [Application of the Rules]

The provisions relating to the Creditors' Committee in Rules 17.1 to 17.29 shall apply to the Arrangement with any necessary modifications.

55.4 [Expenses of members]

The reasonable travelling expenses directly incurred by any member of the Creditors' Committee or their representatives in respect of their attendance at the meetings of the Creditors' Committee, or otherwise on the Creditors' Committee's business, shall rank as an expense of the Arrangement.

56. Use of websites

56.1 [Use of websites]

Where the Supervisor is required to give, deliver, furnish or send a notice or other document or information to any person, that requirement may be satisfied by making the notice, document or information available on a website.

56.2 [Application of the Rules]

The provisions of Rules 1.49–1.51 relating to use of websites shall apply to the Arrangement with any necessary modifications.

57. Power to seek a decision of Creditors

57.1 [Supervisor's power to seek a decision]

The Supervisor may seek a decision of Creditors for any purpose connected with the Arrangement.

57.2 [Choice of Decision Procedure]

A decision of Creditors may be made by any Decision Procedure provided for in Rule 15.3 (the prescribed decision procedures) except that it may not be made by physical meeting unless Sub-paragraph 57.3 applies.

57.3 [Power to require physical meeting]

If 10% in value, or 10% in number or 10 of the Creditors request in writing that a decision of Creditors sought by the Supervisor be taken at a physical meeting, the Supervisor shall, unless relieved by the Court from so doing, convene such a meeting within 21 days from the receipt of such request.

57.4 [Power to requisition a decision]

If 25% in value of the Creditors request in writing that a decision of Creditors be sought, the Supervisor shall, unless relieved by the Court from so doing, initiate a Decision Procedure within 21 days from the receipt of such request. This is subject to any deposit for costs required under Paragraph 59 having been paid.

57.5 [Content of notice requisitioning a decision]

A notice served upon the Supervisor under Sub-paragraph 57.4 shall state the decision of Creditors for which the Decision Procedure is requested.

57.6 [Company request]

If the Company requests in writing that the Supervisor seek a decision of Creditors the Supervisor shall not unreasonably refuse such a request. If the Supervisor considers the request to be reasonable the Supervisor shall convene such Decision Procedure as the Supervisor considers appropriate to consider the decision.

58. Procedure for seeking Creditor decisions

58.1 [Notice of a decision procedure]

Notice of a Decision Procedure shall be given by the convenor to every Creditor whose address is known to the convenor or identified in the Proposal at least 14 days before the Decision Date, or such shorter period as the Court may allow.

58.2 [Contents of notice and procedure]

The notice and procedure shall follow, so far as applicable, the requirements of Rules 15.4 (electronic voting), 15.5 (virtual meetings), 15.6 (physical meetings) and 15.8 (notices to creditors of decision procedure).

58.3 [Convenience of participants]

The convenor must have regard to the convenience of those invited to participate when making arrangements for a Decision Procedure.

58.4 [Time of meeting]

Meetings of Creditors shall be convened for commencement between the hours of 10.00 and 16.00 on a business day.

58.5 [Chair of meeting]

Unless Paragraph 20.3 (chair where no Supervisor acting) applies, the Supervisor, or a person experienced in insolvency matters and nominated by the Supervisor, shall be chair of the meeting.

58.6 [Non-receipt of notice]

Where a decision is sought by a notice in accordance with Sub-paragraph 58.1, the Decision Procedure is presumed to have been duly initiated and conducted, even if not everyone to whom the notice is to be delivered has received it.

58.7 [Exclusions from meetings]

The provisions of Rules 15.36-15.38 relating to persons excluded from meetings shall apply to the Arrangement with any necessary modifications.

59. Cost of requisitioned decisions

59.1 [Security for payment of expenses]

Subject to Sub-paragraph 59.3 below, the cost of requisitioning a decision of Creditors at the instance of the Company or Creditors shall be paid by that person or persons, who shall deposit security for their payment with the Supervisor.

59.2 [Appropriate security]

The sum to be deposited shall be such as the Supervisor determines to be appropriate; and the Supervisor shall be under no obligation to act without the deposit having been paid.

59.3 [Vote for cost to be an expense of arrangement]

Where a Decision Procedure is requisitioned, the Creditors may vote that the expenses of convening and taking it shall rank as an expense of the Arrangement.

59.4 [Repayment of deposit]

To the extent that any deposit made under this Paragraph is not required for the payment of expenses of convening and taking the Decision Procedure, it shall be repaid to the person who made it.

60. Participation in Creditor decisions

60.1 [Conditions for voting]

Subject as follows, in order to be counted in a Decision Procedure other than where votes are cast at a meeting, votes must:

(a) be received by the convenor on or before the Decision Date; and
(b) accompanied by a Proof in respect of the Creditor's claim, unless it has already been provided to the convenor.

60.2 [Unliquidated and unascertained claims]

A Debt for an unliquidated or unascertained amount is to be valued at £1 for the purpose of voting unless the convenor, or in the case of a meeting the chair, decides to put a higher value on it.

60.3 [Secured Creditors]

A Secured Creditor is entitled to vote only in respect of the balance (if any) of Debt after deducting the value of Security as estimated by the Secured Creditor.

(a) [Vote cast not changeable]
(b) A vote cast in a Decision Procedure which is not a meeting may not be changed.
(c) [Decision to be made]
(d) For the decision to be made, the convenor must receive at least one valid vote on or before the Decision Date.

61. Admission and rejection of Proofs

61.1 [Power to admit]

The convenor, or chair in the case of a meeting, has the power to admit or reject a Creditor's Proof for the purpose of entitlement to vote. The power is exercisable with respect to the whole or any part of the Proof, and whether the claim is secured or unsecured.

61.2 [Appeal from decision]

The convenor or chair's decision on entitlement to participate is subject to appeal to the Court by any Creditor, or by the Company, within 28 days of the record of the decision being given, or such longer period as the Court shall, in the special circumstances, allow.

61.3 [Voting subject to objection]

If the convenor or chair is in doubt whether a Proof should be admitted or rejected, it shall be marked as objected to and the Creditor shall be allowed to vote, subject to the vote being subsequently declared invalid if the objection to the claim is sustained.

61.4 [Where decision reversed]

If, on an appeal, the convenor or chair's decision is reversed or varied, or a Creditor's vote is declared invalid, the Court may order another Decision Procedure to be convened, or make such other order as it thinks fit, provided that the Court considers the matter is such as to give rise to unfair prejudice or a material irregularity.

61.5 [Costs of appeal]

The convenor or chair is not personally liable for the costs incurred by any person in respect of an appeal under this Paragraph unless the Court so orders.

62. Majorities required for Creditor decisions

62.1 [Decisions by majority in value]

Subject as follows, a decision in a Decision Procedure is made when a majority of more than half in value of Creditors voting have voted in favour of it.

62.2 [Decisions varying terms of Arrangement]

In the case of a decision varying the terms of the Arrangement, a majority of three-quarters or more in value of Creditors voting in favour of it is required.

62.3 [Votes rendering decision invalid]

A decision is not made if those voting against it include more than half of the total value of Creditors who are not Connected with the Company.

62.4 [Resolution for the appointment of Supervisor]

In the case of a decision for the appointment of a Supervisor:

(a) if on any vote there are 2 nominees for appointment, the person who obtains the most support is appointed, provided that such support represents a majority in value of all those voting; and

(b) if there are 3 or more nominees, and one of them has a clear majority over both or all of the others together, that one is appointed; and
(c) in any other case, the convenor or chair shall continue to take votes (disregarding at each vote any nominee who has withdrawn and, if no nominee has withdrawn, the nominee who obtained the least support last time), until a clear majority is obtained for any one nominee.

62.5 [Resolution for joint appointment]

The chair may put to a meeting a resolution for the joint appointment of any 2 or more Supervisors.

63. Chair of meeting as proxy-holder

Where the chair at a meeting holds a proxy for a Creditor which requires the chair to vote for a particular resolution, and no other person proposes that resolution, the chair shall propose it

64. Suspension/adjournment of meetings

64.1 [Suspension]

The chair may, without an adjournment, declare the meeting suspended for one or more periods not exceeding one hour in total (or, in exceptional circumstances, such longer total period during the same day at the chair's discretion).

64.2 [Adjournment]

The chair may (and must if the meeting so resolves) adjourn the meeting, provided that if the chair is the Supervisor and a resolution has been proposed for the Supervisor's removal, the chair shall not adjourn the meeting without the consent of at least one half in value of the Creditors attending and entitled to vote.

64.3 [Period of adjournment]

An adjournment under this Paragraph shall not be for a period of more than 14 days after the date on which the meeting was originally held, or such longer period as the Court may allow.

64.4 [Use of Proofs and proxies at adjourned meeting]

Where a meeting is adjourned under this Paragraph, Proofs and proxies may be used if lodged at any time up to or at the adjourned meeting.

65. Record of Creditor decisions

65.1 [Record of a decision]

The convenor, or chair in the case of a meeting, must cause a record of the Decision Procedure to be kept. In the case of a meeting, the record must be in the form of a minute of the meeting. The record must be signed by the convenor or chair and retained as part of the records of the Arrangement.

65.2 [List of Creditors participating]

The convenor or chair shall also cause to be made and kept a list of all the Creditors who participated and the amount of their claims.

65.3 [Record of decision made]

The record of the decision shall include a record of the decisions made and how creditors voted.

65.4 [Record of decision to be circulated]

The record of the decision referred to in Sub-paragraph 65.3 shall be sent to the Creditors and the Company.

PART 11: PROVISIONS FOLLOWING BREACH OF THE ARRANGEMENT

66. Breach by the Company of the terms of the Arrangement

The Company shall be regarded as in breach of the Arrangement if:

(a) the Company fails to comply with any obligation under the Arrangement;

(b) information which was false or misleading in any material particular or contains any material omissions:

  (i) was contained in any statement of affairs or other document supplied by the Company or its Directors under Part I of the Act to any person, or

  (ii) was otherwise made available by the Company or its Directors to the Creditors or Shareholders at or in connection with any meeting of Creditors or Shareholders held, or any decision taken, in connection with the Arrangement, or

(c) the Company or its Directors fail to do all such things as may for the purposes of the Arrangement have been reasonably required by the Supervisor

67. Procedure following breach

67.1 [Notice of Breach]

If, at any time, it appears to the Supervisor that the Company is in breach of the Arrangement, then, unless such breach is remedied forthwith or the

Supervisor has already presented a petition for the Company's winding-up, the Supervisor shall as soon as practicable issue to the Company a notice ('Notice of Breach') identifying the breach and requiring the Company within one month of sending the notice:

(a) to remedy the breach if it is capable of being remedied, and,
(b) if the Supervisor thinks fit, to give a full explanation of the breach.

67.2 [Remedy of breach]

If, within the one month period referred to in Sub-paragraph 67.1, or such longer period not exceeding a further one month as the Supervisor shall reasonably allow, the Company:

(a) remedies the breach of the Arrangement;
(b) if so, required in the Notice of Breach, provides a full explanation of the breach, and
(c) pays to the Supervisor such sum (if any) as the Supervisor may reasonably require to compensate the Creditors for any reduction in Dividend caused by the Company's breach,

no further action shall be taken against the Company save that the Supervisor shall report the breach to the Creditors in the next progress and prospects report under Rule 2.41 (Supervisor's accounts and reports), or on the next convenient occasion, if earlier.

67.3 [Notice of Termination/winding-up petition]

If the Company has not done those things specified in Sub-paragraph 67.2 by the time specified or allowed, the Supervisor shall as soon as practicable either

(a) issue a notice ('Notice of Termination') terminating the Arrangement by reason of the Company's breach and present a petition for the Company's winding-up; or
(b) seek a decision of the Creditors to resolve whether or not to do the following things:
    (i) issue a notice ('Notice of Termination') terminating the Arrangement by reason of the Company's breach;
    (ii) present a petition for the Company's winding-up;
    (iii) vary the terms of the Arrangement under Paragraph 72;
    (iv) take no action.

67.4 [HMRC specific]

If the Company's breach of the Arrangement is a failure to comply with paragraph 69, the Supervisor shall work with the Company to remedy this breach. If any such breach is not remedied within 30 days of its occurrence this shall constitute default of the CVA that cannot be remedied and the Supervisor shall petition for a winding-up order, unless HMRC agree otherwise in writing.

67.5 [Supervisor's duty]

If the Creditors decide to issue a Notice of Termination and/or to present a winding-up petition against the Company, the Supervisor shall do so as soon as practicable.

67.6 [Copies of Notice of Termination]

A copy of any Notice of Termination issued by the Supervisor shall be sent to the Company and Creditors as set out in Paragraph 11.

68. Retention of funds by Supervisor

The Supervisor shall, at all times during the course of the Arrangement, retain sufficient of the funds coming into the Arrangement as represents the Supervisor's best estimate of the costs of petitioning for the Company's winding-up should the Creditors so decide under the previous Paragraph hereof. Such costs shall be provided for in priority to any other costs of the Arrangement.

PART 12: CONDITIONS WHERE TAX AUTHORITIES ARE CREDITORS

69. Post approval statutory returns and payments

All statutory returns and payments due to HM Revenue and Customs post approval shall be provided on or before the date they fall due.

70. Overdue accounts and returns

All statutory accounts and returns overdue at the date of the approval of the Arrangement must be provided to HM Revenue and Customs within 2 months of the approval date together with any other information or explanations required.

PART 13: MISCELLANEOUS PROVISIONS

71. Third Party obligations

71.1 [Application of Paragraph]

This Paragraph applies where the Proposal includes any obligation on the part of a person other than the Supervisor or Company to pay moneys, transfer assets or do any other thing.

71.2 [Evidence of agreement]

The third party shall sign the Proposal or such other document evidencing the agreement to be bound by the obligation as the Supervisor shall reasonably require.

71.3 [Enforcement of obligation]

The obligations of the third party shall be enforceable by the Supervisor, or by the Company at the direction of the Supervisor.

71.4 [Failure a default of arrangement]

The failure by the third party to carry out the obligation when due shall constitute a breach of the Arrangement.

72. Variation of the Arrangement

72.1 [Variation with Creditors' approval]

The provisions of this Arrangement may be amended by a Decision Procedure of the Creditors.

72.2 [Consent of Company/third party to variation required]

No variation of the terms of the Arrangement shall be of any effect unless made with the consent of the Company (acting by its Directors) and any third party affected thereby.

72.3 [Saving for certain rights]

No variation which restricts the following rights shall be of effect:

(a) the right of any Secured Creditor to enforce Security, except with the Secured Creditor's consent;
(b) the right of an Ordinary Preferential Creditor to be paid in priority to other Creditors, except with that Creditor's consent;
(c) the right of a Secondary Preferential Creditor to be paid in priority to other Creditors (save for Ordinary Preferential Creditors), except with that Creditor's consent;
(d) the right of a Preferential Creditor to be paid pro rata with other Preferential Creditors in the same class, except with that Creditor's consent.

72.4 [Unfair prejudice and material irregularity]

No variation shall be of effect if it unfairly prejudices the rights of any Creditor or if there has been any material irregularity in the operation of the provisions of this Paragraph.

72.5 [Restriction on variation]

No variation shall be of effect if it causes the Arrangement to cease to be a voluntary arrangement within Part I of the Act.

73. Tax liabilities arising on realisations

Taxation liabilities of the Company arising on the sale or other realisation of any asset subject to the Arrangement shall, in so far as those proceeds are sufficient, be discharged out of the sale proceeds of the asset in question.

74. Invalidity and/or illegality

If any provision or part of the Arrangement is found to be contrary to the Act or Rules, illegal, invalid or contrary to public policy, that will not affect the validity of the remainder of the Arrangement and the provision or part of the Arrangement in question shall be construed accordingly.

75. Shareholders' decisions

75.1 [Supervisor's power to seek a decision]

The Supervisor may seek a decision of Shareholders for any purpose connected with the Arrangement.

75.2 [Decision Procedure]

A decision of Shareholders shall be sought as provided for in Rule 15.41 (Company meetings).

INDEX